ILLINOIS'
GERMAN HERITAGE

Vern,
Alles gute,

Don

German Day at the World's Fair in Chicago, 1893

Illinois'
German Heritage

Edited by

Don Heinrich Tolzmann

Little Miami Publishing Co.
Milford, Ohio
2005

OTHER TITLES BY THIS AUTHOR
PUBLISHED BY LITTLE MIAMI PUBLISHING INCLUDE

German Pioneer Accounts of the Great Sioux Uprising of 1862, edited by Don Heinrich Tolzmann (2002)—The fascinating firsthand reports of two German-American women who were kidnapped as children and survived to tell the story.

New Ulm, Minnesota: J. H. Strasser's History and Chronology, translated and edited by Don Heinrich Tolzmann (2003)—The history of a frontier settlement founded by Cincinnati Germans in the 1850s.

German Heritage Guide to the Greater Cincinnati Area, by Don Heinrich Tolzmann (2003)—A guide that explores the rich German heritage of the Cincinnati, Hamilton County, Ohio, Butler County, Ohio, Northern Kentucky, and Indiana regions, among others.

Wooden Shoe Hollow: Charlotte Pieper's Cincinnati German Novel, edited by Don Heinrich Tolzmann (2004)—The classic German-American historical novel about the community known as Wooden Shoe Hollow. This book is based on real places, events, and people who lived in this region of Cincinnati and how they survived as new immigrants to this country.

Missouri's German Heritage, edited by Don Heinrich Tolzmann (2005)—The history of German immigration, settlement, and influence in the state of Missouri.

German Heritage Guide to the State of Ohio, by Don Heinrich Tolzmann (2005)—A guide that explores the rich German heritage of Ohio.

Little Miami Publishing Co.
P.O. Box 588
Milford, Ohio 45150-0588
http://www.littlemiamibooks.com

Printed in the United States of America
Printed on acid-free paper
First Edition

ISBN-13: 978-1-932250-27-5
ISBN-10: 1-932250-27-1

Library of Congress Catalog Card Number 2005927591

Contents

Acknowledgements   vii

Editor's Introduction   1

PART ONE: AREAS OF SETTLEMENT   3

CHAPTER 1 — Southern Illinois   5

CHAPTER 2 — Central Illinois and Beyond   43

CHAPTER 3 — Chicago   65

PART TWO: GERMAN-AMERICAN LEADERS   91

CHAPTER 4 — Gustav Koerner   93

CHAPTER 5 — Friedrich Hecker   107

CHAPTER 6 — Francis A. Hoffmann   117

PART THREE: CONCLUSION   127

CHAPTER 7 — Illinois' German Heritage   129

Guide to Sources   167

Index   173

Acknowledgements

I would like to thank the following individuals, organizations, and institutions who assisted me in the preparation of this work either by providing me with information, and, or illustrations:

Nancy L. Barta, Site Manager, Hegeler Carus Foundation, LaSalle, Illinois;

Christa Frentz, Brandenburger Schuetzenverein von Chicago, Chicago, Illinois;

Christa Garcia, President, German-American Education Fund;

David Gosdeck, Librarian, Martin Luther College, New Ulm, Minnesota;

Jaci Jasnoch, Germania Place, Chicago, Illinois;

Arnold J. Koelpin, Professor Emeritus, Martin Luther College, New Ulm, Minnesota;

Frank H. Mackaman, Dirksen Congressional Center, Washington, D.C.;

William Milleker, United German-American Societies of Greater Chicago, Chicago, Illinois;

Ernst Ott, President, German-American National Congress, Chicago, Illinois;

Diane Walsh, Koerner Klub, Belleville, Illinois;

Hans Wolf, Rheinischer Verein von Chicago, Chicago, Illinois;

Helga Zettl, Schwaben-Verein, Chicago, Illinois.

Finally, a special word of thanks to the Little Miami Publishing Co. for its support in bringing out my works dealing with German-American history and heritage.

Editor's Introduction

IN HIS GUIDE TO THE HISTORY OF ILLINOIS, JOHN HOFFMANN NOTES that Illinois' German-Americans "have been less studied" than other groups "although surveys of Illinois" and "broader examinations . . . have touched on their experiences in the state."[1] And, Illinois: An Annotated Bibliography, compiled by Ellen M. Whitney, and edited by Janice A. Petterchak, and Sandra M. Stark, lists only forty-five items out of a total of 4,620 that deal with German-Americans.[2] The history of German immigration, settlement, and the role played by the German element in the building of the state, therefore, seems to constitute a major gap in the historical literature pertaining to Illinois, and one that is moreover underscored by the fact that German-Americans amount to one-third of the state's population, thereby making them the largest single ethnic element of Illinois.[3]

There are two general reasons why German-Americans have been overlooked in Illinois, as well as elsewhere. First, much of the source material relating to the German-American experience is in the German language, such as the German-American press, and this, of course, would not be accessible to monolingual historians. Second, the period of the world wars tended to obscure the role played by German-Americans in American history. It has really only been since 1968, when the Society for German-American Studies was founded, that interest in the topic has grown and developed substantially.[4]

This work, therefore, aims to address the gap that exists with regard to the history of the German element of Illinois by providing an introductory survey of the topic. To accomplish this task, I have assembled several articles dealing with Illinois' German heritage. The first two chapters consist of my translations from German of the chapters from Gustav Koerner's history of the German element in America that deal with Illinois.[5] They cover of the beginnings of German immigration and settlement in southern and central Illinois, and are followed in chapter three by Andrew Jacke Townsend's work on how Chicago developed as the major German-American urban center of the state of Illinois.[6] Chapters four through six then focus on three individuals who play a major role in the history of the Illinois' Germans: Gustav Koerner, Friedrich Hecker, and Francis A. Hoffmann.[7] An understanding of their life and work is crucial to an appreciation of the German heritage of Illinois. Chapter seven provides a survey history of the German element of Illinois, bringing the history up to the present time. Reference to sources can be found in the footnotes, as well as in the guide to sources found at the end of this volume.

Don Heinrich Tolzmann
University of Cincinnati

NOTES

1. John Hoffmann, ed., *A Guide to the History of Illinois* (New York: Greenwood Press, 1991), 115.

2. Ellen M. Whitney, Janice A. Petterchak, and Sandra M. Stark, eds., *Illinois History: An Annotated Bibliography* (Westwood, Connecticut: Greenwood Press, 1995).

3. With regard to the Census, see Don Heinrich Tolzmann, *The German-American Experience* (Amherst, N.Y.: Prometheus Books, 2000) 454.

4. For a history of the growth and development of the field of German-American Studies, see Don Heinrich Tolzmann, *German-American Studies: Selected Essays*. New German-American Studies, vol. 24 (Oxford: Peter Lang Pub. Co., 2001).

5. See Gustav Koerner, *Das deutsche Element in den Vereinigten Staaten von Nordamerika, 1818–1848* (Cincinnati: A. E. Wilde & Co., 1880).

6. See Andrew Jacke Townsend, *The Germans of Chicago* (Chicago: Deutsch-Amerikanische Historische Gesellschaft, 1932).

7. These chapters consist of the following articles: Evarts B. Greene, "Gustav Koerner, a Typical German-American Leader," *Deutsch-Amerikanische Geschichtsblätter* 7, no. 2 (1907): 76–83; Alice Reynolds, "Friedrich Hecker," *American German Review* 12, no. 4 (1946): 4–7; D. I. Nelke, ed., *The Columbian Biog. Dictionary of the Representative Men of the U. S., Wis. Vol.* (1895), 540–48.

Part One

———

AREAS OF SETTLEMENT

CHAPTER 1

Southern Illinois

—Gustav Koerner

Illinois – Kaskaskia – Vandalia – Settlement of Ferdinand Ernst – St. Clair County – Friedrich Theodor Engelmann & Sons – Johann Scheel – Gustav Koerner – Karl Schreiber – Dr. Gustav Bunsen – Dr. Adolph Berchelmann – Georg Neuhoff – Eduard Abend – Dr. Adolph Reuss – Dr. Anton Schott – Georg Bunsen – Theodor E. Hilgard & Family – Julius C. Hilgard – Eugen Woldemar Hilgard – Dr. Albert Trapp – German Library Society – The Latin Settlement

IN THE EARLY NINETEENTH CENTURY, THERE WAS NO SINGLE CENTER OF the German element in Illinois that functioned, as did New York, Baltimore, Philadelphia, and Cincinnati as German-American centers in the states they were located. The seat of government was moved in the 1820s from the old French town of Kaskaskia to Vandalia, located in the approximate middle point of the then settled area of the state. The location was a poor choice in every way, especially as the settlement of the northern part of the state proceeded so rapidly thereafter, and so much so that a second move could have been expected, and, indeed, did take place in 1839. Vandalia, therefore, never developed beyond the embryonic stage, and it took more than a decade even for Springfield, the new capital, to rise to any significance.

Chicago, the current business center of the state and the entire northwest, had a population of only about four thousand in 1837, and was only settled by Germans in the 1840s. By 1848, the population may have been slightly more than twelve thousand. For the southern and middle region of the state, however, St. Louis functioned as the real capital city. All business and trade concentrated there, and in Illinois itself the German element settled in the counties adjacent to St. Louis: Madison: St. Clair, and Monroe.

In the meantime, Ferdinand Ernst from Hildesheim, who had trav-eled across the country searching for an appropriate place for a settle-ment, established a colony of Hannoveraners at Vandalia in the hope that the area would thrive. But the colony did not last, and some of the settlers left the recently pioneered area. Those who remained with Ernst were struck down with illness, and Ernst himself died soon thereafter (1820). He left a widow who became the center of society life due to her pleasant manners and fine education, and was held in high regard for many years. The German families that came with Ernst and remained in Vandalia and the surrounding area gradually attained a great deal of suc-cess, as well as the respect of their neighbors.

For Illinois, it was St. Clair County, one of the most fertile counties in the entire state, that became the destination of German immigrants moving west. In 1818, there were already several Swiss immigrants from Aargau in the area, such as the Steiner, Hardi, and Wildi families. The Baumann family followed them in 1822. They had chosen an attractive area consisting of rolling prairie land near to the Kaskaskia River, and their settlement, then known as "Dutch Hill," became one of the best and richest in the county. In 1832, a number of farmers from Hessen-Darmstadt settled along the beautiful chain of hills that extends from Belleville towards the southwest (Turkey Hill). They were well known for their successful wheat farms, and many eventually became well to do, even wealthy as farmers. In 1833 and thereafter, a large wave of highly educated German immigrants came to the area.

In 1832, Theodor Hilgard, Jr., from Speier in the Rheinpfalz, who had studied law in München, Heidelberg, and Paris, immigrated to America with his brother Eduard, a farmer from Hohenheim. Their goal was to become independent farmers in the manner idealized by Gottfried Duden, and they at first stayed with a German farmer in Penn-sylvania by the name of Speyrer, where they tried their hand at farming for a year before moving west. They purchased a four-hundred-acre farm in the vicinity of Belleville, the county seat, in an area that was noted for fertile soil.

Their cousin, Theodor Krafft, also came with them. He had studied law in Heidelberg and was filled with romantic notions of an idyllic life in the American West. Also arriving with them was Gustav Heimberger, a stu-dent of law from Heidelberg and München. He was a stouthearted young man with an enthusiastic zest for life, who later traveled to Mexico and Havana, and then published some very interesting and well-written travel reports. Later, he then returned to Illinois, where he passed away in 1857.

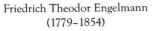

Friedrich Theodor Engelmann
(1779–1854)

Friedrich Theodor Engelmann
in later years.

Photographs courtesy of Mary Armstrong, secretary of the Engelmann Family Association and great-great-great-grandniece of Sophie Engelmann Koerner and her brother Col. Adolph Engelmann.

In 1833, Friedrich Engelmann, the great-uncle of the Hilgards and Krafft, Friedrich Engelmann and his large family and close friends arrived. Engelmann purchased a farm near his nephews located on a hilly slope northwest of Belleville that looked towards Lebanon. Friedrich Theodor Engelmann was born in Bacharach in 1779, and his father, Theodor Erasmus, was the first reformed minister of the city as well as a ministerial inspector. He was a man of exceptional scholarship, of the noblest character, the pride of his hometown, and was deeply loved by his family and revered as a patriarch by his congregation. The brothers of Friedrich Engelmann had obtained important positions from the French in the administration of crown lands, and located jobs for Friedrich, who had been educated by his father and private teachers, in their various offices.

His father, as well as his brothers and sisters, were ardent Republicans who were thoroughly disillusioned with the French Empire. However, they preferred the liberal-minded institutions enjoyed on the left bank of the Rhine under the French occupation to the antiquated feudal conditions in the rest of Germany. Friedrich Engelmann was especially attracted to mathematics and land surveying and as a youth had

Looking Glass Vineyard, Residence of Theodor Engelmann. St. Clair County, Illinois. Illustration from *History of St. Clair County, Illinois* (Philadelphia: Brink, McDonough, & Co., 1881). Provided by Diane Renner Walsh.

Entrance Gate to the Engelmann Cemetery, St. Clair County, Illinois. Photograph courtesy of Mary Armstrong.

already obtained a governmental position as a surveyor. Later on, he concentrated on forestry, and was superintendent of forests at Winnweiler in the Bavarian Rheinkreis at the time of his immigration.

At an early age, he married a lovely and highly educated young lady, and they lived in the most fortunate of circumstances. However, his liberal ideas were quite well known, although he did not wear them on his shirtsleeves. Moreover, his open-mindedness and his close connections with liberal leaders in the Rheinkreis created some definite obstacles to further advancement. They also caused him to fear that he might be transferred out of his beloved little corner of Old Bavaria to some other less desirable area. His concerns increased in the politically excited years following the July Revolution of 1832, as did his disfavor with the prevalent conditions.

He justifiably felt that his sons could find a better future in America. There is no question that the favorable reports of Duden and others, which at that time were circulating throughout Germany, exerted a decisive influence on him, especially due to his idealistic orientation. Although Friedrich Engelmann, who was twenty-five years old at the time of his immigration, was not interested at first in getting involved in public affairs, he nonetheless exerted an irresistible charm on German as well as American circles. That he did so was due to his outstanding character, his honesty and openness, his ever-cheerful spirit, as well as his impressive politeness, something almost foreign to the present time. Moreover, his presence was impressive, and his appearance was very fine even in his most advanced years. Large blazing blue eyes enlivened his features and he had the greatest resemblance to Blücher, only the lower parts of his face were much more nicely formed than those of the general of the Hussars.

He had had his own farm in Germany, and had farmed for many years. Here he concentrated particularly on viticulture and fruit growing. Numerous attempts with German grapes had failed, but he succeeded with the best American grapes, specializing in Catawba and Norton, and his grapes and his wines often received first prize at wine and fruit exhibitions. Later on, he took an active role in political affairs, naturally without consideration of any personal benefits accruing to him. He loved his new homeland with an enthusiasm seldom found among the youth today. The loss of a son, who had sailed to America in March 1854 on board the unfortunate ship *City of Glasglow*, deeply troubled him, and he passed away in the same year after a short illness at the age of seventy-six although appearance-wise he looked much younger. The words of Wilhelm Humboldt that are engraved on his tombstone describe him well: "The hand of time leaves the heart untouched that is firmly and truly led by the genius of youth."

The eldest son, Theodor Engelmann, had just completed his studies of law in Heidelberg, Jena, and München, when the family decided to immigrate to America. In order to pick up a trade, he had gone to Kaiserslautern a year prior to the immigration to learn the trade of tanning. However, in 1833 he got involved in the Frankfurt revolt, and had to flee to France. He arrived at LeHavre before his family's departure for America on 1 May 1833. After trying his new trade in America, he

Tombstone in Engelmann Cemetery for Friedrich Theodor Engelmann and wife Elizabeth (Kipp) Engelmann. Photograph courtesy of Mary Armstrong.

came to the conclusion that the outlook didn't look that promising, especially as he had made no significant progress in it. And for agriculture he had little interest, but did enjoy hunting, which he engaged in with a passion, as did his father and other members of his family. But even the greatest success in hunting couldn't provide the foundation for a livelihood, so he moved to St. Louis, where he opened an advertising office together with a land agency.

He returned to the study of law again and came to the service of his countrymen as a lawyer. He also frequently assisted Wilhelm Weber in the editorial office of the *Anzeiger des Westens* and his reports were noted for their great clarity and skillful style. In 1840, he returned to Belleville, where he continued his law practice and also took over the publication and editing of the *Belleviller Beobachter* in 1844. In the same year, he was appointed assistant Clerk of the Circuit Court, and this did not permit him to continue publication of the newspaper, so that it then moved to Quincy. In 1845, he was appointed Chief Clerk, and was later elected to that office as well, which he held until 1852.

He then took up his law practice again, which he continued until 1860, when he moved to one of the most beautiful farms in the countryside, which he had acquired some time earlier. Here he devoted himself enthusiastically to viticulture and had the largest vineyard and winery in the county by the 1880s. He was an exemplary public official, but had no inclination to play a role in political affairs at all. He corresponded with agricultural authorities and societies in America as well as Germany, focusing on viticulture as well as the problems encountered in grape growing.

The youngest son, Adolph Engelmann, born in 1825, was educated, as long as he was on the farm, by members of his family. From 1836 on, he attended the schools at Belleville, and worked in his brother's office there. He also studied law in Belleville as well as St. Louis, in the office of Fields and Leslie. In 1845, he was admitted to the bar in Illinois, and began a career as a lawyer in Quincy, which at that time had a large number of educated and well to do Germans. When the war broke out with Mexico and the president called for volunteers, he rushed back to Belleville to join the first company of volunteers, and which of course consisted of Germans. It became the First Company of the Second Illinois Regiment. Elected Sergeant by his comrades, he soon had advanced, at the age of twenty-one, to the rank of a noncommissioned lieutenant.

The regiment was in the brigade of General Wool that marched through New Orleans, Texas, and then crossed the Rio Grande, and moved on to Santa Rosa in the state of Coahuila. There they learned that General Taylor was threatened at Saltillo by the main army of Santa Anna. In fast marches (forty miles per day) they got to Buena Vista, where Taylor had taken up a position. In a very bloody battle (21 February 1847) Engelmann was severely wounded in the left shoulder. In May, the regiment was mustered out after having served its time, and Engelmann returned to St. Louis, where the bullet was finally removed. It took almost an entire year before he was fully recovered, after which he moved to Chicago to practice law.

After Friedrich Hecker came through Chicago on his way to Germany in June 1849, where he spoke with such great enthusiasm and hopes about the revolution, Engelmann then decided to go to Europe. On arrival in London he learned that the revolution had failed in Baden and in the Palatinate. Being so close to Germany, where he had so many relatives, he decided to go to Germany anyway and spent a year in Berlin, Frankfurt and München. When Schleswig-Holstein was deserted by other powers in its battle with Denmark, he joined the service of the Fourth Volunteer Infantry Battalion as first lieutenant. The battalion

Col. Adolph Engelmann (1825–1890
Photograph courtesy of Mary Armstrong.

was not involved in the terrible battle of Idstedt, but did take the field at
the battle of Missunde and for the storming of Friedrichstadt.

Engelmann returned to Illinois after Schleswig-Holstein was forced
by Austria and Prussia in 1851 to end the war. After his brother, who
had run the farm, drowned at sea, Engelmann decided to take over the
job of running the farm. When war broke out in 1861, he was tending
the farm as fruit grower and was especially successful with viticulture.
But he then left his farm and young wife to heed the call to arms, and
was elected first lieutenant. Of the Forty-third Infantry Regiment of Illi-

nois, whose superior, Julius Raith, had also been his captain the Mexican War.

This was a German-American regiment, consisting especially of the American-born sons of the immigrant generation. It was first ordered to Missouri, and then placed under the command of General Grant in the spring of 1862. It first saw battle at Fort Henry and was in the bloody battle at Shiloh, where Raith was killed and where the regiment suffered heavy losses (one-fourth wounded or killed). Engelmann then advanced to captain of the regiment, and from then on, as long as the regiment served (three years), led a brigade. There was a famous battle at Jackson, Tennessee against Forrest's cavalry, which was decisively defeated, and then it took part in the failed siege of Vicksburg. It was then ordered to Arkansas where it took park in the capture of Little Rock, which had been occupied for a long time. In March 1864, it formed a unit of the army of General Steele that moved through Arkansas to unite with the army of General Banks at Shreveport at Red River. As often happens with such marches from afar that aim to join together at some point, so too did it happen here that before Steele could reach him the Confederates attacked, and threw everything they could at him, so that Steele was forced to beat a hasty retreat back to Little Rock.

At Jenkins Ferry at Saline River the Confederates caught up with Steele, who was trying to cross the river. General Friedrich Salomon led the rearguard action, and the brigade led by Adolph Engelmann covered the end of it. A bloody battled ensued. The Forty-third Regiment, a Wisconsin and an African-American regiment covered their crossing. They not only succeeded in this, but also beat back the enemy lines for several miles and captured two of their canons. Only by means of the greatest efforts of the officers were the Blacks stopped from granting no pardon, and killing the wounded enemy soldiers. With the battle cry "Remember Fort Pillow," they pounced on the enemy as if raving mad. After completing his service, Engelmann was decommissioned with the rank of brigadier general. Thereafter, he lived quietly at his farm, and was an active member of the agricultural society. His character is sufficiently described by stating that he was the son of his father.

Along with the Engelmanns, a young man came with the family, Johann Scheel, who had studied forestry in Aschaffenburg and had been appointed to a position by forester Engelmann. He was very kindhearted, practical, skillful, and a good worker. Soon after his arrival he found a good position as a surveyor and also assisted the county sur-

Johann Scheel as pictured in *History of St. Clair County, Illinois*.
Illustration provided by Diane Renner Walsh.

veyor as well. In 1836, Scheel obtained a position as assistant engineer when Illinois undertook the gigantic task of covering the state with a railway system by means of public funds, a position he held until the collapse of the system in 1839. He then returned to his previous position as assistant surveyor and later held the offices many times of county treasurer and tax officer.

Then, for eight years he was elected to office as Clerk of County and Probate Court. In 1858, St. Clair County elected him to the state legislature on the Republican ticket while he and his family were visiting Germany. And in 1860, he was unanimously named as candidate for state senator, but was defeated. Although he received the majority of the votes in his county, the other county in the district voted almost exclusively for the Democratic candidate. He therefore was defeated by only a few votes. In 1862, President Lincoln appointed him to an important position as tax assessor for the congressional district, in which Belleville is located, a position he held until his death in 1864. It should be noted that he won the popular support of Germans as well as Americans.

The author of these lines, Gustav Koerner, was born 20 November 1809 in Frankfurt am Main, and arrived in Illinois with the Engelmanns (3 August 1833). He stayed on their farm for a year, studied law, and then attended law school in Lexington, Kentucky (1834–1835). Thereafter, he was admitted to the bar as a lawyer at the state supreme court, in 1835, and opened a law office in Belleville. In 1836, he married Sophie Engelmann. In 1840, the Electoral College of Illinois sent him to Washington, D.C., to deliver the official results of the presidential election to the vice president.

There he came to know Van Buren, Richard M. Johnson, and many senators and representatives. He also heard the most important speakers of the time, such as Webster, Clay (whom he had personally gotten to know in Lexington), Calhoun, and Preston of South Carolina, Benton and others. In 1842, he was elected to the state legislature of Illinois, and in 1845 was appointed by the governor a member of the state supreme court, and was then overwhelmingly elected to the same position in 1846. In 1852, he was elected to a four-year term as lieutenant governor of Illinois, but in 1856 he retired from public life and devoted himself to his law practice until the Civil War brought him back into public service.

He organized the Forty-third Illinois Infantry Regiment, and was appointed captain of the Volunteer Army by Lincoln in August 1861. He was then commanded to the staff of Fremont and, after Fremont's recall, was ordered to the staff of General Halleck, but a protracted illness caused him to retire in March 1862. Later on in 1862, he was appointed minister to Spain, an office he held until 1 January 1865, when he resigned for financial reasons. In the same year, he served as a member and as president of the commission that aimed to build an orphanage for the children of soldiers, an honorary office that nonetheless consumed a great deal of his time. In 1871, he served as a member and as president of the railway commission, but resigned in January 1873. In 1872, he was nominated as the candidate for governor by the state conventions of the liberal Republicans as well as the Democrats against Governor Oglesby, but was defeated in the election.

Karl Schreiber of Meiningen also joined the Engelmann family. As a member of the *Burschenschaft* he had feared persecution and, therefore, fled. He was a young man with a calm and affable nature. He studied law, and remained for some time with the Engelmann family. Thereafter, he roamed about in the mountains as a hunter and trapper, returned and wrote a very interesting story about his adventures, finally settling down on a farm in St. Clair County, where he lived out the rest of his life. In like manner, a young minister, Michael Ruppelius, purchased a farm near the Engelmann farm, but later moved to Peoria, where he worked for many years as a preacher and teacher.

Soon thereafter, other refugees arrived in the area: Dr. Med. Gustav Bunsen from Frankfurt, who had been actively involved in the Frankfurt revolt, where he had been wounded. He was a man of action, sharp wit, and resolute courage, but was disinclined to taking extreme positions. In 1830, he went to Poland as a doctor, where he was captured by the Russians, then later released. In 1836, he joined a volunteer group to assist Texas in attaining its independence, and was unexpectedly killed in an attack by the Mexicans.

Dr. Med. Adolph Berchelmann, who also participated in the Frankfurt revolt, practiced medicine first in the country near the Hilgard brothers, then in Belleville, where he lived until his death (1873), and where he attained the love and respect of fellow citizens. He was as an easygoing, friendly, and magnanimous man, who was devoted to his profession.

Georg Neuhoff of Frankfurt, a farmer, arrived with him. He had also participated in the Frankfurt revolt, and fled as a result. He purchased a farm, and later moved to Belleville, where he owned a hotel for some time before moving to a farm in the Belleville area. In the same fall, Karl Friedrich, who had studied public affairs and agriculture in Leipzig, also arrived. At the same time, Eduard Haren from the Rheinkreis and Heinrich Sandher from Rheinhessen, where both had been officials, purchased farms by the Hilgards. In 1834, the following immigrants sought refuge at the hospitable home of the Engelmanns: Wilhelm Weber, Ernst Decker, and Mirus.

The family of Heinrich Abend of Mannheim arrived in St. Louis at the same time the Engelmann family arrived in Illinois. The head of the family, as well as the two oldest children, died soon thereafter, and the widow purchased a farm near the Engelmann farm. Later the family moved to a large farm bordering on Belleville. One of the sons, Eduard Abend, who had been eleven years old at the time of immigration, obtained the customary school education, and then spent some time at the college in Lebanon where he studied law. In 1842, he was admitted to the bar, but soon had to take on the responsibility of administering the affairs of his mother, and related business, so that he had no time for his law practice. However, he proved to be good at finance and acquired property. He also took an active role in public affairs, and was elected on the Democratic ticket to the state legislature, and was elected four times to the office of mayor of Belleville. For many years, he held the position as county estate administrator in St. Clair County, and was president of several commercial and business associations, including the Belleville Savings Bank, which he founded in 1859.

Adolph Reuss, M.D.
Illustration from the *History of St. Clair County, Illinois*, and provided by Diane Renner Walsh.

Adolph Reuss came from an old Frankfurt family of stature. He was a very efficient doctor and scientist, and soon built up an extensive practice, but really excelled as a farmer. Physically he was quite strong and clearing a forest and plowing a field was a joy to him. Up into his later years, he spent his free time away from his practice on the farm. He was interested in politics, but never ran for office himself. He was friendly, but frank, and was given to pithiest kinds of expressions. He founded the Medical Society of St. Clair County, and kept well informed with what was going on in the scientific world. He died in 1878 at the age of seventy-six, and his death was considered a great loss in the long list of German immigrants to the area.

Dr. Kehl, who had been an assistant teacher at the Frankfurter Gymnasium, returned for familial reasons after having spent a few years in Europe.

Anton Schott, who had been professor of history at the Frankfurter Gymnasium, had studied theology and philology at Halle and Jena. The

Public Library of St. Clair County can thank him for having been established. He served as its librarian for many years out of a unique sense of devotion and determination. Public education was especially important to him and he was elected director and administrator of the public schools, devoting a great deal of his time to the faithful execution of his duties and responsibilities. He was one of the most important and respected persons of the county. He followed the politics of the country with great interest, without ever showing, however, any interest in running for office. Only one time did he allow his name to be offered by the Democratic Party as a candidate for the state legislature, although the candidacy did not have a chance given the great Republican majority of the time. His calm, modest, manly, and thoroughly honest character, together with his active participation in all endeavors devoted to the welfare of the community, brought him the respect of all parties and nationalities. He passed away in 1869.

Residence of Adolph Reuss, Shiloh, St. Clair County, Illinois.
Illustration from *History of St. Clair County, Illinois*, courtesy of St. Clair County Historical Society, Belleville, Illinois.

Reuss and Schott, both indivisible friends since their youth, purchased a large, beautiful farm with a fine farmhouse on it, located about a mile northeast of the Engelmann farm. They later divided it, as Germans usually concerned themselves first with providing the best home for their family that was available given the conditions at hand and then proceeded from there, and such was the case with Reuss and Schott.

In the same year, Georg Bunsen immigrated, and settled about two miles from the Hilgard farm. The Bunsen family was part of the failed Giessen Immigration Society, and they preferred to settle in Illinois. Georg Bunsen, the head of the family, was born 18 February 1793 in Frankfurt am Main. His father, a director of the municipal mint, was considered outstanding in his field, and was related to the famous diplomat and scholar Josias Bunsen and the outstanding chemist Robert Wilhelm Bunsen. Georg Bunsen received his education in his hometown, and then studied philosophy in Berlin in 1812, where he attended the lectures of Wolf and Fichte. He then joined the Frankfurter Voluntary Infantry, and participated in the campaign of 1814 against France.

After the end of the war, he returned to Berlin to complete his philosophical and philological studies and found a position in the well-known Lauter School at Charlottenburg, which was based on the principles of Pestalozzi. After he had been in a similar institution in Wiesbaden, he founded a school in Frankfurt in 1820 in the spirit of Pestalozzi that blossomed and lasted until 1834. His freethinking republican principles, as well as his desire to find a more appealing home caused him to immigrate.

He quickly got involved in public affairs, and was elected justice of the peace by his neighbors, a position he held for many years. But he did not remain untrue to the teaching profession for a minute. He undertook the education of his own children, and soon the children of his neighbors as well. In 1847, St. Clair County elected him as delegate to the state convention to draw up a new constitution, which was a highly regarded and respected position. In 1855, he moved to Belleville and opened a model school, where he could put his views regarding education into practice. The public school teachers were invited from time to time to observe his teaching methods and it wasn't long until they willingly became his students. In 1856, he was elected director and inspector of the public schools of Belleville, and several years later he was elected superintendent of the schools of the entire county. He was likewise a member of the state board of education, and a founder of the state normal school (teachers' college) at Bloomington. He brought an entirely new spirit into the local school system, and almost found a greater following and respect among American than German teachers. Memory work and formulas were banned, and replaced by thought exercises and self-development programs. He greatly contributed to the educational system of the state of Illinois. In a memorandum about him by an American educator, it was stated that:

Georg Bunsen
Photograph courtesy of the St. Clair County Historical Society, Belleville, Illinois.

He was made of special stuff. Selfless to the highest degree, of impeccable character, and clean cut, his life was worthy of emulation and admiration. His outstanding service as a teacher, director of schools, superintendent of the county schools, member of the state board of education, and as an ever active and energetic proponent of education are of inestimable value, and will long remain in our memory.

He passed away in 1874. A schoolhouse in Belleville was named in his honor as the Bunsen School; others there bear the names of Franklin, Washington, and Lincoln.

In 1836, Theodor E. Hilgard, Sr. (the father of Theodor, Jr., who had immigrated earlier), and his family from Zweibrücken settled down on a nice farm bordering the city of Belleville. Hilgard, born at Mannheim in the Rheinpfalz, the son of a respected minister, was the nephew of Friedrich Engelmann, and received his education during the French occupation partly from private teachers, the gymnasium at Grünstadt, and the Lyceum at Metz. At the latter, he planned to prepare himself for the polytechnic school in Paris, and was especially interested in mathematics, a field in which he excelled. His shortsightedness, however, caused him to give up the plan of becoming an artillery officer or engineer and, therefore, he decided to study law, and studied at Göttingen, Heidelberg, and then attended the law schools at Koblenz and Paris. At the age of twenty-two, he became a lawyer at the Imperial Supreme Court at Trier, and also at the appellate court in Zweibrücken, since a part of the left bank of the Rhine had fallen to Bavaria later on. After a very fortunate and successful practice at this court, and after having served as a member of the district magistrate in the Rheinkreis, he was appointed chairman of the appellate court in 1824, and held this position until 1836, when he took his leave.

He was undoubtedly one of the foremost jurists in the country and chaired the presidium of the assizes many times. He also excelled as an author of legal works. For several years, he edited the highly regarded *Annalen der Rechstspflege in Rheinbaiern*. But even the most strenuous kinds of professional activities could not satisfy this lively spirit. He remained a devoted student of mathematical studies and of classical antiquity, and greatly enjoyed reading the Roman and Greek poets and authors well up into his latter years. He also dedicated a great deal of his time to French and German literature, and read and wrote in French as if it was his mother tongue. So thorough was his knowledge that he instructed all of his sons, who had immigrated with him as boys and only had moderate amount of knowledge from their schooling. Indeed, he taught them so well that the two younger ones went directly to German universities, while the eldest, Julius, obtained a position as a surveyor on the coast. He is the second highest officer in the Bureau, but in fact really functions as its head, and has attained a reputation as one of the foremost mathematicians in the United States and Europe.

The following factors played a role in Hilgard's decision to exchange his homeland for America. First, he always had a preference for rural life, especially as his health had suffered as a result of his rigorous intellectual endeavors. Second, like all members of his family, he had a strong admiration for the republican form of government. And, finally, he was deeply offended by the attempts of the Bavarian government, especially after the events of 1832–33 in the Palatinate, to infringe upon the rights of the democratic institutions that had arisen as a result of the French Revolution. Moreover, its attempts to reform the courts struck him as symptomatic of a suspicious and bureaucratic government.

The thought of providing his large family with a secure and solid foundation in the land across the sea blended together with a touch of Romanticism, something altogether unusual for such a serious and practical man, but strengthened the idea he had long held of immigrating to the United States. In the meantime, he carefully examined the prevailing conditions in America, and accomplished this sooner than others might have, as many of his relatives had been settled for years in Illinois, and had provided lively and illuminating reports containing the plain truth with regard to the advantages and disadvantages of the New World.

In the fall of 1835, Hilgard left his beautiful Rheinpfalz, and arrived in St. Louis in the spring of 1836 with his large and interesting family. He purchased a nice farm near Belleville with substantial and, for their time, almost elegant buildings on it, as well as a beautiful fruit garden. He concentrated on viticulture and fruit growing, in particular. Not long thereafter, he laid his land out in building sites, which he gradually sold as Belleville blossomed. In other parts of the state he acquired a great amount of land, partly from the government, partly from private parties. The town of Freedom in Monroe County, fourteen miles from Belleville, was founded by him, as was West Belleville. After the death of his first wife, who was an excellent wife and mother, and his second eldest son, who was the only one of his children interested in farming,

Hilgard began selling off his properties with the intention of spending the rest of his life in Germany. However, he only sold his home in Belleville after all his children had established a home.

In 1850, and again in 1852, family affairs brought Hilgard to Germany for a brief stay. In 1854, he and his second wife moved to Germany and made Heidelberg their place of permanent residence. In 1863, he returned to Belleville to finalize business affairs, and remained there for a year until he finally said farewell forever to his second homeland that he loved so much. He died at the age of eighty-two in 1872, surrounded by a newly blossoming family.

During his latter years, Hilgard was able to devote more time to writing. As soon as he got an idea, he became restless, as this was not only the case with Goethe, but rather with all gifted people who want to express their thoughts in writing in a pleasing manner, as is their custom. In Belleville, he completed excellent translations of *Die Feueranbeter* by Thomas Moore and Ovid's *Metamorphosen* in eight-line stanzas. Both authors must have attracted him, as both were masters of a beautiful style of writing without which the greatest and most elevated thoughts were of decidedly lesser value in Hilgard's view. Later attempts at translating *King Lear* and the *Nibelungen* and making them accessible to the German-reading public testify to his deeply held feeling that beauty, rather than its opposite, should be stressed in literature. He, himself, wrote as a youth in Germany, as well as in America. And he continued to write in his later years, just like Friedrich Muench who, however, was altogether different temperamentally as well as intellectually.

However, he was not only concerned with literary writings, but also matters relating to public affairs, especially in the years around 1848. In 1847, he published a pamphlet that aroused considerable interest, *Zwölf Paragraphen über den Pauperismus und die Mittel ihn zu steuern*, which was favorably reviewed by a number of journals, including the *Westminster Review*. It appeared in French translation as *Essai sur le droit au travail et les questions qui s'y attachement*. In 1849, he published *Eine Stimme aus Amerika, über verfassungsmässige Monarchie und Republik*. In the same year, he published a pamphlet *Ueber Deutschlands Nationaleinheit und ihr Verhältnis zur Freiheit*. All of these works were written with extraordinary clarity and transparency in a noteworthy style reminiscent of the French, and which express a love of freedom, but tempered by sense moderation. They contain a trace of idealism that never disappeared in his work even though he encountered nothing in America but a sharp sense of realism in matters pertaining to public affairs.

No one could convince Hilgard to get involved in local politics. Although he was fully grounded in the English language, he lacked the ability to quickly come up with the appropriate expression. At the same time, he was a skilled speaker in German as well as French, and didn't want to risk losing these skills by trying to become an English-language public speaker. In German circles he was quite influential. Also, he quickly became acquainted with the institutions of this country, and was naturally quite able to come to the right conclusions in this regard. He wrote a great deal for German-American newspapers, and soon dealt with important political issues in the English-language press of Belleville as well. He corresponded with county officials and legislators, discussing and suggesting various legislative matters. His influence extended accordingly in both directions: he worked for the edification and enlightenment of German-Americans by means of the German-American press, and discussed his views on serious and important questions in the English-language press as well, thereby reaching an American audience.

He had not held a public office since he left Germany, so one cannot try to come to a mathematical summation of his influence by counting the offices he held during his lifetime, as this would not reflect the impact that he had. However, it is obvious that a man of such in-depth knowledge and education in the areas of law, politics, and history, who expressed himself widely in the press, clearly didn't live and work in vain. His name, which still is well known by means of his descendants, must be mentioned in all present and future discussions of the influence of the German element. We have mentioned the name of his son, Julius, and his contributions, as well as those of his brother, Eugen, and they are important enough to merit a short description of their work.

Julius E. Hilgard was born 5 January 1825 at Zweibrücken in the Rheinkreis, where he obtained an excellent education. After he had immigrated at age eleven with his father, who provided a regular and methodical education for all his children, Julius was instructed in both classical as well as modern language, and soon helped his father teach his brothers and sisters. He was especially gifted in mathematics, and one could say that he had an almost instinctive comprehension in this area. His father, himself an adept mathematician, soon had to dispense with teaching the topic to his son, and had to admit that he had been surpassed by him. It was only natural that he decided to become a civil engineer, and for that reason moved to Philadelphia in 1843. There he worked at the Norris Company, which constructed locomotives for the domestic market as well as for export abroad. At this company he worked with two outstanding engineers, Roberts and Trautwein. After having been introduced into the family of Judge Kane, he made the acquaintance of Dr. Patterson and Professor Alexander Dallas Bache, as well as other members of the Philosophical Society of Philadelphia. His thirst for knowledge and his outstanding mathematical abilities were quickly recognized.

After Bache became head of the United States Coast Survey, he immediately turned to Hilgard, enlisted his service, and entrusted him with important responsibilities. Bache, a great-grandson of Benjamin Franklin, had previously been in the United States Corps of Engineers, a professor of mathematics at the University of Pennsylvania and then served as president of Girard College. In the journal, *Popular Science Monthly* (September 1875) it was said of Hilgard:

> Hilgard soon became known as one of the masterminds in his field. By means of his indefatigable efforts and the improvements that he instigated, he advanced to become head of the Bureau of Coastal Surveys (1862), with headquarters in Washington, D.C. Hilgard's scholarly research concentrated on surveying and physical geography and the development of the related methodology and instruments. The annual reports of the Bureau (several large quarto-sized volumes, richly illustrated with maps of all kinds) contain many of his articles, and dealt with surveying, the determination of longitude and latitude, the earth's magnetism, etc. His treatise on the ebb and flow of harbor tides first appeared in *The American Institute*, and demonstrated his clarity of expression as well as his command of mathematical principles.

He was also responsible for the determination of weights and measures, and was instrumental in their recognition throughout the United States. Due to his knowledge in this area, he was appointed by the United States Government as a delegate to the international metric commission that met in Paris. As a result, an international bureau was established in Paris to regulate weights and measures for the metric system, and Hilgard was appointed to the board. He was a member and secretary of the National Academy of Science, and also became an honorary member of the American Philosophical Society of Philadelphia and the Academy of Arts and Sciences in Boston. His correspondence with scholarly journals was extensive. Outside of his professional field, he also engaged on a work of the greatest interest—the magnetic survey of the United States. The costs of this great undertaking were covered by a fund, which the late Professor Bache had donated to the National Academy of Sciences. Hilgard also visited Europe on various occasions due to his research interests, and which resulted later in various scholarly publications.

Eugen Woldemar Hilgard was born in Zweibrücken on 5 January 1833 and arrived with his father in Illinois in 1836. He then worked on his father's farm, and received an outstanding education from his brothers and sisters. At an early age, he became interested in the natural sciences, especially botany, something for which the forest and field of the area offered a wealth of possibilities.

In the fall of 1848, he went to Philadelphia and took a course in chemistry. In the following spring, at the age of sixteen, he went to Heidelberg where his elder brother, Theodor, was studying medicine. Eugen then decided to move to Zürich, where he continued his studies of the natural sciences for three more semesters. In 1850, he left Zürich to attend the Berg Academy in Freiberg in Saxony, as he had decided to concentrate on metallurgy and mining as his area of specialization. Here he studied for two years with the following teachers: Plattner, Weisbach, Cotta, and Scherer. The influence of poisonous vapors at smelting works, which he unfortunately had to endure as part of his course of studies, impaired his health to the extent that he found it necessary to give up this line of study. He left Freiberg, visited his brother Theodor in Vienna, and took a trip to Switzerland to regain his health. He then returned to Heidelberg, finished his studies in chemistry in the laboratory with Bunsen, and in 1853 received his doctorate. The strenuous work in the laboratory had, however, exerted a negative impact on his health, and he found it necessary to spend the winter in an area with a milder climate. So he traveled to southern France to Marseilles, and from there took a ship to the harbor cities of Spain, finally staying in Malaga. There he remained for eighteen months, studying the geology and flora of the area. After visiting Portugal, he sailed to New York, and arrived there in July 1855.

Shortly after his arrival, he became director of the chemistry laboratory of the Smithsonian Institute in Washington, D.C., a post he soon left to accept a position as an assistant with the Geological and Agricultural Survey of the state of Mississippi. When this work was halted briefly in the winter of 1856, he returned to his former position in Washington, D.C. Here he devoted himself to the research of various chemical and technical topics, and taught a course on medical chemistry at the National Medical College in Washington, D.C. in the winter of 1857–1858.

By this time, the work in Mississippi had been continued, and Hilgard was then appointed Chief State Geologist. For two years he devoted his complete energy to this task. He collected data for geological maps, paying particular attention to their agricultural, as well as practical, use. The results of this work brought him to the attention of the state legislature, which provided a solid foundation of support for his work and also assured the printing of his work, *Report on the Geology and Agriculture of the State of Mississippi.* (Jackson: E. Barksdale, 1860). While the manuscript was waiting to be bound in St. Louis, a blockade was declared, and so it actually was not published until after the Civil War. This book contains a complete geological map of the state and provides information on the various geological formations and the nature of the soil and an analysis of their economic implications. The second part of it contains a description of the various kinds of soil and their value, and is based on extensive analysis. At the time, Hilgard was almost the only person to recognize the importance of such research, as well as its value and applicability, as other attempts in the field had basically been superficial and practically worthless. Since that time, soil research became his specialty and he also contributed greatly to the field by means of the construction of the mechanical apparatus necessary for this kind of study and research.

In the fall of 1860, he traveled to Spain, to marry the daughter of the daughter of the Spaniard, Captain Bello, whose acquaintance he had made while he had been in Malaga. He then traveled with his young bride to France and Germany, finally returning to Mississippi, which had already seceded from the Union. During the war, he was occupied with the preservation of the collections and apparatus, as well as other materials at the university in Oxford, Mississippi. As he still held the office of State Geologist, he continued on with that job as much as was possible given the conditions of the time.

With the reopening of the university after the war in 1865, he resigned his office, and took a position as professor of chemistry, a position he held until 1871. However, he still managed to continue his geological research during this time. In 1868, he undertook a geological study of the coast of Louisiana on behalf of the Smithsonian Institute, which also had the goal of investigating the salt deposits that had been discovered in Vermillion Bay during the war. At the same time, he investigated and described the unusual phenomenon of the Mississippi River delta which formed the main deterrent to the development of the shipping industry, and which in his view formed an obstacle to the main artery of the river.

He organized an expedition in 1869 to complete the geological survey of the state. This received the support of the state's scientific society, as well as the state immigration bureau of Louisiana. He then led a thirty-day-long research trip throughout the state, which enabled him to complete the first geological map of Louisiana, which has been changed only with a few minor details. The results of this research were published in the *Smithsonian Institute*, the *American Journal of Science*, as well as in the reports of the United States Department of Engineers. The New Orleans Academy of Science also had this published as a pamphlet to make it available to the general public.

In 1872, the legislature turned over half of the Morrill fund to the university. This fund had as its purpose the establishment of an agricultural and polytechnic school, and Prof. Hilgard was charged with its organization while at the same time serving as state geologist. But the political conditions provided little hope for the successful completion of the project. In June 1873 he, therefore, accepted an offer that he had received several times for a position as professor of chemistry and natural sciences at the state university in Ann Arbor, Michigan. The climate, however, was not particularly amendable to someone who had lived so long in the south. In the fall of that year, he received an invitation to hold a series of lectures on agricultural chemistry at the state university of California, which he accepted, and found the climate and country to his liking. He then accepted a position at the university at Berkley, and the entire family moved there in the spring of 1875.

Prof. Hilgard published numerous articles in the *American Journal of Science* dealing with geology and chemical topics and many of his lectures relating to education and agriculture appeared in the appropriate journals as well. Moreover, he also published articles for *Johnson's Encyclopedia*. He was a member of the National Academy of Science. In spite of his poor health, he worked tirelessly for the advancement of science, and attained an enviable reputation in scholarly circles, as well as affection among those who came to know him well.

At this time, and several years later, Belleville and the surrounding area became the gathering place for many political refugees, especially members of the German student movement known as the *Burschenschaft*, as well as for those who were simply fed up with conditions in Europe. Heinrich Schleth, a jurist from Holstein, was exiled from Switzerland. Albert Trapp, an outstanding physician who got actively involved in politics, had acquired a thorough knowledge of the political history of the United States, had such a good memory that he was known as a walking political library. In 1858, he was elected to the state legislature from St. Clair County, but later on moved to Springfield where he continued his medical practice. Trapp, born in 1813 in Saxony-Meiningen, attended the gymnasium at Schleusingen, and then studied medicine at Jena in 1832 and 1833, and later also at Berlin and Halle.

However, he then got entangled in the investigations against earlier members of the *Burschenschaft*, and fled to Switzerland, where he continued his studies at Zürich, becoming an enthusiastic student of Schoenlein. However, he was also exiled from there, and traveled across France on his way to London in 1836. In the following year, he landed in America, and headed for the well-known destination of St. Clair County where his selfless, straight, and amenable character was highly valued, and later on in Springfield as well.

August Konradi, a physician from Augsburg, was a man of gifted but somewhat unsteady and stormy temperament who also settled down in St. Clair County. The following also arrived: August Hassel, a jurist also from Augsburg, who also became active in politics; the two brothers Karl and Eduard Tittmann from Dresden, young men who were jurists with the best education; August Dilg, a theologian, who became a farmer; Herman and Heinrich von Haxthausen from Westphalia, both educated at German universities; Dr. Adolph Wislizenus, a physician; Dr. Vinzens from Rheinbaiern; Dr. Nette from Hannover; Dr. Wichers from Cologne; Dr. Georg Engelmann, a nephew of Friedrich Engelmann, who was already on his uncle's farm in 1833, settled in St. Louis after several trips to the West. Ewald von Massow came because of his involvement in the *Burschenschaft* at Jena, as did thirty-six others, including Fritz Reuter, who had been condemned to death but had escaped the prison at Colberg. He and his family also settled in the vicinity of the Engelmann farm.

Under such circumstances it is not at all surprising that the German settlement in St. Clair County came to be known as "the Latin Settlement" and that the term "Latin farmers" also derives from this settlement. This term is widely used in the United States to refer to immigrants who have chosen farming after arrival in this country. The Latin Settlement consisted of a great number of energetic, mostly young and highly educated individuals, who were all active in their particular fields of interest, as well as many other educated Germans, who were engaged in farming, business, the trades, etc. One might think that such an area would have felt isolated from the rest of the world. However, that was not the case, as the Latin Settlement won many good friends from the American population and thereby exerted a great deal of influence on the customs, thought, and way of life of the population that had settled there earlier.

In 1836, a German Library Society was formed that was incorporated several years thereafter. The founders were: Schott; Reuss; Engelmann; Theodor, Eduard, Fritz and Otto Hilgard; Koerner; Fritz and Hermann Wolf; Georg Bunsen; Adolph Berchelmann; Joseph Ledergerber; and J. L. Hildenbrandt. Generous gifts from the many private libraries that had been brought to Illinois provided the foundation for the society's library. By means of annual contributions, the collection of the German classics was expanded. The most significant American historical works, memoirs, and biographies of American statesmen were also acquired, as well as the most recent German and English novels. The first work that was acquired consisted of the collected writings, letters and dispatches of George Washington, edited by Sparks, which was followed sooner thereafter by the purchase of the collected works of Thomas Jefferson. The first German journals that were ordered included the *Morgenblatt* and the *Literatur-Blatt*, published by Cotta, and then the *Blätter fuer literarische Unterhaltung*, published by Brockhaus. In the course of time, literature relating to American statesmen was substantially increased.

From the district's members of Congress, the society's library acquired all the important documents of Congress, which numbered more than several thousand volumes. From the very beginning, some of the best German periodicals were acquired, as were the most significant English and American review journals. In 1863, the society numbered more than two hundred members and, by 1879, the number of volumes had reached fifty-five hundred (excluding government documents). In the first years, the library was located in the home of Dr. Schott in the countryside, but was later moved to Belleville. Americans also became members now and then. Meetings were held several times a year, and became popular social events, and as the families of members often attended, it often happened that after the meeting a social get-together would follow.

Each summer, several picnics also took place at selected spots in the Latin Settlement, and became so well known that they attracted German families from nearby St. Louis. The Puritan Sunday hypocrisy was done away with, as even neighboring Americans showed up and participated in German social events, and which were always noted for the good behavior of everyone there.

The Germans of St. Clair County held a meeting in Belleville and appointed Wilhelm Weber of St. Louis as their delegate to the Pittsburgh Convention that was held in Pennsylvania to discuss matters relating to the German heritage, including the establishment of a teacher's seminary. Weber was informed that it should be emphasized that although the convention should focus on the preservation and advancement of the German heritage, "that students should receive an education that would enable them to teach in English. They should become American teachers, and not just German teachers. However, they should of course be able to teach rationally in accordance with German teaching methodology." Moreover, it was emphasized that German-Americans should not separate themselves off in any way, but rather as good citizens should fuse their love of their new homeland together with their love of the German heritage.

Of course there were many private German schools in St. Clair County at this time, and although there were no *Turnvereine*, nonetheless, there were many Turner-like activities going on, especially when one considers that the predominant element in the area was German. This included a great deal of singing as well as other kinds of musical events and functions.

NOTES

1. Koerner refers here to several German-American urban centers as a means to compare and contrast with the situation in Illinois, where there really was no major urban German-American center, but rather one that was located across the Mississippi River in Missouri. The German element in southern Illinois developed due to its proximity to St.

Louis, which, as Koerner notes, functioned as the capital city for southern Illinois. In the following chapter, he traces German immigration to the state, and the emergence of other areas of settlement, including the growth and development of Chicago as a German-American center in northern Illinois.

For Illinois' German element there were, therefore, really two major urban centers, with Chicago in the north and St. Louis to the south, and with many settlements throughout the state. Although St. Louis functioned as an urban center, southern Illinois, especially St. Clair County became a stronghold of the German element. The history of the German element of southern Illinois is, therefore, closely interwoven with that of St. Louis, and both areas need to be considered in relation to one another

For further information about Cincinnati, one of the German-American urban centers mentioned by Koerner, see Don Heinrich Tolzmann, *German Heritage Guide to the Greater Cincinnati Area* (Milford, Ohio: Little Miami Pub. Co., 2003). For references to other German-American areas of settlements, see Don Heinrich Tolzmann, *German-Americana: A Bibliography* (Metuchen, N.J.: Scarecrow Press, 1975), and also by the same author *Catalog of the German-Americana Collection, University of Cincinnati* (München: K. G. Saur, 1990).

2. For the history of the German element of St. Louis, see Ernst D. Kargau, *The German Element in St. Louis: A Translation from German of Ernst D. Kargau's St. Louis in Former Years: A Commemorative History of the German Element* trans. William G. Bek, ed. Don Heinrich Tolzmann (Baltimore: Clearfield Co., 2000), and for Missouri, see Don Heinrich Tolzmann, ed., *Missouri's German Heritage* (Milford, Ohio: Little Miami Pub. Co., 2003).

3. For further information regarding the arrival of Ernst in Illinois, see H. A. Rattermann, "Wann kam Ferdinand Ernst nach Illinois," *Deutsch-Amerikanische Geschichtsblätter* 3, no. 2 (1903): 59–62, and for information about his descendants, as well as those who accompanied him, see Emil Mannhardt, "Die Nachkommen von Ferdinand Ernst und seiner Begleiter," *Deutsch-Amerikanische Geschichtsblätter* 3, no. 1 (1903): 9–11.

4. Due to its significance in German-American history, several articles have appeared in German-American historical journals about St. Clair County. See, for example, the following articles: "Deutsche Ansiedlung in St. Clair County, Ill.," *Der Deutsche Pionier* 13 (1881): 107–110; "Deutsche Einwanderung in St. Clair Co., Ill.," *Der Deutsche Pionier* 13 (1881): 340–344; G. E. Engelmann, "Zur Geschichte der frühesten deutschen Ansiedlungen in Illinois: Die deutsche Niederlassung in Illinois fünf

Meilen von Belleville," *Deutsch-Amerikanische Geschichtsblätter* 16 (1916): 248–279.

Gustav Koerner himself wrote two articles focusing on St. Clair Co.: "Erste deutsche Ansiedlung in St. Clair Co., Illinois," *Der Deutsche Pionier* 1 (1869): 113–118; and "Zur Geschichte der frühesten deutschen Ansiedlungen in Illinois: Beleuchtung des Duden-schen Berichtes über die westlichen Staaten Nordamerikas," *Deutsch-Amerikanische Geschichtsblätter* 16 (1916): 280–333.

Another historian, who wrote a great deal about the Illinois' Germans was Emil Mannhardt, and two of his articles deal with St. Clair Co.: "Die ältesten deutschen Ansiedler in Illinois," *Deutsch-Amerikanische Geschichtsblätter* 1, no. 4 (1901): 50–59; and his "Die Besiedlung von St. Clair County von 1814 bis 1840 durch Deutsche und Nachkommen von Deutschen," *Deutsch-Amerikanische Geschichtsblätter* 3, no. 3 (1903): 53–57.

According to the 1869 article by Koerner cited above, St. Clair County had a population at that time of sixty thousand, of which two-thirds were German (German- or American-born). Moreover, many towns, such as Mascoutah, Centreville, and West-Belleville, were almost exclusively German. Many towns usually had elected officials, who were likewise almost exclusively German, as was the case with, Belleville, which had a population at the time of twelve thousand.

By 1888, Belleville's population had grown to about twenty thousand, which was a substantial growth from the population it had in the early 1830s of about four hundred. According to Ruetenik, its influence statewide was substantial, as it had given Illinois by that time: three governors, two lieutenant governors, two senators, and numerous legislators and other officials. See H. J. Ruetenik, *Berühmte deutsche Vorkämpfer für Fortschritt, Freiheit und Friede in Nord-Amerika: Von 1626 bis 1898: Einhundertundfünfzig Biographien, mit sechzehn Portraits* (Cleveland: Forest City Bookbinding Co., 1888), 168. A list of these officials can be found in the second article cited in this footnote.

5. Regarding Hilgard, see Koerner's article cited in footnote no. 4 that appeared in *Der Deutsche Pionier*. Hilgard immigrated with his brother in 1832 and was followed in 1836 by their father, Theodor Erasmus Hilgard. The sons had been drawn to the idea of immigration as a result of their father's correspondence with Duden. See Marlin Timothy Tucker, "Political Leadership in the Illinois-Missouri German Community, 1836–1872," (Ph.D., Diss., University of Illinois, 1968), 45. Theodor Erasmus Hilgard's brother, Friedrich Hilgard of Speyer, was married to Gretchen Engelmann, thus linking the Engelmann and Hilgard families

together. As Tucker notes: "The relationships between the Engelmann and Hilgard families have been imperfectly and only with great difficulty unraveled from scattered information in Koerner's memoirs and other sources. Friedrich Engelmann evidently had at least twelve children, and the family was tied by marriage to the Hilgards, the Eduard Abend family, the Theodor Krafft family, and to Gustav Koerner." See Tucker, "Community," 69. See also, A. S. Wilderman and A.. A. Wilderman, eds., *Historical Encyclopedia of Illinois and History of St. Clair County* (Chicago: Munsell Pub. Co., 1907), 2:1039-40, for a biography of Th. Hilgard Jr.

6. For further information on the Engelmann family, see Ruetenik, *Biographien*, 166-174. See also, A. S. Wilderman and A. A. Wilderman, eds., *Historical Encyclopedia*, 2:1007-08.

7. Regarding conditions in the German states during the Napoleonic era and thereafter, see Don Heinrich Tolzmann, "Understanding the Causes of the German Immigrations: The Context of German History," in Don Heinrich Tolzmann, ed., *Das Ohiotal–The German Dimension* (New York: Peter Lang Pub. Co., 1993), 3-19.

8. Duden's book about his life in Missouri has often been called the most influential book in the history of the German immigration to America. For further information about Duden's book and its imporance for German immigration, see Dorris Keeven Franke, "Gottfried Duden: The Man Behind the Book," in Don Heinrich Tolzmann, ed., *Missouri's German Heritage*, 85-95.

9. Viticulture was also quite successful among the Missouri Germans. See Tolzmann, *Missouri's German Heritage*, 7, 10, 14, 32.

10. Regarding Theodor Engelmann, see note 6 above.

11. For a biography of Wilhelm Weber, see Ruetenik, *Biographien*, 229-334. For information on the *Anzeiger*, see Tolzmann, *Missouri's German Heritage*, 42-46.

12. The *Beobachter* was published from 1844-46 and was an "independent weekly, with some Democratic leanings." See Karl J. R. Arndt and May E. Olson, *The German Language Press of the Americas: Volume 1: History and Bibliography, 1732-1968: United States of America* (München: K.G. Saur, 1976), 49

13. Regarding Engelmann, see note 6.

14. For further information on Friedrich Hecker, see Tolzmann, *Missouri's German Heritage*, 80-81, 84, which includes further references to works about him. Also, see Ruetenik, *Biographien*, 338-342.

15. For further information about Schleswig-Holstein, and the German emigration from there, see Joachim Reppmann, *North Germans in America, 1847–1860* Schriften zur Schleswig-Holsteinischen Amerikaauswanderung (Wyk: Verlag für Amerikanistik, 1999).

16. Wilhelm Kaufmann writes with regard to Julius Raith: "Born in Göppingen, Württemberg, raised in the Belleville Latin Settlement, he participated in the Mexican War. In 1861 he was colonel of the Forty-third Illinois Regiment, which consisted largely of Belleville Germans. In the first large battle of the Civil War, he commanded a brigade at Shiloh on 6 April 1862. He was severely wounded in one foot. His men wanted to carry him away, but Raith forbade it. He did not want even one man able to fight to leave the battle. But the Union troops were dispersed, and Raith lay for the entire night in the woods. A fire started, and the brave man soon died in it. Next to him fell a nephew, a boy who had just immigrated from Göppingen." See Wilhelm Kaufmann, *The Germans in the American Civil War, With a Biographical Directory*, trans. Steven Rowan, ed. by Don Heinrich Tolzmann (Carlisle, Pa: John Kallmann, 1999), 315.

17. For information on Johann Scheel, see Koerner, *Memoirs*, 1:265, 281, 324, 419, and 2:68–69, 101, 103, 397, 645. See also, A. S. Wilderman and A. A. Wilderman, eds., *Historical Encyclopedia*, 2:1111–12.

18. See Gustav Koerner, *Memoirs of Gustave Koerner, 1809–1896, Life-Sketches Written at the Suggestion of His Children*, 2 vols., ed. Thomas J. McCormack (Cedar Rapids, Iowa; The Torch Press, 1909). This autobiographical work provides a wealth of information not only on Koerner's life, but also on the history of the Germans in Illinois. A detailed biography of Koerner can be found in H. A. Rattermann, "Gustav Koerner: Deutsch-Amerikanischer Jurist, Staatsmann, Geschichtsschreiber und kritischer Schriftsteller," *Gesammelte ausgewählte Werke* (Cincinnati: Im Selbstverlage, 1911), 11:219–386.

For further information on Koerner, see Karl J. R. Arndt, "Gustav Koerner, Lieutenant Governor of Illinois, Honored Fugitive and Champion of German Unity: On the 150th Anniversary of the Frankfurt Drive of April 3, 1833," *Yearbook of German-American Studies* 18 (1983): 83–85. Regarding the fiftieth anniversary of Koerner's doctoral degree, see "Gov. Koerner's 50 jähriges Doktorjubiläum," *Der Deutsche Pionier* 14 (1882): 74–75, and for an article on the wedding anniversary of the Koerners, see "Ein Ehrentag eines berühmten Deutsch-Amerikaners," *Der Deutsche Pionier* 18 (1886): 43–44. For a brief biography of Koerner, see Ruetenik, *Biographien*, 373–377. For further information and references to works about Koerner, see Tolzmann, *Missouri's German Heritage*, esp. 1–5.

19. For information on Michael Ruppelius, see Koerner, *Memoirs*, 1:271, 289.

20. For further information on Gustav Bunsen, see Ruetenik, *Biographien*, 180.

21. For information on Adolph Berchelmann, see Koerner, *Memoirs*, 1:200, 226, 310, 339, 578. See also, A. S. Wilderman and A. A. Wilderman, eds., *Historical Encyclopedia*, 2:838.

22. Information on most of the individuals mentioned here can be found by consulting the index of Koerner, *Memoirs*.

23. For information on Heinrich Abend, see Koerner, *Memoirs*, 1:258, 288, 577.

24. Information on Adolph Reuss can be found in Koerner, *Memoirs*, 1:369, 2:371, 512, 631. See also, A. S. Wilderman and A. A. Wilderman, eds., *Historical Encyclopedia*, 2:836.

25. For information on Anton Schott, see Koerner, *Memoirs*, 1:412.

26. Regarding Georg Bunsen, see Ruetenik, *Biographien*, 178-181.

27. Johann Heinrich Pestalozzi was a Swiss educator "who advocated Rousseau's natural principles (of natural development and the power of example), and described his own theories in *Wie Gertrud ihre Kinder lehrt/How Gertrude Teaches Her Children*, 1801. He stressed the importance of mother and home in a child's education." See *The Wordsworth Dictionary of Biography* (Ware, Herfordshire: Wordsworth Editions, 1994), 339.

28. See the biography of Theodor E. Hilgard in Ruetenik, *Biographien*, 175-76 and the references to him in Tolzmann, *Missouri's German Heritage*, 62. See also, Helmut Hirsch, "Early Days in West Belleville, Illinois: Letters from Theodore Erasmus Hilgard," *American-German Review* 9, no. 5 (1943): 11-13. For a biographical article together with a selection of poetry by Hilgard, see H. A. Rattermann, "Theodor Erasmus Hilgard: Deutsch-Amerikanischer Dichter und juristischer Schriftsteller," in H. A. Rattermann, *Gesammelte ausgewählte Werke*. (Cincinnati: Im Selbstverlage, 1911), 12:467-486. Most of the poems in Rattermann's article originally appeared in the *Belleviller Beobachter*. See also, Hilgard's autobiography *Meine Erinnerungen* (Heidelberg: Durck von G. Mohr, 1860). A translated edition of this work would no doubt contribute a great deal of information on the early history of St. Clair County.

29. For further information on Muench, see Siegmar Muehl, "A Visit with Friedrich Muench," in Tolzmann, *Missouri's German Heritage*, 97-108. Also, see Ruetenik, *Biographien*, 175-76.

30. Regarding Julius E. Hilgard, see Ruetenik, *Biographien*, 176. Among his works, see *Methods and Results: Formulae and Factors for the Computation of*

Geodetic Latitudes, Longitudes, and Azimuths (Washington, D.C.: Government Printing Office, 1877).

31. Regarding Bache, see Hugh Richard Slotten, *Patronage, Practice, and the Culture of American Science: Alexander Dallas Bache and the U.S. Coast Survey* (Cambridge: Cambridge University Press, 1994).

32. For information on Eugen W. Hilgard, see Ruetenik, *Biographien*, 176.

33. The *Burschenschaft* was a patriotic German student organization, which had affiliates across the German states, and which had visions of a united Germany under a republican form of government.

34. For information on Heinrich Schleth, see "Heinrich Karl Theodor Schleth," *Der Deutsche Pionier* 13 (1881): 402–403.

35. For further information on Albert Trapp, see Koerner, *Memoirs*, 1:421, 447, 458, 533 and 2:747.

36. For further information on most of the individuals Koerner mentions here, see Koerner, *Memoirs*.

37. Regarding the Latin Settlement, see "Das lateinische Settlement bei Belleville, Illinois," *Deutsch-Amerikanische Geschichtsblätter* 3, no. 2 (1908): 57–58. Carl Wittke writes the following with regard to Latin Settlements: "Some German intellectuals of the 1830s, with more of a flair for the romantic than the practical, became 'Latin farmers,' a title bestowed upon them by their skeptical neighbors who discovered that the newcomers knew more about art, music, literature, Virgil, and Cicero than agriculture. Many such misfits lost their entire investment after years of toil and sacrifice. Some succeeded, and others moved in time into the cities to practice their professions and skills for which they were really fitted. Belleville, in St. Clair County, Illinois, one of the best-known 'Latin' settlements, included such distinguished refugees of both 1830 and 1848 as the Koerners, Engelmanns, Bunsens, Hilgards, and Heckers." See Carl Wittke, *Refugees of Revolution: The German Forty-Eighters in America* (Philadelphia: University of Pennsylvania Press, 1952), 13–14.

Carl Schurz wrote: "Some of the notable men of the early '30's, the Engelmanns, Hilgards, Tittmanns, Bunsen, Follenius, Koerners, and Muenchs, settled in and around Belleville in Illinois, near the Mississippi, opposite St. Louis, or not from from St. Louis, on the Missouri, there to raise their corn and wine. Those who, although university men, devoted themselves to agriculture, were called among the Germans, half sportively, half respectfully, the 'Latin farmers.' One of them, Gustav Koerner, who practices law in Belleville, rose to eminence as a judge, as a lieutenant governor of Illinois, and as a minister of the United States to Spain. Another Friedrich Muench, the finest type of the 'Latin farmer,' lived to a venerable old age in Gasconade County, Missouri, and remained active almost to the day of his death, as a writer for newspapers and periodicals, under the name of 'Far West.' These men regarded St. Louis as their metropolis and in a large sense belonged to the 'Germandom' of that city." See Carl Schurz, *The Reminiscences of Carl Schurz: Volume 2, 1852–1863* (New York: Doubleday, Page, & Co., 1908), 40.

38. Other libraries founded by German-Americans in Illinois together with the dates of their establishment were: the German Library Society in Peoria (1856); the Concordia Turnverein Library in Moline (1861); the German Farmers' Club Library in Spring Bay (1861); and the German Library Society in Peru (1869). Although there is a catalog of the Belleville Public, *Classified Catalogue . . . With Dictionary Catalogue or Index of Authors, Titles & Subjects* (Belleville, Illinois: Belleville Public Library, 1900), it is not only out of print, but difficult to locate. The completion of a catalog of the German collection would make its contents accessible and would be most useful for historical research. Koerner wrote of the Library: "So our library founded in 1836 became the nucleus of our present highly useful and popular public library. Save when I was absent in Europe, I was always an active member and usually a director of the institution; and I may say I take as much pride in the exertions I made during all this time in securing success for our library as in anything else to which I have devoted myself during my long life." See Koerner, *Memoirs*, 1:413. See also, A. S. Wilderman and A. A. Wilderman, eds., *Historical Encyclopedia*, 2:750–51.

39. The Pittsburgh Convention of October 1837 was an important event in German-American history as it represented the first national meeting of German-American community leaders and representatives. There were thirty-one delegates from seven states (Ohio, New York, Virginia, Maryland, Missouri, and Illinois). As a result of the meeting, a German-American educational institution was established at Philipsburg, Pennsylvania. See Heinz Kloss, *Um die Einigung des Deutschamerikanertums: Die Geschichte einer unvollendeten Volksgruppe* (Berlin: Volk und Reich Verlag, 1937), 198ff. Kloss also quotes the instructions given to Wilhelm Weber by the Belleville Germans, 199–200. He cites as his source a Pennsylvania German newspaper, the *Reader Adler* (7 November 1837). This means that the "Belleville Instructions" were most likely widely published in the German-American press. The formulation of these "Instructions" was no doubt greatly influenced by Koerner.

40. German-Americans exerted a great deal of influence on the growth and development of social life in America. Koerner himself was quite influential with regard to the introduction of German Christmas customs. In

1833, he set up a Christmas tree and with no decorations available, he adorned the tree with candles, apples, ribbon, nuts, as well as bits of brightly colored paper. For further information on how Koerner celebrated Christmas in 1833, see Koerner, *Memoirs*, 1:330.

APPENDIX

The names listed below are from an article by H. A. Rattermann dealing with German immigration and settlement in St. Clair County: "Deutsche Einwanderung in St. Clair Co., Illinois," *Der Deutsche Pionier* 13 (1881): 340–344, Rattermann notes that he compiled this information from an article in the *Anzeiger des Westens* (19 October 1881). As is the case with such lists, this one most likely is incomplete, and probably contains spelling errors. Nonetheless, the names were copied as listed to supplement Chapter 1. For a list of naturalizations, 1838–49, see also, A. S. Wilderman and A. A. Wilderman, *Historical Encyclopedia*, 2:682–83.

Pre-1830 Settlers

Friedrich Germann	Jakob Hardy
Samuel Holtz	Philipp Merker
Matthias Schillinger	Bernhard Steiner
Daniel Schultz	Rudolph Wildy

Post-1830 Settlers

Ackermann	Adam Bopp
Bornmann	Busse
Georg Fischer	Funk
Thomas Heberer	Georg Hehret
Balthasar Knobloch	John Knobloch
John Wendelin Knobloch	Thomas Knobloch
Georg Merger	Merkel
Georg Meser	Jakob Mohr
Balthasar Müller	Jakob Müller
Obermüller	Siebert
Jakob Weber	

Naturalizations, 1833–1841

Ed. Abend
J. H. Aggemann
Anton Amrein
Karl Barth
Conrad Beelman
Heinrich Bergkotter
Conrad Bornmann
Georg Bremer
Jos. Briesacher
Georg C. Bunsen
August Conradi
Peter Diehl
Joh. Deschner
Albert W. Dönnewald
J. G. Eckert
Philipp Eckert
Friedrich Engelmann
Aloysius Ewers
Matthias Finklang
Michael Flick
Ferdinand Friedrich
Adam Fritz
Martin Funk
Joh. Geiger
Friedrich Glaser
Christian Grünerwald
Heinrich Harwarth
F. A. M. Hasel
Johann G. Heberer
Gustav Heimberger
Cornelius Hennig
Michael Hild
Theodor Hilgard
Jos. Hock

Jos. Abend
David Ameiss
Friedrich Aul
Philipp Baum
Adolf Berchelmann
Jos. Biermann
Michel Bossle
Georg Briesacher
Heinrich Buff
Georg Busch
Ernst W. Decker
Christian Delsch
Bernh. Dingworth
Georg Eckert
J. Wendel Eckert
Heinrich Eidmann
Ludwig Engelmann
G. P. Fein
Georg Fischer
Jos. Freivogel
Heinrich Friedrich
Georg Funk
Michael Funk
Friedrich Germann
Karl Grossmann
Adam Haas
Wilhelm Harwarth
Georg Heberer
Georg Hehr
Georg Henckler
Nikol. Hertel
Eduard Hilgard
Theodor Erasmus Hilgard
J. L. Höreth

Naturalizations, 1833–1841

Philipp Hoff

August Holzappel

Jacob Huber

Michael Junger

Peter Kalbfleisch

Heinrich Kaysing

Jos. Keck

C. H. Kettler

Joh. Knobloch

Heinrich Knöbel

Karl Knöbel

Gustav Koerner

W. Kracht

J. G. Kratsch

J. Adam Krick

Georg Kriechbaum

Georg Kuntz

Bernhard Lake

Jos. Ledergerber

Heinrich Lintz

Johann Maus

Valentin Metzler

Georg Mittelstadter

Balthasar Müller

Michael Müller

Georg Neuhoff

Philipp Pfadler

Sebastian Pfeifer

Christian Probst

Georg Rauch

Lorenz Reichert

Chrisoph Reinhold

B. Robker

Peter Sauer

Adam Hoffmann

Peter Horst

Philipp Jeckel

Samuel Just

Christian Kaysing

Jacob Kaysing

Joh. Kehrer

Michael Kleinschmidt

Friedrich Knöbel

Jakob Knöbel

Franz Knötz

Jos. Kopp

Theodor J. Krafft

Friedrich Kress

Joh. Krick

Jacob Kumm

Kaspar J. Kurtz

Jaakob Läuffert

Conrad Liebig

Joh. Massmann

Christian Metzler

Jacob W. Michel

Heinrich Möser

Conrad Müller

J. G. Neubarth

Franz Oppmann

Heinrich Pfeffer

Georg Adam Popp

Peter Rappauf

Philipp Rauch

Seb. Joh. Reichert

Georg Ritter

Jos. Roos

Adam Schäfer

Naturalizations, 1833–1841

Joh. Schäfer

Julius Scheve

J. N. Schmalenberg

Joh. W. Scholl

Conrad Schrag

Martin Sieber

Franz Stolz

Joh. P. Trautwein

Franz Urban

Ludwig Vierheller

Johann Weilbacher

Nicolaus Werner

Jakob Wetzer

Anton Wichers

Georg Winter

Hermann Wolf

Wilhelm Zimmermann

Johann Scheel

H. C. T. Schleth

Peter Schneider

Heinrich Schraer

Franz Schulheiss

Peter Steinheimer

Karl Tittmann

Heinrich Unnigmann

Christian Vierheller

Balthasar Weber

Martin Weilmünster

Conrad Westermann

Franz Wezel

Joh. Wiesenborn

John Winter

Heinrich Zieren

CHAPTER 2

Central Illinois and Beyond

—Gustav Koerner

Political Life in Illinois – Elections in 1836 and 1840 – German Newspapers – Captain Hugo Wangelin – Julius Raith – Madison County – Julius A. Barnsbach – Dr. H. Ch. Gerke – New Switzerland – Highland – The Koepfli & Suppiger Famlies – Alton – Dr. Friedrich Humbert – J. H. Jaeger – Bishop Heinrich Damian Juncker – Cass County – Beardstown – Dr. Georg Engelbach – Joseph Kiefer – Heinrich Goedeking – Franz Arenz – J. A. Arenz – Quincy – Dr. Stahl – Chicago – Chicago German Meetings, 1843–44 – German Newspaper, 1844 – Franz A. Hoffmann

IN ST. CLAIR COUNTY AND THE SURROUNDING GERMAN SETTLEMENTS an active political life soon developed. This was partly due to the nature of the German immigration, as well as the liberal election laws of Illinois, which were in effect until 1848 when the state constitution was changed. Anyone who lived in the state was immediately granted voting rights in accordance with the constitution. Only the constitution of Texas, which dated only from 1846, had a similar kind of liberal provision. With few exceptions, voting rights in all other states were contingent upon citizenship, which in the best of cases could be attained only after five years residency. And, in the states where this was not required (New Hampshire, Vermont, Virginia, Ohio, and South Carolina), it required a much longer period of time, the payment of taxes, or the possession of land as a precondition.[1]

It is obvious that the native-born population would relate to the immigrant-born differently if it was empowered with voting rights than if it would have remained politically powerless for five years. No candidate had a chance of success in Illinois, which was so heavily settled by immigrants, and no one would have had the slightest chance of victory of the polls who was suspected of not being favorably inclined to the immigrant vote. This explains the reason why so many Germans were elected to public office early on, as citizenship was not required. We, therefore, find many Germans in the 1830s who had been elected as justices of the peace, as well as to other county offices in various parts of Illinois.

In 1836, Germans actively took part in the presidential elections and especially in the elections for Congress. Moreover, the candidates themselves were also issuing German-language position statements. In 1840, during the hotly contested election between Van Buren and Harrison, Germans threw their now considerable weight on the scale and saved the state for the Democrats. It hardly needs to be said that the Germans in Illinois almost without exception voted for the Democrats and remained loyal to the Democratic Party until 1854 when the questions arose as to the introduction of slavery into the territories and the nullification of the Missouri Compromise. This resulted in the great majority of Germans moving into the Republican camp.[2]

The first German newspaper, *Der Freiheitsbote für Illinois*, a campaign journal, was published in Belleville (although printed in St. Louis), and dealt extensively with the issues of the day, and strongly attacked the anti-immigrant nativist movement.[3] German political societies and debating clubs were formed in Belleville and in the countryside, and speakers from Illinois and St. Louis held German speeches in St. Clair, Clinton, Madison, and Monroe Counties. German politicians didn't confine themselves to German newspapers, but expressed their views in the English-language press as well as extending their influence to the rest of the electorate. In 1844, the *Belleviller Beobachter* appeared, a newspaper that was mentioned earlier, and in 1849, the *Belleviller Zeitung* appeared and soon became one of the most influential organs of publication for the German element of southern Illinois. Its founder was also Theodor Engelmann.[4]

Before departing St. Clair County, reference must be made to two men who greatly contributed to bringing honor and praise to the German name: Hugo von Wangelin and Julius Raith. Mention was made earlier regarding the immigration and residency of the former in Ohio. Von Wangelin was the son of a Saxon officer whose family originated in Mecklenburg, and who had lived with his mother (from the von Kamptz family) in Berlin where he attended a military school, prior to which he attended a cadet school in Kulm, from age eleven to fifteen.[5] At the age of sixteen, he immigrated to America, and lived and worked on a farm near Cleveland until he was twenty-one. In 1839, he came to St. Clair County, where several of his friends had already settled, and purchased a farm in the Latin Settlement. In 1846 he moved to Lebanon, where he opened a store, and later on a mill.

At the outbreak of the Civil War, von Wangelin wanted to join the ranks of the volunteers, but since the quotas had been filled, he went to St. Louis along with other young men from Illinois. There he joined the Twelfth Infantry Regiment commanded by Major General Osterhaus, who had also lived in Lebanon.[6] The regiment, which consisted almost exclusively of Germans, was probably one of the best in the Union Army. During its three years term of service, it fought in twenty-eight battles and skirmishes. At the Battles of Pea Ridge (March 1862), the regiment fought gallantly under Sigel's command.[7] Thereafter, Osterhaus was promoted to the rank of brigadier general and von Wangelin, who had been appointed to the rank of major, advanced to the rank of colonel.

From fall 1863 on, von Wangelin was always in command of a brigade. At the failed storming of Vicksburg (May 1863) the regiment suffered a loss of one-third of its troops. Later on, it served with the army of Tennessee under Sherman at the battles of Lookout Mountain and Missionary Ridge. It caught up with the fleeing enemy forces at Ringgold (27 November 1863), but lost many men and several of its best officers in one of the bloodiest battles of the war. Lt. Joseph Ledergerber, a grandson of Friedrich Engelmann, a young man of exceptional talent who had just returned from the polytechnic school in Zürich, and his brother, Major Fritz Ledergerber, were also wounded at the time.[8] Captain Heinrich Kircher, son of Joseph Kircher of Belleville, an outstanding young man, lost his right arm and a leg, Col. von Wangelin his left arm.[9] Many of the best of the young people of St. Clair County met a heroic end at this battle.

Von Wangelin's physical stature enabled in him to quickly get back into action, and in March 1864, he again took over his brigade, and participated in the fighting around Atlanta. He served until his regiment was mustered out after completing its term of service, after which he was promoted to the rank of brigadier general. He was hardly home, when General Price broke into Missouri. At the time Sherman was on his march to the sea and Thomas could hardly fight off the enemy that Sherman had left behind him. The president, therefore, issued a call for

Julius Raith

volunteers to serve for one hundred days to defend Missouri. From across the country new regiments were formed, and von Wangelin was placed in supreme command of these troops, most of which were veterans, and which were assembled in St. Louis. The victories of Sherman and Thomas meanwhile had caused the Confederates to abandon western Missouri and the new troops were therefore dismissed from duty. In 1865, Lincoln appointed von Wangelin as postmaster of Belleville, an office he held for many years. He had a decidedly military appearance, and was in excellent physical condition. He was completely devoid of any pretense, was noted for his impeccable honesty, loyalty, and enjoyed the respect of his compatriots.

In 1837, Julius Raith arrived in St. Clair County with his parents who purchased a farm six miles east of Belleville.[10] He was born in Göppingen, Württemberg, and had attended the first classes of a trade school there, where his mechanical talents had been recognized early on. After a short stay at his father's farm, he became apprenticed with a millwright and soon became one of the most skilled in the trade.

At the outbreak of the war with Mexico in 1846, he joined the ranks of the volunteers and was appointed to the rank of 1st Lt. of the First Company of the Second Regiment. As the captain soon advanced to a higher rank, Raith moved into his position and led the company with distinction during its campaigns. Untiring in service, as well as good-natured, he was highly regarded by the entire regiment. In the bloody battle of Buena Vista he was noted for his cold-blooded courage, as well as his well-tempered reason. After completing his term of service he returned home, and continued on with his business. His reputation as a skilled millwright and engineer spread throughout the entire region, and he built many of the largest commercial mills in St. Clair and surrounding counties. Not long before the outbreak of the Civil War he built a mill for himself, and carried on business with a co-owner at O'Fallon in St. Clair County. Although a staunch Democrat, he nonetheless offered his services to the Union, and was appointed Col. of the Forty-third Illinois Regiment.

After the regiment was engaged in the fall and winter with the defense of the railways in Missouri against guerilla attacks, he moved on to a position in Grant's army at the Tennessee River and participated in the Battle of Shiloh (6 April 1862). Col. Raith, who commanded a brigade, was so seriously wounded at the very beginning of the battle that he died several days thereafter. He was a brave soldier, and such a good, widely respected man that his passing was sincerely mourned not only by his regiment, but also by the community at large. As a testimonial of the deep sympathy of the entire population of Belleville his body was brought to his father's farm, where he was laid to rest with military honors.

In the neighboring county of Madison, one of the first German settlers was Julius A. Barnsbach.[11] He was the son of one of the most respected families of Osterode and had received a good education there. Working and living at a local business, he decided to leave the same without the permission of his parents, and in 1797 at the age of sixteen took to the sea, and landed in Philadelphia. However, he soon made his way to Kentucky and apparently worked as an overseer on a plantation, which hardly seems plausible given his age. Seized by homesickness, he boarded a ship headed for Hamburg after a two-year stay in America, but his ship sank near Dover.

Surviving with nothing but the shirt on his back, he was heartily welcomed by his family. Nevertheless, he didn't remain there long. By

1802, he was already back in Kentucky, where he acquired a farm and built a distillery, but by 1809 Kentucky had become too crowded for him, so he moved with his family to Illinois, to what today is Madison County. Here he settled down on congressional land, and became a successful farmer. In the War of 1812, he served with the volunteers who protected the frontier against the Indians, who had sided with the English, and was said to have been with the Rangers for two years. In 1825, he went to Germany to claim an inheritance, and upon his return decided to go to Missouri, where he purchased a larger farm in St. Francois County. It appears that he acquired his revulsion for slavery there, and after having his fill of it, he moved before 1830 to Madison County to take up residence there. Here he felt more at peace with himself and concentrated on the success of his farm, so that at the time of his death he had one of the best.

Barnsbach was a tall and muscular man with a countenance emanating energy, and even as an old man had a rather imposing presence. Although he took an active role in public affairs. he did not seek personal advantages. However, contrary to his wishes, he held several county offices. In 1846, he was elected to the state legislature, which was also against his expressed wishes. He donated his salary to the county for the support of those in need. He was exacting in all his dealings, and saw to it that what was due to him was paid. He was just as conscientious in relations with others, and it was reported that he never demanded the standard interest rates, but only asked half that amount. This most likely explains the reason that at his death in 1869 (at age 89) he did not leave a large estate, but only the reputation of an undeniably honest man.

After his second trip to Germany, several close relatives, nephews actually, immigrated and settled in the vicinity of their uncle. One of them, Julius Barnsbach, became justice of the peace by the early 1830s and enjoyed considerable influence and a highly respected reputation in the county.[12] Julius moved to Edwardsville, where he opened a successful store, but which later on failed for several reasons, especially as a result of his failing health. He passed away without having reached an elderly age. A co-owner, Friedrich Krafft, a brother of Theodor Krafft in Belleville, played a significant political role in the county.[13] He had a sharp wit and a practical sense of business knowledge. Theodor was often elected to the office of sheriff in the 1840s. However, he then lost a great fortune as a result of speculation and, because of his failing health, he also passed away in the best years of his manhood.

In 1831, Dr. H. Ch. Gerke purchased a farm and settled down in one of the most beautiful area of the county, the so-called Marine Settlement. He was an extraordinarily well-educated, liberal minded man with the best of intentions, who possessed, at least theoretically, an extensive knowledge of agriculture. He was quite well known for *Der Nordamerkanische Rathgeber*, a comprehensive work he published in Hamburg in 1833 with the publishers Perthes and Besser. It dealt with all phases of American life and was in many respects an instructive compilation of informational facts from the best works that had appeared dealing with the U.S. He was the father of the talented painter, Philip Gerke of St. Louis, and his family flourished in Madison County.[14]

Not far from the Marine Settlement in the northeastern part of the county, where today one finds the prosperous town of Highland, the Koepfli and Suppiger families from the Swiss canton of Luzern, settled in 1832.[15] Both families contributed greatly to the elevation of the German element of the area, which became the center of a thriving colony. Several quite well educated families from French Switzerland, of which mention is made here only to the Bandeliers, Rilliers, Constants, and Bautiers, also contributed to the growth and development of the area.

Among the sons of Dr. Kaspar Koepfli, the head of the family, Salomon Koepfli was especially noteworthy. Clever, thoughtful, and action-oriented, all of his endeavors aimed to advance the settlement, especially the town of Highland. He offered a helping hand to every business undertaking, worked tirelessly to improve the area's road, and in later years worked for the establishment of railway connections with Highland. He knew how to make the best possible use of county offices and state legislative committees for these purposes, and his extraordinary efforts usually met with success even though they were time-consuming efforts and often involved temporary setbacks.

Such a person obviously soon attained great influence. Americans valued him highly and perhaps more so than Germans, as he always was on the go, and never tired in his efforts. His energy was ascribed to greed by many of the latter, and envy always led some to question his motives. It may be that he asserted himself too strongly, and might have repelled some by his determination, and often-hasty approach. However, he was the right man at the right place, and the rapid growth of the settlement, and the reputation it came to enjoy throughout the state is largely the result of his work, as well as that of the Suppigers. They also contributed greatly to the growth of the area by means of their enterprising activities, good judgement, and integrity.

Salomon Koepfli also took an interest in politics, but not for the reason of obtaining offices. It was only in 1862 that he allowed himself to be elected as a member of the convention that prepared a new constitution for the state. The work on this project, however, proved to be so exhausting that it adversely affected his health, and he never recovered fully, and was sick on and off thereafter. Nevertheless, he did make several trips to Germany. E. Zschokke, the son of Heinrich Zschokke, the pastor at Aargau, wrote of him:

> His last visit in Zürich was devoted to his favorite plan of establishing a university in Highland. But he could not carry it out, or his plan of publishing the history of the Swiss colony his family had founded, although he had done some preliminary work on it. His death brought both plans to naught, for after he returned to Illinois in 1869, he became quite sick and passed away in August after suffering a two-day illness.

He deserves special merit for his important work for the improvement of the schools. Zschokke wrote that he was "like a second Pestalozzi. He himself sat for days with the children, teaching them, and raised capable teachers and provided for the necessary instructional materials with significant expenditures out of his own pocket."[16] If anything, Germans-Americans can probably take the greatest pride in the fact that leading members of their community have done so much to advance the cause of education at all educational levels. In this are alone, the German element has made a valuable contribution to America.[17]

Alton, located in the same county, became the most important business center of the state in the 1830s, even flattering itself that it might surpass St. Louis. If the state railway system had been completed, the city might have advanced more rapidly, as all trains headed in the direction of the Mississippi River Valley had Alton as their starting point on paper. With the collapse of the system the best hopes of its citizens were dashed. Nonetheless, a good number of Germans moved to the town, and among them were many well-educated and hard-working individuals. One of those who settled in Alton (Ober-Alton, or Upper Alton) was Dr. Friedrich Humbert from Frankfurt am Main who came in 1836. In December 1833, he arrived in St. Louis, probably as a result of participation in the Frankfurt Revolt of 1833.[18] He established a large practice there. He was a politician "body and soul," a hundred percent Demo-crat, but did not have any aspirations for political office. According to a highly interesting lecture that he presented (4 July 1876) on the history of the Germans of Alton, the most influential citizens of Alton at the time were the following gentlemen: Schweppe, Homann, and Weigler, all of whom became members of the state legislature.[19]

One of the younger Germans who made a name in the state of Illi-nois was John H. Jaeger (Yager), who was born in 1833 in Sachsen-Weimar and came with his parents in 1834 to St. Louis.[20] He had the misfortune of losing his father in 1840, but received a good education in the public schools of St. Louis. At first he was employed in local stores as an assistant, but then moved in 1854 to Edwardsville in Madison County, where he studied law and later on continued his studies in Chi-cago as well. Thereafter, he settled down in Alton as a lawyer. He actively participated in politics, and in 1858 obtained a position in the legisla-ture as secretary and in 1866 was elected as representative from Madison County. He declined the office of tax collector for his congressional dis-trict that was offered him by President Grant (1871) and was elected to the state senate. He was quite lively, had a quick grasp of issues at hand, and fulfilled his duties and responsibilities skillfully and efficiently. Although he came to this country at a young age, he was fluent in Ger-man and well versed in German literature. Moreover, in spite of the English spelling of his name, which by the way is pronounced the same in both languages, Yager remained a German in every sense of the word.

In 1857, Alton was named seat of the Roman Catholic episcopate and Heinrich Damian Juncker was appointed the first bishop of the dio-cese. He was born 1810 in Finstingen in Lothringen, and came to Amer-ica in 1824 with his parents, studied theology in Cincinnati and was ordained a priest in 1834 at the first German Catholic church there and founded German Catholic churches in Chillicothe, Circleville, Colum-bus, and other places in Ohio. In 1857, he was named bishop of Alton, and passed away there on 2 October 1868.[21]

Part of the Giessen Immigration Society went to St. Louis, but another part moved to Morgan County, one of the richest counties in central Illinois.[22] Some settled in the small town of Beardstown by the Illinois River, and some in the surrounding area. The most prominent members of this group were: Dr. Georg Engelbach, Karl Coerper, J. L. Cire, W. L. Schneider, Th. A. Hoffmann, as well as Joseph A. Kircher and Heinrich Goedeking, the last two of which later moved from Beardstown to Belleville, where they established a flourishing store.[23]

Joseph Kircher from Fulda, Kurhessen, studied law in Marburg and München, leaving the latter in 1831.[24] He was noted for his congenial nature and integrity. Heinrich Goedeking from Berlin, the son of the mint-master Goedeking, had an excellent education, and was an energetic man known for his common sense and outgoing personality. Unfortunately, he passed away in 1865, still in the best years of his manhood, and was deeply mourned by his many friends and the entire community, which he had served as mayor.

Almost all of these men were Latin farmers at first until they found more suitable fields of endeavor, after having some rather unsuccessful experiences with farming. It is not surprising that more and more Germans gradually joined this settlement, and Cass County, as this part of Morgan County where Beardstown is located is now called, came to be one-third German (German- and American-born) by the early 1880s. Of course, they all now have established themselves in respectable positions and occupations. At the same time, the foundation was laid for German settlements in neighboring Scott and Mason Counties.

The first German settler in this area, and probably the drawing point for the entire colony was the well-known Franz Arenz.[25] He was born in Blankenburg in the district of Köln on 30 October 1801, where he received a good education and became a salesman. In 1827, he immigrated to America and spent his first two years in Kentucky. Slavery repelled him so much that he moved to Beardstown in 1829. Although he didn't find any Germans there, he became an active member of the community, and participated in local politics. It was unusual but he was a Whig, which, however, is not surprising due to his stay in Kentucky, which was then under the influence of the well-known statesman Henry Clay.[26]

In Beardstown, he established the first newspaper in the state west of Springfield, *The Chronicle*. In 1837, he laid out the town of Arenzville, where he lived until his death. Like Salomon Koepfli, Arenz was an active and energetic man, especially when it came to the community's welfare. He worked industriously to encourage immigration to Illinois, and he is responsible for the fact that many German families settled in the region where he lived. He built the first schoolhouse in Beardstown and donated it to the community as a gesture of goodwill. He also built the first flour and sawmill in Arenzville.

Not surprisingly, he soon became one of the most important men in the county and was elected to the state legislature by a great majority, earning him statewide attention. Even the agricultural society of the county was a result of his work and he served as its president for many years. In 1844, he established a German newspaper in Springfield, the *Adler des Westens*, which he edited, but which ceased publication after the presidential election.[27] In 1854, he enthusiastically joined the Republican Party, as he was an implacable foe of the institution of slavery.[28] He was thoroughly acquainted with American politics, an eloquent speaker and a man of the sharpest intellect. Life here had not deprived him by any means of his German idealism and his spirit of *Gemuetlichkeit*, and he enjoyed the highest regard of Americans and Germans alike. Moreover, he enjoyed great influence in his own political party, and was well trusted by members of the party. He died in 1856. A brother of his, J. A. Arenz, served as the first mayor of Beardstown, as well as a county judge, and was as widely respected as his brother.

In the 1830s, many Germans had also settled in the nicely situated town of Quincy in Adams County, which is located about 150 miles above St. Louis along the Mississippi River.[29] If we are not mistaken, there was a German military company there as early as 1842. The number of Germans increased and the town flourished at the same time. Germans soon played important roles as merchants, business, and tradesmen. Both political parties did their utmost to attract them to their fold. However, there were a number of outstanding personalities among the Americans at that time, which enjoyed a great deal of influence due to their wealth, hard work, and intelligence, and belonged to the Whig Party. They were especially popular with the Germans, which thereby depleted the ranks of the Democratic Party.

The presidential election of 1844 was a hotly contested one. Dr. Stahl stood at the head of the German Democrats, and was a man of the sharpest wit and great enthusiasm. He organized German mass meetings together, invited speakers, and campaigned on behalf of a great Democratic victory. As a result, the power of the Whigs was broken forever, and Quincy became a Democratic stronghold. However, Dr. Stahl himself later on joined the Republican Party, passing away in later years in Germany.[30]

A German newspaper, *Stern des Westens*, was established in Quincy in April 1845 by Bartholomaeus Hauck.[31] In 1846 a German General Beneficial Society was formed. After 1848, Quincy became one of the richest, most beautiful, and flourishing towns in Illinois with a large, influential, and hard-working German element. Even in the county itself, where Pennsylvania Germans had settled earlier, many Germans settled down. Adams County came to form a central point from whence German settlements spread out into the fertile neighboring counties of the region.

In Peoria, also one of the most prosperous towns of Illinois, Germans settled as they did in Quincy, but at a later date.[32] The large German settlements in Peru, Lassalle, Ottawa, and Joliet owe their origin to the completion of the Michigan and Illinois canal, and also are of a later date.[33]

We noted earlier that there were only a few Germans in Chicago in the 1830s, and the first signs of life of a German element there date from 1843.[34] On 18 May of that year, a meeting of the German citizenry of Chicago was held, presided over by Karl Sauter, and with Karl Stein serving as its secretary. A committee was appointed consisting of Valentin A. Boyer, Johann Pfund, Kaspar Walter, Martin Straussel, and Georg Scheirer, which drew up two resolutions that were approved by the meeting. The first expressed gratitude to the German representative from St. Clair County for the passage of a law that resulted in the completion of the Illinois and Michigan Canal. The second also thanked the same representative for his vigorous stance against a tax assessment law, as well as for his courageous defense of the legality and sanctity of contracts, noting that his work was worthy of the praise of all citizens of the state. This commendation probably took place because the German representative from St. Clair County had taken a strong stand in the legislature against other representatives of southern Illinois during a vote on the first matter, and had also taken a position against other representatives of the state on the second issue, and had firmly stood his ground in both cases.[35]

In 1844, a meeting of the German citizenry of Chicago was held that aimed to take a stand against the nativist movement of the time.[36] Mr. Brehl and Mr. Baumeister held speeches. Several decisions were made, including the following the following resolution: "Since no distinction is made in the U.S. Constitution between the rights of the native-born and immigrant citizens, we feel it our duty to protect our rights and to decisively combat even the tiniest attempt made to encroach upon them."

By 1845, the German population had grown to such an extent that Höfken established a German newspaper, the *Chicago Volksfreund*.[37]

From it, the *Illinois Staats-Zeitung* emerged in 1847, which was first edited by Franz A. Hoffmann, and then for a short time by Hermann Kriege.[38] Later on, it was taken over by Georg Hillgaertner, and became a very influential newspaper under the editorship of Georg Schneider, Brentano, and others until it finally became one of the best edited German newspapers on both sides of the Atlantic under the editorship of Hermann Raster.[39]

One of the most important Germans at that time in Chicago was Franz A. Hoffmann, who was born in Herford, Westphalia, where he had received his education at the local gymnasium.[40] What actually motivated him at the young age of seventeen to immigrate to America in 1839 alone and without a trade remains a mystery today. However, he made it to Buffalo by means of the Hudson and the Erie Canal and was then came across the lakes to Chicago on a little schooner. There he found himself in the midst of a Yankee town without knowledge of English, and with precious little money. Fortunately, there was a German settlement not far from Chicago in DuPage County called Dunkley's Grove that was seeking a German teacher. The salary was fifty dollars per year, with food and lodging provided by the families of the pupils.[41]

However, after a time, he decided that the ministry offered better prospects for the future, so he studied theology at a German Lutheran seminary in Michigan, and was ordained by the synod there. He accepted a call to serve a pastorate embracing Cook, DuPage, and Will Counties in Illinois, as well as Lake County in Indiana. The region was larger than a German grand duchy and there were no real connections among the sheep in his flock other than him. He learned the English language rather easily and spoke it with the greatest ease and fluency. Early on, he participated in public affairs and in 1842 represented DuPage County in the once so famous River and Harbor Convention in Chicago. He actively contributed to the betterment of the community, obtaining for it a post office, showing great interest in education and for a time served as preacher, postmaster, school director, and township secretary, all rolled up in one person.

He also edited a religious monthly, the *Missionsbote*, for a time, and wrote extensively for the *Chicago Democrat*, which was then the state's major Democratic journal.[42] In 1851, he decided to resign the ministry due to poor health, and move to Chicago. He soon became an influential citizen of the city and in 1853, was elected to the city council, and also opened up a quite successful real estate office. In the momentous battle (1854–60) against the introduction of slavery into the new territories, he made the important decision to move into the Republican camp. As an eloquent speaker in both English and German, he traveled across the state, thereby contributing as much as anyone to the Republican victory at the polls.

In 1856, Hoffmann was nominated as the candidate for lt. governor by the Republican state convention. However, he had to decline, as the constitution required that candidates for the office of governor and lt. governor both have held United States citizenship for at least fourteen years, and Hoffmann with ten years citizenship was, therefore, still ineligible. However, by 1860, he met the requirement and was unanimously nominated by acclamation and was elected lieutenant governor by an overwhelming majority. This was very responsible position during the Civil War, and Hoffmann earned the respect and admiration of all parties by means of his nonpartisan approach, his dignified manner, and the great intelligence he displayed in all his actions. In 1864, he was appointed as a presidential elector for the state of Illinois, and worked wholeheartedly for the reelection of Lincoln, traveling throughout the state and holding numerous addresses in both languages.[43]

Chicago is especially indebted to him for his successful work of attracting Germany's attention to the business potential of the area. At his own cost, he published an annual survey regarding the business, industry, and progress of the city, and thousands of copies were sent to he major business centers of Germany. Great sums of money were invested in Chicago due to his endeavors. Moreover, for many years he held several consular offices representing the various German states.

In 1862, Hoffmann obtained a position as superintendent of the Foreign Land Department of the Central Railroad of Illinois, which owned great stretches of land it had obtained from the state, a position he held for many years.[44] In 1867, he organized the International Bank of Chicago on behalf of German businessmen, and which became one of the major banks in the northwest, and which he served as cashier and president.[45] For years, he had been suffering from poor health as a result of his hectic life; causing him to decide to retire to a rustic life on a farm in Wisconsin, where he thought he could peacefully spend the rest of his days.[46]

In conversation Hoffmann conveyed a genuine sense of frankness, but was also quite easy going, often enlivening discussions with his good humor. A life in politics had not made him a wishy-washy kind of person, nor did his highly successful business experience make him aloof or arrogant. When he once stood alone as a boy in the midst of the noisy business district of Chicago without friends or funds, only a good lucky fairy could have predicted that one day he would not only make it here, but also would rise to the top. For him the motto certainly rings true: "By my own efforts."[47]

NOTES

1. For a history of Illinois in the early ninteenth century see Lois Carrier, *Illinois: Crossroads of a Continent* (Urbana: University of Illinois Press, 1993). See also, Robert P. Sutton, ed., *The Prairie State: A Documentary History of Illinois* (Grand Rapids, Michigan: Eerdmans, 1976).

2. Until the 1850s, German-Americans voted predominantly Democratic. For further information on the political situation at the time, see Don Heinrich Tolzmann, *The German-American Experience*, 187–208.

3. The *Freiheitsbote* was published and edited by Gustav Koerner. See Arndt & Olson, *The German Language Press*, 1:49.

4. The *Belleviller Zeitung* was published from 1849 to 1919. See Arndt & Olson, *The German Language Press*, 1:49–51. See also, A. S. Wilderman and A. A. Wilderman, eds., *Historical Encyclopedia*, 2:852–53.

5. Wilhelm Kaufmann provides the following biography of von Wangelin: "He came from a Mecklenburg noble family, was trained in a Prussian military academy, but emigrated with his parents at the age of 16 in 1834. Hugo von Wangelin entered a Missouri regiment in 1861, soon becoming major in Osterhaus's 12th Missouri Regiment and fighting with particular distinction in the storming of Elkhorn Pass (Pea Ridge). Von Wangelin was the true friend and comrade in arms of Osterhaus. He followed Osterhaus in promotions, first as colonel of the 12th Missouri, then as the leader of the old Osterhaus Brigade (3rd, 12th and 17th Missouri and 44th Illinois Regiments). Almost all of the fights Osterhaus had were also waged by Wangelin. The two were inseparable throughout the entire war. Wangelin's brigade distinguished itself at Vicksburg, then Lookout Mountain, Missionary Ridge, and in the bloody Battle of Ringgold, George, where Wangelin lost an arm. The surgeons had to amputate the arm, but when they came with drugs, Wangelin refused them, saying that a soldier could stand a little cutting. He whistled 'Yankee Doodle' as the saw went through his bones. . . . On the March through Georgia, he fought brilliantly. He beat back a severe

attack at New Hope Church on 28 May. During the fighting around Atlanta, Wangelin's men discovered the body of General McPherson, commander of the Army of the Tennessee, shot while on a reconnaissance, and captured the rebels who had killed McPherson and taken the general's saber, uniform and important papers . . . Wangelin held Bald Hill in a brilliant manner in this battled. Wangelin was wounded there several times, but he remained with his troops. Unfortunately, all of Wangelin's war deeds cannot be recounted here, continuously at the front (his 'leaves' were the weeks needed for the healing of his wounds), and among German heroes of the Western army, the name of Wangelin must be remembered immediately after that of Willich." See Wilhelm Kaufmann, *The Germans in the American Civil War*, 328. For further information, see H. A. Rattermann, "General Hugo Wangelin," *Der Deutsche Pionier* 15 (1883): 408–10.

6. In his biographical directory of German-American Forty-Eighters, A. E. Zucker indicates that Peter Joseph Osterhaus (1823–1917) "studied at military acdemy in Berlin and became an officer in the Prussian reserves. He was enthusiastically on the side of the Revolution and was made commandant at Mannheim. In 1849 he came to the U.S. as a political refugee and settled in Belleville, Ilinois, and later moved to St. Louis where he became a bookkeeper for a hardware firm. At the outbreak of the Civil War he volunteered as a private but rose rapidly in rank in as highly distinguished a military career as any Forty-Eighter. . . . He served in Lyon, France from 1866 to 1877. He then returned to St. Louis and engaged in the hardware business. In 1898 he was appointed consul in Mannheim and served until 1900, when he resigned. By special act of Congress he was appointed brigadier general on March 3, 1905. All reports on General Osterhaus stress his gallant and chivalrous character." See A. E. Zucker, ed., *The Forty-Eighters: Political Refugees of the German Revolution of 1848* (New York: Columbia University Press, 1950), 323. For further information see Emil Mannhardt, "General Peter Joseph Osterhaus," *Deutsch-Amerikanische Geschichtsblätter* 4, no. 3 (1904): 54–62.

7. Zucker writes of Franz Sigel (1824–1902) that he "graduated from the military academy in Karlsruhe and served as lieutenant in the army. His liberal political views brought about his resignation in 1847. In both insurrections in Baden he was one of the leading military commanders. Forced into exile, he spent two years in England and arrived in New York in 1852. He taught at first in Dr. Dulon's school in New York and later in another school of that city. After his Civil War service . . . he edited the Baltimore *Wecker* for two years and then served in turn as

pension agent, collector of internal revenue, and editor of the *Deutsches Volksblatt*. While his military career was not highly successful, Sigel deserves credit for his prompt and ardent espousal of the Union cause, which helped enormously in bringing the large German population solidly behind the Union. He published his memoirs of 1848–49 and was a prominent lecturer." See Zucker, ed., *The Forty-Eighters*, 343. See also, Don Heinrich Tolzmann, ed., *The German-American Forty-Eighters, 1848–1998* (Indianapolis: Max Kade German-American Center, Indiana University—Purdue University & Indiana German Heritage Society, 1998).

8. Regarding Ledergerber, see Kaufmann, *Germans in the American Civil War*, 306.

9. Regarding Kircher, see Henry A. Kircher, *A German in the Yankee Fatherland: The Civil War Letters of Henry A. Kircher*, ed. Earl J. Hess (Kent: Kent State University Press, 1983).

10. Kaufmann writes of Raith: "In the first large battle of the Civil War, he commanded a brigade at Shiloh on 6 April 1862. He was severely wounded in one foot. His men wanted to carry him away, but Raith forbade it. He did not want even one man able to fight to leave the battle. But the Union troops were dispersed, and Raith lay for the entire night in the woods. A fire started, and the brave man soon died in it. Next to him fell a nephew, a boy who had just immigrated from Göppingen." See Kaufmann, *Germans in the American Civil War*, 315. See also, chap. 1, n. 16.

11. Regarding Barnsbach, see Ruetenik, *Vorkämpfer*, 164–65.

12. For further information on Barnsbach, see Koerner, *Memoirs*, 1:371.

13. Regarding the Krafft family, see chap. 1.

14. For further information on the Gerke family, see Emil Mannhardt, "Die Familie Gerke," *Deutsch-Amerikanische Geschichtsblätter* 5, no. 3 (1905): 52–56.

15. Regarding Highland, see Norman Bettis, *The Swiss Community of Highland, Illinois: A Study in Historical Geography* (Macomb: Western Illinois University Pr., 1968). See also, Adolf Eugen Bandelier, "Highland, Illinois," *Der Deutsche Pionier* 11 (1879): 210–14; E. Z. Zschokke, "Caspar und Salomon Köpflie und die Gründung der Schweizerkolonie 'Highland' in Illinois," *Der Deutsche Pionier* 11 (1879): 43–50, 97–104; and "Die Schweizer-Kolonie Highland in Illinois," *Deutsch-Amerikanische Geschichtsblätter* 5, no. 1 (1905): 1–36.

16. For further information on Pestalozzi, see chap. 1, n. 27.

17. For further information on German-American contributions to Ameri-

can education, see Tolzmann, *The German-American Experience*, 386–92.

18. For further information on the Frankfurt Revolt of 1833, see Koerner, *Memoirs*, 1:216–42.

19. Regarding Alton, Illinois, see Koerner, *Memoirs*, 1:586 and 2:123.

20. By means of his discussion of Jaeger/Yager, Koerner aims to demonstrate an example of how the German heritage was being maintained by the American-born generation. For a study of German ethnic identity in an Illinois, see Timothy John Fiedler, "Ethnic Identity in Later Generations: The Case of German-Americans in Waterloo, Illinois—A Preliminary Investigation," Ph.D. Diss., Southern Illinois University at Carbondale, 1980).

21. Regarding Juncker, see Don Heinrich Tolzmann, *Cincinnati's German Heritage* (Bowie, Md.: Heritage Books, Inc., 1994), pt. 1, 62.

22. Regarding the Giessen Immigration Society, see Tolzmann, ed., *Missouri's German Heritage*, 7–8, 10, 14, 20, 30, 39, 105.

23. Some of these names are referenced in: Koerner, *Memoirs*.

24. For further information on Joseph Kircher, see Koerner, *Memoirs*, 1:142, 308, 413; and 2:145.

25. Regarding German settlement in this area of the state, see Emil Mannhardt, *Deutsche und deutsche Nachkommen in Illinois und den östlichen Nord-Central-Staaten* (Chicago: Deutsch-Amerikanische Historische Gesellschaft von Illinois, 1907).

26. For information regarding Henry Clay, including Koerner's visit with him, see Koerner, *Memoirs*, 1:348, 487, 589.

27. The *Adler* had the following motto: "Wo Freiheit thront, da ist mein Vaterland." For further information, see Arndt & Olson, *The German Language Press*, 1:105.

28. Regarding German-American views on slavery, see Kaufmann, *Germans in the American Civil War*, especially chap. 1. See also, Tucker, "Political Leadership in the Illinois-German Community, 1836–1872," 193–237.

29. For further information on Quincy, see H. A. Rattermann, "Geschichte von Adams County, Illinois und seiner Hauptstadt Quincy," *Der Deutsche Pionier* 6 (1874): 406–11, 450–54; 7 (1875) 18–23. See also, Heinrich J. Bornmann, *Bornmann's Sketches of Germans in Quincy and Adams County*, trans. Lester Holtschlag and Lenore Kimbrough (Quincy, Ill.: Great River Genealogical Society, 1999), which consists of translations of forty articles by Bornmann that appeared in the journal, *Deutsch-Amerikanische Geschichtsblätter*.

30. Regarding Dr. Stahl, see Koerner, *Memoirs*, 1:43.

31. The *Stern des Westens* was a Democratic weekly that was published from 1846 to 1848. See Arndt & Olson, *The German Language Press*, 1:103. See also, A. S. Wilderman and A. A. Wilderman, eds., *Historical Encyclopedia*, 2:855, 858.

32. Regarding Peoria, see F. B. Bek, *Eine populäre Geschichte der Stadt Peoria* (Peoria, Ill.: W. H. Wagner and Sons, 1906), as well as the following two articles: "Der erste deutsche Ansiedler von Peoria," *Der Deutsche Pionier* 3 (1871): 243–44, and Friedrich Frendel, "Geschichtliche Mittheilungen aus Peoria," *Deutsch-Amerikanische Geschichtsblätter* 1, no. 1 (1901): 22–24.

33. For further information regarding German settlements mentioned by Koerner.

34. For histories of the Chicago Germans, see Andrew Jacke Townsend, *The Germans of Chicago* (Chicago: Deutsch-Amerikanische Historische Gesellschaft von Illinois, 1932), and Rudolf Hofmeister, *The Germans of Chicago* (Champaign, Ill.: Stipes, 1976).

35. Although Koerner does not mention the German-American representative from St. Clair County by name, the person in question was actually Koerner himself.

36. Regard nativism, see Tolzmann, *The German-American Forty-Eighters*, 43.

37. The *Volksfreund* was published from 1846 to 1848. See Arndt & Olson, *The German Language Press*, 1:85–86.

38. Hermann Kriege (1820–1851) was a Forty-Eighter who, according to Ernest Bruncken, "was a writer and speaker of some ability, but very extreme views. He had been in the United States several years, but returned to Germany when the revolution broke out, and was conspicuous in the Democratic congresses held at Frankfurt and Berlin during the year 1848. Soon he returned to the United States, was for a while editor of the *Illinois Staatszeitung*, but died at New York, December 31, 1851, little more than 31 years old." See Ernest Bruncken, "German Political Refugees in the United States, 1815 to 1860," in Tolzmann, *The German-American Forty-Eighters*, 34. See also, Zucker, *The Forty-Eighters*, 312.

39. Georg Schneider (1823–1905) was a Forty-Eighter who came to America in 1849, first settling in St. Louis, where he edited the *Neue Zeit*. In 1851, he moved to Chicago to where he took over the *Illinois Staats-Zeitung*. According to Zucker, "he transformed this conservative weekly into a daily and perhaps the most influential German newspaper in the politics of the fifties. Schneider, in addition to making his influence felt as an editor, played a very aggressive part in politics. On January 29, 1854, he called a public meeting to draft resolutions against the Kansas-Nebraska Bill and took a leading part in the anti-Douglas meeting. . . .

He was one of the leaders in organizations the Republican Party in Illinois, and at the state convention in Bloomington of 1856 he proposed a plank condemning the Know-Nothing policy of discrimination against naturalized citizens. When opposition arose, Schneider appealed to Lincoln, who had appeared at the convention. The latter read the paragraph very carefully and then said: 'Gentlemen, the resolution introduced by Mr. Schneider is nothing new. It is already contained in the Declaration of Independence.' Schneider was a friend of Lincoln's, did much to win the German vote for him in 1860, and was sent by the President as a consul to Elsinore with the special mission of influencing public opinion in northern European countries in favor of the Union cause; he returned to the U.S. in 1862, after achieving considerable success. Lincoln appointed him collector of internal revenue for the Chicago district. . . . Next to Carl Schurz he was probably the foremost political leader among the Forty-Eighters." See Zucker, *The Forty-Eighters*, 339–40.

Lorenz Brentano (1813–1891) was a Forty-Eighter, who came to the United States in 1850, and lived in Pennsylvania and Michigan before moving to Chicago in 1859, where he first tried practicing law, and then edited the *Illinois Staatszeitung*. According to Zucker, "Under his sensible, forceful leadership, the paper became the leading Republican organ among the Germans of the Middle West. Through the sale of his land in Michigan, Brentano was enabled to buy a half partnership in the *Staatszeitung* when its value was not very great, and later the vastly increased circulation made him moderately wealthy. His able leadership attracted wide attention and brought him into political life: in 1862 he was elected to the Illinois State Legislature and in 1876 to Congress." See Zucker, *The Forty-Eighters*, 282.

Hermann Raster (1827–1891) was a Forty-Eighter, who came to the United States in 1851, and after writing for various German-American newspapers came to Chicago in 1867 to edit the *Staatszeitung*, and also contributed to its statue and influence. According to Zucker, he "was very active in Republican national politics and was appointed by President Grant collector of internal revenue for the Chicago district." See Zucker, *The Forty-Eighters*, 329.

40. For a biography of Hoffmann, see Lore Blanke, *Franz Arnold Hoffmann (1822–1933): Politiker auf deutschamerikanischem Kurs = Francis A. Hoffmann (1822–1903): German-American Opinion Leader* (Stuttgart: Verlag H-D Heinz, 1993).

41. Regarding DuPage County, see Emil Mannhardt, "Die Deutschen in DuPage County," *Deutsch-Amerikanische Geschichtsblätter* 1, no. 4 (1901): 33–40.

42. The *Democrat* was an English-language publication.

43. For a discussion of Hoffmann's role as a German-American leader, see Victor R. Greene, *American Immigrant Leaders, 1800–1910: Marginality and Identity* (Baltimore: Johns Hopkins University Press, 1987). Greene provides insight into Hoffmann's German-American heritage philosophy, noting that his basic message was always the same: "to be active in preserving German culture while also being an involved American." He "rocketed to ethnic preeminence, and in the process he realized early the need of his countrymen and himself to deal with Anglo-Americans. From soon after his arrival about mid century until his death almost fifty years later, he was the region's leading German-American mediator, recruiting waves of newcomers and easing their adjustment. His major means of reaching and maintaining that position, and the advice that he gave to his followers, was to learn English quickly and become active in politics." Also, Hoffmann often discussed the matter of German-American identity, and "the philosophy expressed was similar to that of other German-American mediators, to retain *Deutschtum* but still be involved citizens. . . . 'Germans we are and Germans we wish to remain in this free land.' The American society, he said, needed the cultural polish that only German could give." Hoffmann maintained that German-Americans "could make such a contribution and still be American because it is entirely possible to have a cultural identity that is separate from the civic and political one." According to Hoffmann, "they would always be true Americans, too. . . . Yet again, culture and nationality are divisible. It would not be necessary to 'expel from our hearts' the love of our Fatherland . . . the land of Hermann . . . Schiller . . . Goethe . . . Mendelssohn . . . (and) Mozart; the land that is bright and great in art and literature." German-Americans could, therefore, combine their German heritage with their American citizenship, as both complemented one another. See Greene, 54–58.

44. As head of the Land Department of the Illinois Central Railroad, Hoffmann attracted thousands of German settlers to the state of Illinois. Rudolf Hofmeister notes that Hoffmann was asked in 1862 "by the Illinois Central Railroad to colonize the area between Mattoon and Effingham, and parts of Marion, Washington and Clinton Counties with German settlers. German place names of towns in those areas, such as Sigel, Teutopolis or Germantown, and Augsburg attest to his phenomenal success. A small town in Clinton County on Route 161 perpetuates his name as well as Hoffman Estates, northwest of Chicago." See Rudolf Hofmeister, *The Germans of Chicago*, 23.

45. J. H. A. Lacher notes with regard to Hoffmann's banking accomplishments: "After the outbreak of the Civil War his bank failed owing to the repudiation of the bonds of the Southern states. Later, when he became commissioner of the Foreign Land Department of the Illinois Central Railroad, settling thousands of persons on their grants in the state, he used his large earnings mainly to liquidate obligations incident to the bank failure. In 1866 he established the International Bank, which soon took a leading place in business affairs. After the great fire of 1871, Hoffmann was chairman of the committee of bankers, through whose efforts the banks were promptly reopened, thereby averting a panic. He was likewise prominently active in restoring Chicago's necessary business establishments." See J. H. A. Lacher, "Francis Arnold Hoffmann," *Dictionary of American Biography* Base Set, American Council of Learned Societies, 1928–1936, reproduced in *Biography Resource Center* (Farmington Hills, Mich.: The Gale Group. 2004), http://galenet.galegroup.com/servlet/BioRC.

46. Greene notes regarding Hoffmann's retirement: "Even after his so-called retirement in 1875 to his Jefferson, Wisconsin home for health reasons, he continued to be a significant German guide. It was from here, at Riverside, until his death in 1903 that he wrote a long series of instructive and immensely popular articles for Germans under the pen names 'Hans and Grete Buschbauer.' The essays, later a widely circulated newspaper supplement called *Der Haus- und Bauernfreund* . . ." These essays were written in an everyday style that appealed to German-American farm families and aimed "specifically to educate them in the advanced farming techniques and practices. Actually, the pieces were engagingly written advisories counseling farm families on personal problems. The column appeared in Milwaukee, Chicago, and Buffalo newspapers with a huge readership of 150,000. As German-American observers put it at the end of his life, Hoffmann was a person of 'remarkable personal magnetism' whom German farmers 'greatly admired.'" See Greene, *Leaders*, 56.

47. For an example of one of Hoffmann's works, see his collection of advice and recipes for German-American families: *Der Familienschatz: Eine Sammlung werthvoller Rezepte und Rathschläge für den Familienkreis, die Hauswirthschaft, den Ackerbau, den Gartenbau, die Thierzucht und andere Interessen des menschlichen Lebens: Aus den Aufzeichnungen von Hans Buschbauer und anderen Schriftstellern* (Milwaukee: Geo. Brumder, 1888).

CHAPTER 3

Chicago

—Andrew Jacke Townsend

CHICAGO WAS NOT AN IMPORTANT ASSEMBLY POINT FOR GERMANS before 1850. All signs indicate that the number in the city before that date was small. To be sure the census reports for 1830 and 1840 do not give the number of Germans in Chicago, but Gustav Koerner, the able political leader of Belleville, Illinois, says that there were few.[1] Each of a number of writers who have made special efforts to obtain information about the Germans of the thirties, mentions a few names, but the sum total is very small.[2]

Mathias Meyer and John Wellmacher were two of the first Germans to settle permanently in Chicago in the early thirties; probably they were the first two.[3] Other early Germans are Friedrich Mattern, son-in-law of Meyer; Louis Malzacher; Moritz Baumgarten; Peter Cohen; Anton Berg; Clement Stose; Joseph Marbach; Karl Sauter; Charles Wesenheft; Anton Gehler; J. J. Nahler.[4] The individuals named left no great mark, although three of them became aldermen. Among the voters choosing the first mayor of the city in 1837 there were a total of twenty-nine Germans. Of these twenty-nine, ten came from the second ward and ten from the sixth, indicating the only small number of German settlements of the city at that time.[5] The number of Germans in the city was small, but it was growing and in 1839 there was elected an alderman from the second ward, Clement C. Stose.[6]

The forties saw an increase, but the number remained small. Two more German aldermen were chosen, Joseph Marbach and Karl Sauter, both of whom were born Catholic, though Sauter married in an Episcopal church and was buried in the common cemetery. This election of German Catholic aldermen indicated that the Catholic element may have been stronger than the Protestants among the Germans of this early period.[7]

By 1846 the number of Germans in Chicago was appreciably large, and they were taking their part in the economic life of the community.

Six out of twenty-five boot and shoe makers had names that were obviously German; also two out of three brewers, one out of three confectioners, two out of five men in the hat, cap, and fur business, five out of fifteen in the market business, two out of seven tobacconists, three to five out of nineteen builders, three or four out of fifteen wagon makers. There were also a few Germans who were coopers, druggists, dry goods and grocery proprietors, insurance agents, livery men, lock and white-smiths,[8] packers, ornamental and miniature painters, tailors, clothing men, blacksmiths and bakers.[9]

In the forties the Germans were also beginning to take a part collectively in public affairs. On 25 April 1840, a mass meeting of Democrats was held in a saloon to choose delegates to a state convention. Fourteen Germans were among those chosen.[10] A mass meeting was held in 1843 to praise the German-American member of the legislature from Belleville, Gustav Koerner, for his part in getting the legislation for the completion of the Illinois and Michigan canal passed. Sauter was president of the meeting, a committee of five drew appropriate resolutions, and Koerner was also otherwise praised for his services as a legislator.[11]

One of the most prominent German-Americans of the forties in the vicinity of Chicago was Francis A. Hoffmann. Influenced to leave Germany and come to Chicago by letters from a friend who had left the homeland for political reasons, he reached the United States in 1840, when he was eighteen years of age. Having had a classical training, he became a teacher at Dunkley's Grove; soon he took up the study of theology. After his ordination he was for a number of years an active Lutheran pastor, serving Dukley's Grove and vicinity, but his interests were not confined to spiritual needs of the community; he became an active, public-spirited citizen. He was editor of the *Volksfreund* for a time, later a business man in Chicago and a politician, and lieutenant governor in 1860.[12] More will be heard of him later. While not yet a citizen of Chicago proper, he was a force in the life of the community.[13]

While the German population of Chicago was small before 1850, after that date it shot ahead by leaps and bounds. It seems certain that the largest single factor in the rapid increase was the failure of the revolutionary movements in the German states, a story unnecessary to tell here, fascinating as that story is. It is sufficient to remember that the rebels did fail in their two great objectives, the establishment of liberty in Germany, and German unity. In the wake of these movements a reaction to a more conservative government took place, forcing the leaders to suffer prosecution for treason or to flee. Many did flee to all parts of Europe; some remained in Switzerland; France soon became an uncongenial place for them, as it too was in the throes of reaction; England, as ever, became a haven for many of them, where a number of them gathered who lived in daily hope that a chance in fortune would make possible their return to Germany to complete their work. It is, of course, natural that many should be attracted to the republic in the west where at least in theory the principles of "liberty, equality, and fraternity" prevailed. These Forty-Eighters came, then in considerable numbers, and became American citizens, eager to take active part in our problems.[14]

Besides leaders themselves many others left Germany because they were in sympathy with the movement. Some of them had taken no active part in the revolts, but political conditions in Germany were unpleasant for them. Examples of such men who came to Chicago were Frederick Wacker, Sr. and Henry Claussenius.[15]

As at all times, the economic motive entered largely into the migration. Forty-Eighters themselves would naturally go to places where the economic opportunities were sufficient for making a livelihood. Some Forty-Eighters, even though pardoned, found it hard to make a living in Germany, because of their radical views.[16] For those who were not leaders of the revolutionary movements, but who were dissatisfied with political conditions, the economic motive was of course an important one driving them to the United States.

Conditions remained favorable for heavy emigration from Germany throughout the decade, though the first half of the sixties saw a decline due to the Civil War. In 1850 the German population of Chicago was 5,035; that of Illinois was 38,160. In 1860 there were 22,227 in Chicago and 130, 804 in Illinois.[17]

There were several factors causing a large number of the German immigrants of this period to come to Illinois; for example, Friedrich Hecker, leader of the revolt in Baden, led many to the state, most of them reaching the German settlement in the vicinity of Belleville, and guidebooks, such as those of John Mason Peck and others, pictured the advantages of the state. Early in 1854 some Chicago businessmen sponsored a movement for an office of commissioner of immigration to travel in Germany and direct emigration to Illinois, a step opposed by the *Illinois Staats-Zeitung* as a sharp business and political maneuver. Such a commissioner was not chosen, but the Chicago Germans did organize a society for the protection of German immigrants, the German Aid Society of Chicago. In this they were following the example of the Irish. With a full time agent to look after the interests of the newly arrived immigrants, it must be true that many stayed here who would not otherwise have done so. The various agencies of German culture— the German theater, musical clubs, churches, parochial schools, and newspapers—must have attracted many also. The economic development of the city drew people, not only from other parts of the United States, but German artisans and laborers as well.[18]

Not nearly all, not even a majority of the immigrants of the fifties were active Forty-Eighters. Nevertheless it is fair to call this the period of the Forty-Eighters, for this group occupied the center of the stage. Most of the Germans here before 1850 were of the artisan class, therefore, relatively uneducated. On the other hand, a large share of the Forty-Eighters were university men or at least men of considerable education.[19] Quite naturally, by virtue of their superior education, the Forty-Eighters assumed the leadership over the German group, becoming its chief spokesmen. For example, they became the newspaper editors.[20] A study of the careers of certain typical Forty-Eighters will further show how they became leaders of their people in Chicago.

Georg Schneider, a native of Bavaria, a journalist, having participated in the Bavarian revolutionary movement, fled first to France, then to the United States in 1849. Though he lived for a short time in Cleveland, he started his career in St. Louis, where, together with his brother, he established the *Neue Zeit*, a liberal paper with anti-slavery tendencies. After destruction of the plant by fire in 1850, Schneider became professor of foreign languages and literature in a college near St. Louis. About this time, Hoeffgen, owner and publisher of the *Illinois Staats-Zeitung* in Chicago, was in search of a partner and editor; to this post he called Schneider in 1851. In a few months the then tri-weekly paper was converted into a daily. In his new place, Schneider was in a position to influence his fellow German-Americans. Liberal and anti-slavery advocate that he was, he went into the fight with the vigor characteristic of the crusading Forty-Eighters, taking an extremely prominent part in the anti-Nebraska struggle. He believed in the nascent Republican Party, but he was unwilling that it fall in the hand those former Whigs who had Know-Nothing tendencies. Lincoln agreed with him, and their joint activity resulted in the recognition of the rights of the foreign-born citizens by the state convention of the party, and example followed by the national Republican convention in 1856 and again in 1860. His support of Lincoln after his nomination was whole-hearted, though he had been for Seward, as had been most of the Germans. Lincoln appointed Schneider consul to Denmark in 1861, in reality to carry on Union propaganda among the states of Northern Europe.

Because back at home the *Illinois Staats-Zeitung* was bitterly criticizing Lincoln for being too mild, Schneider was forced to return. But when he could not quiet the paper, he sold his share. In his later life, Schneider was collector of internal revenue for four years, president of a state savings institution, president of the National Bank of Illinois, elector-at-large on the Garfield ticket, president of the German Society for the Protection of Immigrants. He declined the ministry to Switzerland in 1877. He was an advocate of Civil Service Reform. It is thus seen that Schneider's public career was confined chiefly to the decade 1851–1861, after which time he lost much of his influence. Perhaps his influence was greater in political circles throughout the nation than among the Germans of Chicago. Yet it seems certain that the decade of his control of the *Staats-Zeitung* must have done much to lead his fellow German-Americans in the direction of anti-slavery.[21]

Caspar Butz, a native of Westphalia, was another Forty-Eighter who became prominent in Chicago. He was a man of good education, fond of literature, in fact, something of a poet. For a time he was a clerk and a commercial traveler in Germany. During the revolution he was editor of a strong democratic paper and a participant in the rising in Rhenish Bavaria. He fled first to London, but soon reached Chicago. He life was divided between his mercantile business, the pursuit of literature (he was writing continually), and politics. In 1864 and 1865 he edited *Deutsch-Amerikanische Monatshefte*. This was a popular scientific and literary journal. All his life he contributed to leading journals. Butz entered enthusiastically into the new Republican Party and was a popular and effective campaign speaker in 1856, 1858, and 1860, but was a strong critic of Lincoln during the war and an advocate of Fremont in 1864. He was very active in the Liberal Republican movement in 1872, and a leading member of the convention in Cincinnati that year.

In local politics, besides being a member of the legislature in 1858, he was later clerk of the Superior Court. Beginning in 1870, he served for a time as member of the Board of Penitentiary Commissioners at Joliet. Butz's importance lay in the field of political leadership. He was usually somewhat radical, especially in his opposition to Lincoln.[22]

Dr. Ernst Schmidt was born in 1830 in Oberfranken. His father, a druggist, gave him a good education at the gymnasium at Nürnberg and at the universities in Würzburg, Zürich, Heidelberg, and München. Ernst was a student all his life. He was a radical, socialistic in point of view. After an active part in the revolutionary movement, he was pardoned through influence of relatives on his mother's side. He went to work with a will and took his doctor of medicine examination at the age of twenty-two. He became privatdozent at the University of Würzburg, and in a short time he was physician of the university hospital. Though Schmidt's professional ability could not be gainsaid, he was looked upon with distrust because of his radical views, as a result of which he failed to receive his expected advance to a professorship; two or three other positions also failed to materialize.

Then Schmidt decided to strike out for the United States, where, he hoped, the freer atmosphere would enable him to pursue his profession more successfully. He married and lived in London for six months in order to perfect himself professionally and in English. He chose Chicago as his place of residence, where he found numerous friends from his revolution days and practice came to him readily at first. But even in the United States, the radical was looked on askance. Subordinating his socialistic views, he became a rabid abolitionist. At the memorial celebration after the execution of John Brown, Schmidt made an address in German. This lost him many patients, so he decided again to hunt a new field. In St. Louis he became a teacher in a school founded by German physicians. Soon, however, the war broke out, and Schmidt became a regimental physician of the Third Missouri Volunteer Regiment, where he stayed in this position till his health broke down. His hearing was permanently impaired.[23]

He tried his fortunes in Chicago again, where his radical beliefs were now welcomed. A large practice followed, but Schmidt devoted much to charity. For many years he was head physician of the Alexian Brothers Hospital and of the Michael Reese Hospital. He was chosen coroner in 1864. It seems, however, that certain interests wanted him to rob the graves in the cemeteries. This he refused to do, and resigned his office in disgust. Schmidt then revisited Europe, where he helped put down cholera and a small epidemic. He had an offer of a full professorship at Würzburg with his rank determined by reckoning his years of absence as if he had been there, but America offered him, he thought, better opportunities. Schmidt's old radicalism remained, at least in large part. As Socialist Labor Candidate for Mayor in 1879, he drew many votes, probably more from the Republican than the Democratic candidate; he thus may be credited with having helped to elect the senior Carter H. Harrison for the first time.

Schmidt was organizer and treasurer of the defense committee for the anarchists after the Haymarket Square riot.[24] But by this time Schmidt's respect among the people was so great that he lost very little practice in spite of the strong public opinion against the anarchists. Schmidt gave four sons to the life of the city. All have attained reasonable prominence and success. Dr. Schmidt stands as typical of the well trained, educated Forty-Eighter; he was ever literary in his inclinations. He was always a radical, important especially in Chicago as an abolitionist and a socialist. But "der rote Schmidt," so-called from his red beard, did not spend most of his time in political or other propaganda. He devoted his life to his profession, but was always interested in and even active in public affairs as well.[25]

Lorenz Brentano, Hermann Raster, and Wilhelm Rapp were three Forty-Eighters who played a great part in the life of the *Illinois Staats-Zeitung* in the sixties and seventies. They, like their predecessor, Georg Schneider, were typical of the Forty-Eighters in journalism. Brentano became part owner and member of the editorial staff in 1859, was made chief editor in 1862, at which time he bought out Schneider's share, and sold out to A. C. Hesing in 1867. He was a well-educated man, a master of the subject of law as well as of journalism. He died in 1891 after several years of poor health.[26]

Hermann Raster was a trained student in philosophy, philology, and history, having attended the universities of Leipzig and Berlin. He became first editor of the *Illinois Staats-Zeitung* upon the retirement of Brentano in 1867, but had previously won a reputation as a writer. His editorial writings appealed to the intellectual; his style was considered excellent. Like most Forty-Eighters, he took a prominent part in the public life and was something of a figure in the national Republican Party. He died in Europe in 1891.

Wilhelm Rapp was from Württemberg. He had been a student of theology in a Protestant Seminary at Tübingen and had been active in public life, especially at the time of the revolutionary activities of 1848–49. He was tried on the charge of high treason, but was acquitted. His chief journalistic activities besides those on the *Illinois Staats-Zeitung* were as editor of the *Turnzeitung*, 1855–56, and of the *Wecker* in Baltimore 1857–61 and 1866–72. He was always interested in Turner affairs, and at one time was president of the Turnerbund. After 1872, he was second

editor and co-manager of the *Staats-Zeitung*. While Raster appealed especially to the intellectual class, Rapp wrote more for the masses . . . . He
was less in political life than either Brentano or Raster, but he was a
prominent figure of the city till his death in 1907.

Frederick Wacker and Henry Claussenius were men who, while not
strictly Forty-Eighters, came to the United States chiefly because they
were dissatisfied with political conditions in Germany. Wacker's chief
line of business was that of a brewer; he may be regarded as typical of the
German leadership in that important industry. He was also one of the
originators of the German singing society and of the old sharp shooter's
association. Claussenius was also interested in the German singing society, as well as in the German Relief and Aid Society, and the Germania
Society. He was a draftsman, a consul, and then in the passenger ticket,
foreign exchange, and collecting house business. These two men were
successful businessmen and at the same time to some extent leaders of
their people.[29]

Since the Forty-Eighters were leaders of their pepole, it will be interesting to inquire what their various points of view were. In one sense
Forty-Eighters were radicals. Politically they wished the overthrow of des-
potism in Europe. It is natural that radicals on economic organization
should to some extent be drawn into the movement, but the most consistent followers of Karl Marx were little likely to waste their time on
what seemed to be purely a political struggle. Examples of socialists
drawn into the ranks of the revolutionist movement are Karl Heinzen
and Friedrich Hassaurek[30] who believed that the land should be free,
wages increased, and rich men be taxed to the utmost.[31] Besides that,
they wanted the federal state without a president, abolition of slavery,
employment of German teachers in the schools, even establishment of a
German university at the expense of the government. They wished that
the United States would intervene in favor of the European republics.
They were especially hostile to the papacy and the priesthood. These
views were not typical of a large number, but only of a very noisy minor-
ity, many of who had little patience with the existing social customs.[32]

There were some socialists in Chicago, but the number was not
large; for instance some of the German Turners here were at first socialistic. Established in 1852, they had no doubt had some Forty-Eighters
among them.[33] Dr. Ernst Schmidt was the best-known socialist among
the Forty-Eighters, although his public activities in his first years were
devoted more to abolition.[34] Most of the German radicals came later to

Chicago in the seventies and the eighties.[35] Those who were socialistic or otherwise extremely radical became more conservative after a time.

The Civil War seemed to settle many of the Forty-Eighters, although how much credit should be given to the Civil War and how much to the fact that the men were getting older, is problematical. But it is indisputable that they became more conservative. The German Turners were no longer predominantly socialistic, though there remained some local organizations of that character.[36] The Forty-Eighters had revolted against authority and some were atheistic, or at least agnostic, rejected the authority of the church and held the papacy in contempt.[37] The Forty-Eighters were leaders in many phases of life among their people, but we find them absent in church leadership.[38]

It was in the realm of political life that the leadership of the Forty-Eighters was especially marked. The early Germans were for the most part Democrats, for the Whigs were suspected of nativism. When the Forty-Eighters arrived in the United States they, too, at first tended to affiliate with the Democrats. They followed the example of the earlier Germans, although strongly conscious of their own views as they were, they would scarcely admit that they were doing it. They liked the sound "Democratic"; it seemed in harmony with their political views, and as new immigrants they too were afraid of the Whig nativism. As proof of the Democratic leanings of the Germans, the German mass meeting for Douglas in 1852 in Chicago can be cited. But Forty-Eighter adherence to the Democratic Party was short-lived.[39]

Know-Nothingism was the first great force in opposition to which German sentiment was united. The Irish and the "Dutch" were looked at askance by those who regarded themselves as the only real Americans. The Germans were not willing to stand by and allow the movement to proceed without registering their discontent. At all times German-Americans took a prominent part in combating the movement.[40]

In Massachusetts there was an attempt to amend the state constitution to prohibit the vote to naturalized citizens until two years after their naturalization, which aroused the ire of German-Americans throughout the country. At a meeting held in Cincinnati in 1858 to fight the amendment, the Forty-Eighter, Anneke, of Chicago, was invited to assist in issuing a manifesto. Though the manifesto was not actually drawn up, the occasion was one for uniting German-American opinion.[41]

The Republican Party was a mixture of antislavery Whigs, anti-Nebraska Democrats, and Free-Soilers. Since the Whigs were an impor-

tant element of the new party, what attitude should Republicans therefore take as to immigrants? Was the vote of the Germans, who by 1856
were tending toward the Republican Party, important enough to offset
the possible loss of Know-Nothing sympathizers if nativistic sentiment
should be alienated? The Republican Party in Illinois decided that it was
worthwhile to please the Germans rather than the nativists. For this,
Georg Schneider was largely responsible. Likewise the national Republican Party in 1856 and 1860 took a stand against nativism. There is no
doubt that strong German opinion dictated these positions.[42]

In spite of the action of the Republican Party, the Democrats were
freer from Know-Nothingism than the Republicans. The Irish Catholics
were Democrats, and the party could not afford to antagonize them. For
this reason the German Catholics largely remained Democratic.[43]

The Forty-Eighters came to the United States enthusiastic supporters of their own ideals. In free America, they thought, these ideals were
already being tried out; but the slavery controversy, in the midst of
which they landed, seemed like disillusionment to them. It was seen that
even in this country, work was to be done, that the millennium did not
exist even here. Their idealistic sense was appealed to, so they threw
themselves into the struggle with youthful vim. This conflict helped to
Americanize them in that it substituted interest in an American question instead of a European one. The Forty-Eighters were, therefore,
always antislavery; usually vehemently supporters of the cause.[44] German-Americans throughout the country became prominent anti-slavery
agitators.[45] Butz, Schneider, and Schmidt took up the cudgels in Chicago.[46]

It was the Kansas-Nebraska bill that called forth the first strong German sentiment. One of the first mass-meetings against the bill was one
held by the Germans of Chicago, 29 January 18544, for which Georg
Schneider and Georg Hillgaertner, also of the *Illinois Staats-Zeitung*
signed the call.[47] Another protest meeting was held 28 February in Chicago. Though some Germans signed the call, this one was chiefly American in composition. On 16 March, a mass meeting of Germans was
held in South Market Hall, probably called at the behest of Edward
Schlaeger, editor of the *Deutsch-Amerikaner*. Francis A. Hoffmann,
Schlaeger, and James Breck spoke. Strong resolutions denouncing Douglas and the bill were drawn up. After the meeting Douglas was burned
in effigy by part of the crowd.[48]

Why did the Germans so consistently oppose the Kansas-Nebraska

Bill? According to Paul Selby they felt that the slavery question threatened the principles upon which the Union was founded.[49] The refugees from Europe were especially strong for the Union. They felt also that white and slave labor could not exist together in the Far West without making ordinary labor impossible for the Germans. Furthermore, the South had opposed two policies in which the Germans were particularly interested: the Germans welcomed The Homestead Acts because they were land hungry, and recognition of the revolutionary governments in Europe. That the Germans could be appealed to on the grounds that occupation of the new land would be well nigh impossible if slaves were allowed there is borne out by the Appeal to the Independent Democrats. In the Appeal the German and other foreign language newspapers were asked specifically to stress this argument.[50] The Clayton Amendment to the original bill in March particularly roused the Germans. While the original bill granted the suffrage in Kansas both to citizens and to those who had declared their intention of becoming citizens, the Clayton amendment confined it to citizens. The Germans regarded this as nativistic. They also argued that the pro-slavery men were afraid to give them the vote in the Far West.

It seems that the opposition of the Germans to the original bill granted the suffrage in Kansas both to citizens and to those who had declared their intention of becoming citizens, the Clayton amendment confined it to citizens. The Germans regarded this as nativistic. They also argued that the pro-slavery men were afraid to give them the vote in the Far West. It seems that the opposition of the Germans to the Kansas-Nebraska Bill was almost unanimous. The *Illinois Staats-Zeitung* strongly opposed the bill, as has been already noted.[51] Nearly every German paper of the state was against the Kansas-Nebraska bill. It is worthy to note that these were edited by Forty-Eighters.[52] The anti-Nebraska views of the Germans led them to flock to the Republican party in large numbers.

Carl Schurz, the Forty-Eighter, and Gustav Koerner, a political exile of the thirties and a prominent Democrat of Belleville, Illinois, typify the Germans throughout the country. Butz, Pruessing, Schneider—in fact all Forty-Eighters of Chicago about whom any record can be found—became Republicans.[53] Among the Germans, only the Catholics remained Democrats in any large numbers. The rest seem to have voted with the Republican Party from 1856 to 1860. In Illinois Koerner and Schneider had a considerable part in the formation of the state Republican organization. Schneider was also a member of the Republican National Convention, both in 1856 and 1860.[54] Germans became prominent campaigners in 1856, 1858, and 1860. Schurz and Koerner were very important ones outside of Chicago.[55] Francis A. Hoffmann and Caspar Butz from Chicago were considered in demand; both earned names for themselves by their active work for the party.[56]

The *Illinois Staats-Zeitung*, as would be expected from the point of view of Schneider, was strongly Republican.[57] It was for Fremont in 1856.[58] This was the attitude of the Germans generally, even before his nomination.[59] In 1860 the paper was for Seward, as were indeed the most of the Germans. But Lincoln received its warm support during the campaign. The German attitude in the summer and fall of 1860 seems to have been quite generally that of the *Staats-Zeitung*.[60] Yet the strength of the German Catholics must not be under emphasized. They formed a considerable part of the total German vote.[61]

The importance of the German vote was recognized in Illinois in the framing of the state tickets. Francis A. Hoffmann of Chicago was nominated by the Republicans and elected Lieutenant Governor. The Democrats also courted the German vote by nominating Bernard Arnzten for state auditor.[62]

No attempt will be made to detail the part of the Chicago Germans in the military events of the Civil war because the chief interest here is in the points of view that they held. Many Illinois Germans enlisted in Hecker's First or Second regiment. The Forty-third Infantry was an independent regiment recruited by Gustav Koerner. Other Germans joined the Missouri German regiments because the Illinois regiments were not promptly organized. However, the Chicago Jaeger, the Turner Cadets, and the Lincoln Rifles had German organizations ready from the start. It was estimated that six thousand Germans from Illinois were in the federal army by June 1862,[63] the Germans of Chicago kept on enlisting throughout the war, and as late as 1864 a German regiment was recruited in the city.[64]

If the Germans supported Lincoln generally in 1860, it cannot be said that all of them were always his admirers during the war. They were radicals on the question of slavery; from the outbreak of hostilities they thought the war should be fought to end slavery. The Germans seem to have favored Fremont's attempted emancipation move. For instance, a large mass meeting of Chicago Germans was held at North Market Hall, 10 November 1861. Caspar Butz showed his radical anti-Lincoln tendencies in a speech that he made moving the appointment of a committee to draft resolutions. Support of an loyalty to the government were promised, but the administration was condemned severely for displaying "nothing but indecision and vacillation and a desire to shirk the true issue of the contest," the suppression of slavery.

Fremont's emancipation proclamation, though "unfortunately mutilated by the order of the President." Was hailed as "a harbinger of better days and the surest means to bring this war to a speedy close." The removal of Fremont, which "incredible news," they "were loath to believe," caused them to bow their "heads in silence before a proceeding so unparalleled in history and so detrimental to the best interests of the country." The charges against Fremont were improved and "in every word" bore "the stamp of the malignity of the accuser." People think his (Fremont's) only crime is that he stood in the way of the ambition of other men. They resolved that, "by the act of the removal of Gen. Fremont" they had "lost all confidence in the administration-heads and that the people" would "hold them responsible for the evil consequences." Cheers were given for Fremont, the next president of the United States.[65]

The *Illinois Staats-Zeitung* had come out for Fremont for president nearly two months before this meeting. In an editorial announcing their advocacy of Fremont, they said that "through proclaiming him as future President, the people will protest in the most vigorous manner against the weak-hearted and weak-sighted acts of the present government."[66] In subsequent editorials, Lincoln was criticized severely for his refusal to abolish slavery. Many issues had articles on Fremont, his conduct, his ability, and his relations with Lincoln; and for nearly a year the *Staats-Zeitung* regularly had on its editorial page the caption, "John C. Fremont, our next presidential candidate."[67]

Lincoln was assailed for his refusal to discharge Cameron, in answer to which the president defended himself by claiming that the demand was due to the prejudice of the people, but the *Staats-Zeitung* bitterly attacked this attitude.[68] In the summer of 1861 there was an editorial on vigor in the war.[69] The tendency to compromise was deplored, as also the inactivity in Virginia and elsewhere. While by the fall of 1862 the opposition to Lincoln was quieting down somewhat, an editorial criticizes him for his attempt to do everything by himself and for not listening to advice, especially from his cabinet, and alleged it to be "one of the causes of Lincoln's mal-administration."[70]

Schneider had been forced to come home from his consular position to try to quell the noise against Lincoln made by the paper in which he was so largely interested. He was not as successful as he had hoped to be and as a consequence sold out his share to Brentano. Nevertheless in the fall of 1862 the paper stopped printing Fremont's name as next candidate for the presidency; after the emancipation proclamation there was cautious support of many of his policies; in 1864 the *Staats-Zeitung* was a warm supporter of Lincoln. In 1862 the *Staats-Zeitung* called for the election of the Union ticket, the full carrying out of the emancipation proclamation, all means to be used to put down the rebellion, and the south to bear a large part of the cost of the war.[71] The *Illinois Staats-Zeitung* was not pleased with the policy of conscription in the spring of 1863. However, it did not advise against obeying the law.[72]

With the strong views of a large number of Germans on the question of slavery it is not surprising that the emancipation proclamation was approved by the *Staats-Zeitung*. In an editorial it said that the old union of Republicans and Douglas Democrats had given way to a new party of abolitionists and unionists.[73] Germans of the city joined with others in an emancipation demonstration in the Metropolitan Hall on 12 January 1863 (though an exclusively German meeting was first planned), at which appropriate speeches were made and resolutions drawn up.[74]

In the election of 1864 the Germans were distinctly divided, especially at the first of the campaign. Many continued to distrust Lincoln and denounced him. A German radical meeting was held in Chicago, 26 March 1864, in Ullich's block, North Clark Street. Ernst Pruessing acted as chairman and Caspar Butz, another Chicago Forty-Eighter, and visitors from Missouri and Wisconsin were speakers. Lincoln was assailed as a half-radical, his emancipation proclamation was called double-dealing because it had to be appealed to the Supreme Court, and Fremont was enthusiastically endorsed for Pesident. Butz was especially bitter in attacking "the weakest and worst man that ever filled the Presidential chair." In fact, said Butz, Lincoln had "no more sense than a child," and was "a perfect imbecile." The resolutions condemned electing any man for more than one term, called for Lincoln's withdrawal, and proclaimed Fremont as the first choice of the group.[75]

Butz and Pruessing continued their opposition to Lincoln. The *Illinois Staats-Zeitung* was a bitter opponent of Butz, claiming that he held the position of deputy clerk of the Superior Court as a sinecure, that he had sold himself for it, and that his opposition to Lincoln was factional. Pruessing took Butz's part in the controversy.[76] Butz, Pruessing, and Ernst Schmidt of Chicago were among the signers to the call of a radical meeting in Cleveland to be held 31 May 1864. In the convention that nomination Fremont, Pruessing was vice-president and Butz served as a member both of the committee on permanent organization and of the committee on resolutions.[77] The *Illinois-Staats-Zeitung*, however, continued its strong support of Lincoln in spite of his mistakes.[78]

It was probably at the time of the election that the Germans on the whole supported Lincoln. The factional opposition was lost in enthusiasm over the Union victories. The candidacy of Fremont proved to be a fiasco; but the radical Germans could not support the mild Democratic candidate, McClellan, though some Illinois Germans were reported to be for him.[79] The *Chicago Tribune* assigned an important share of the Union victory to the German vote.[80]

Of course, the problem of reconstruction interested the Germans. In 1864, the proposed Ashley bill provided for military districts under authority of the federal government, the ten per cent plan with specific reservations as to franchise, and the repeal of southern laws against the Negroes. Further, it set limits according to which men disloyal and unfriendly to emancipation could be sworn officials; it extended the repeal of slavery to Tennessee and the expected districts of Louisiana and Eastern Virginia. The paper favored this plan, proclaimed by the *Staats-Zeitung* as the Lincoln plan with modifications. Colonization and deportations of Negroes were opposed.[81]

If Lincoln's plan was favored with reservations and modifications, not so that of Andrew Johnson. He was the target of bitter opposition by the Chicago Germans. A mass meeting of German Republicans and war democrats of anti-Johnson views was held in the winter of 1866 to consider questions of reconstruction.[82] The *Illinois Staats-Zeitung* approved the calm, yet worthy and firm attitudes of Congress toward "the shameless attacks of the president."[83] In June 1866, a rumor was afloat that the administration was about to try to win over Hesing, editor of the *Staats-Zeitung*, either by appointment of himself to office or by throwing its weight toward the election of Hesing's colleague, Brentano, to Congress. The *Staats-Zeitung* regarded this as absurd. The only way for that paper to follow Johnson was for him "to go hand in hand with the radical majority of Congress."[84] This same organ of German opinion came out many times for the impeachment and removal of Johnson.[85] In February 1868, an advertisement of a German mass meeting to urge the removal of Johnson was published in the *Staats-Zeitung*.[86]

Since the Germans so bitterly opposed Johnson, it is to be expected that they would favor Grant in 1868, which, in fact, they did, if the *Illinois Staats-Zeitung* is a fair measure of German opinion. Even as early as the fall of 1867, Grant was mentioned, his good qualities praised, and he was spoken of favorably for the presidency.[87] As radical Republicans, Germans naturally went with the party. In 1872, however, the story was far different. The incompetence of Grant, and the corruptness of many connected with the party machine, led to a formidable movement against his reelection, in which many Germans took part.

Some of the most conspicuous German leaders of the Liberal Republican movement were Carl Schurz, Gustav Koerner, the Liberal Republican nominee for governor of Illinois, and Rummell, nominee for secretary of state. Caspar Butz of Chicago was an active leader in the new party.[88] The *Chicago Tribune* estimated that of the forty thousand Germans in Illinois outside of Chicago, "we have the most trustworthy evidences that six-sevenths are for Greeley and Koerner. Five thousand more German Republicans in Chicago will vote the same ticket." It seems that the Germans of Illinois did quite generally support Greeley. Possibly they were influenced to do so by the places of Koerner and Rummell on the ticket. However, the *Illinois Staats-Zeitung* opposed the Liberal Republicans. It agreed with Schurz in his opposition to Grant's San Domingo policy and in his demand for civil service reform; but it did not think the situation would be remedied by a new party. It may be worthy to note that Caspar Butz was an old enemy of the *Staats-Zeitung*, and that he was on the other side. At any rate, it stood for Grant throughout the campaign. Although the majority of Germans voted, they were considerably divided.[89]

In 1876 also the Germans were divided. German mass meetings were held in July, both in support of Hayes and of Tilden. A German-American Tilden Reform Club was formed. In support of Hayes were Wilhelm Vocke, Richard Michaelis, Ernst Pruessing, Lorenz Brentano, Georg Schneider. Brentano was a campaign speaker, and Butz, candidate for city clerk. The *Illinois Staats-Zeitung* claimed to be neutral; certainly it professed no enthusiasm for Hayes. In fact, early in the summer he was spoken of as a second Franklin Pierce, rather than a second Lincoln. The *National Demokrat* favored Tilden in repeated editorials throughout the year. This paper opposed Hayes on the grounds that he was temperance and a Know-Nothing advocate and that he was supported by those elements. There was undoubtedly a tendency at this time on the part of some Germans to leave the Republican Party because it was believed to favor temperance legislation, though the tendency was more marked in local than in national politics.[90]

In 1880 there was no special German appeal. Many Germans who had voted outside the Republican Party for a time returned. The *Illinois Staats-Zeitung* was for Garfield.[91]

The local question of this period on which the Germans took the most decided stand was that of temperance. Everywhere they resented the attempts of their "puritanical" fellow citizens to interfere with their personal habits on Sunday or at any other time. On 8 June 1871, a German antitemperance meeting was held in a Turner hall. The following winter a bill was passed by the legislature of Illinois, known as the "Ohio Temperance Law." This bill made the owner of a store where liquor was sold responsible for all damages caused by drunken men. This was opposed by the *Illinois Staats-Zeitung* with a threat that the Germans would bolt the Republican Party if the bill were not vetoed. A German mass meeting was held at which strong resolutions against the law were drawn up.

Likewise, Germans opposed all efforts at Sunday closing. When Mayor Medill attempted to enforce the Sunday closing law in 1872, he was assailed by the *Illinois Staats-Zeitung* with great bitterness. This paper recommended that saloonkeepers keep the front doors closed and wait on their customers as usual. Following the first Sunday of the attempt, the *Tribune* claimed that the law-abiding saloonkeepers kept the law no matter how much they regretted it. At a German mass meeting 24 October 1872, it was resolved to work for "the repeal of such laws as are in restraint of individual freedom;" to unite on candidates for state, city, and county offices favorable to their views; to request the council and mayor not to enforce the law that had been a dead letter; to ask suspension of enforcement till a new council could be elected; and to call on the German papers to strike from the list of endorsed candidates those not favoring the repeal of temperance and Sunday closing laws. The *Chicago Tribune*, while generally favoring the mayor, who was a stockholder in it, suggested that beer might be excepted from the operation of the law for the sake of the Germans.[93]

The Germans determined to make temperance a test question in 1873. In April the *Illinois Staats-Zeitung* opposed the reelection of

Lawrence to the superior court on account of temperance fanaticism. There were repeated editorials in that paper in the spring of 1873 on the subject of temperance. In September the temperance law was called a kind of Know-Nothingism. The anti-temperance forces claimed to stand for an honest, economical city and county administration; for temperance and morals to be promoted by good rearing, not by coercive laws; for official inspection of drinks and confiscation of those impure and unwholesome; for preservation of the services of God on Sunday, but no coercion; against tavern concessions to people of bad repute; for reorganization of the local police; against imprisonment for violations of city ordinances where these violations were punishable by fine; for rejection of the state law holding the owner responsible for offenses of the tenant instead of the drunkard; for law and order, but not for intolerance and tyranny; and for independence of judicial elections from party questions.[94]

In order to participate in the local elections, the so-called "People's Party" was started in May 1873. Under its auspices an open air mass meeting, attended by about fifteen thousand, was held on 4 October. Anton C. Hesing of the *Illinois Staats-Zeitung*, was the German leader of the movement. The Germans combined with the Irish, headed by O'Hara, in this attempt to put in a "wet" administration. The *Chicagoer Freie Presse* in general supported the Hesing candidates, but demurred in specific cases where it thought the "Citizens" candidates were better if the offices had nothing to do with temperance. The *Illinois Staats-Zeitung* naturally favored the whole ticket. It appealed to the German voters to register and to aliens to be naturalized. In return, the *Chicago Tribune*, which opposed the "Sample Room ticket," charged that Hesing was engineering fraudulent naturalizations of hundreds and even thousands of foreigners.[95]

The People's Party was triumphant; Colvin was chosen mayor, O'Hara, treasurer, the city and county candidates of the party were successful, and a majority of the council gained. The *Illinois Staats-Zeitung* was exultant, claiming defensively that the election was fair; that the party was not a "subjugation of the Americans by a horde of foreigners," but "a victory of honorable and true American citizens over a smaller number of American citizens;" and that improvement in the city government would follow. Likewise the *Freie Presse* gloated over the victory over the "puritanical nativists and Know-Nothings."[96]

The question of attempt to enforce Sunday-closing and temperance laws by the city administration was settled for a long time to come. German and Irish liberalism had won. Many Germans returned to the fold of the Republican Party. But the German-Irish combination was not entirely dead. In the summer of 1875 the *Chicago Tribune* charged a foreign Know-Nothingism by those two groups, referring to their attempt in the council to defeat an American born man for city marshal. The leaders of the People's Party became publicly Democratic, thus disgusting the Liberal Republicans, according to the opinion of the *Freie Presse*.[97]

It had been noted that the Germans tended to vote on the temperance question in local elections, but in national elections to regard national issues, which even for some time after the Civil War were chiefly questions growing out of it.[98] Yet by 1875 there was undoubtedly a tendency for some Germans to be alienated permanently from the Republican Party because they believed it fanatical on temperance.

Although the following editorial comment of a German newspaper is couched in rather extreme terms, it is probably fairly typical of what Germans regarded as Puritanism:

> The nation owes nothing to Puritanism. We owe our religious freedom to Catholic Maryland, our free states' existence to the freethinking men of Virginia, Pennsylvania, etc., standing at the top of European culture. The day was an unfortunate one in which New England attained power in the hypocritical role of champion of humanity and could lay its hands, soiled with usury on the necks of the people.[99]

Mr. Hesing's anti-temperance propaganda was not entirely disinterested, for he was not only a newspaper editor, but he had financial interests in a distillery. In June 1876 he, in conjunction with a number of others, was convicted of conspiracy to defraud the government in a Chicago Whiskey Ring scandal. Hesing's punishment was set at a five thousand dollar fine and imprisonment in the county jail for two years. There was a feeling abroad in the city that Hesing was not as much to blame as the others. A meeting, largely of Germans, was held in Romer's Hall, 45 North Clark Street, in sympathy for Hesing. They thought the penalty of two years was extreme and requested the president to pardon him or reduce his punishment. Petitions for his pardons were signed by twelve thousand citizens of Chicago, another by six thousand and still another by many from outside the city. The president commuted his term to three months on 23 September. As his time was up, he was released the following day.[100]

The Germans in America were, of course, greatly interested in all national questions. As Germans, they took part collectively in some local struggles. It would be altogether unnatural, however, if Germans of the country should not also notice the foreign relations of the United States and foreign questions in general. The attitude of the *Illinois Staats-Zeitung* was probably fairly typical; in others, opinion was divided.

In 1864 Lincoln's policy in Mexico was approved. The *Staats-Zeitung* was glad to see that more attention was being paid to Louis Napoleon's designs there; but Lincoln's policy was defended against the attacks of the anti-Lincoln Germans because the rebellion must be put down first. The paper also disapproved the desire of some for the annexation of Mexico.[101]

At the same time the new Prussian premier, Otto von Bismarck, was engaged in his famous constitutional struggle with the Reichstag. Secretary of State Seward could have no official part, but the *Illinois Staats-Zeitung* deduced from correspondence laid before Congress that he was on the side of the people in the struggle, and that the United States desired the unity and freedom of Germany. This attitude was, of course, approved.[102] Two years later the *Staats-Zeitung* decried the "Ich bin der Staat" attitude of the Prussian king.

In 1864 the policy of Austria and Prussia toward Schleswig-Holstein was called treacherous. It was said to be designed to end the national and liberal movement in Germany. In 1867 the refusal to hold a plebiscite was condemned.[104]

The *Staats-Zeitung* regarded the Austro-Prussian War in 1866 as brought on by Bismarck, but nevertheless in reality unavoidable. It was predicted that the effects on the United States would be a rise in the rate of exchange. If the war lasted long enough, immigration of capital and labor to the New World would be "sufficient to move the industrial and commercial gravity to the United States."[105]

The Franco-Prussian War was the occasion for a great outburst of German sentiment in the United States. In 1867, the *Illinois Staats-Zeitung* asserted that Napoleon wanted war, in proof of which the Luxemburg situation was cited. It was claimed that Germany sought only a natural development of power. When the war broke out meetings of Germans were held in all parts of the United States. The *Illinois Staats-Zeitung* guaranteed two hundred thalers to the German soldiers who could capture the first French colors. Called to a mass meeting on 30

July 1870, the German women of Chicago responded handsomely. War relief work was engaged in. The establishment of the German Empire was also the occasion for the expression of German enthusiasm.[106]

After the war, some of the hostility of German liberals in this country to Bismarck died down, as it did in Germany. The *Illinois Staats-Zeitung* approved of his policies in general in 1873. In 1874, however, it deplored the lack of self-government in Germany.[107]

It is now time for a backward look at the generation from 1850 to 1880. The Germans were in Chicago in small numbers before 1850; after that date German immigration shot up rapidly, not only in Chicago, but throughout the country. Among these people, the Forty-Eighters assumed the leadership. They became the editors of the German-American papers, leaders in political movements and leaders in German life. The Forty-Eighters especially played an important part in the formation and early history of the Republican Party. They were enthusiastic, anti-slavery men. In Chicago Schneider, Butz, Pruessing, Schmidt, and Dietsch were especially important. Francis A. Hoffmann should also be included; though not a Forty-Eighter, his sympathies were with them.

After the Civil War, the German-Americans of Chicago remained true for a time at least to the Republican Party. Three important exceptions must, however, be noted. First, many joined the Liberal Republican movement in 1872. Secondly, the Catholics, for the most part, remained with the Democrats on the temperance question. During this same period the German newspapers devoted considerable time to foreign news and expressed opinions on foreign questions.

The leadership of the Forty-Eighters was notable indeed. The year 1880 is a fairly good dividing line, though of course an approximate one. The political issues growing out of the Civil War were dying down. The Forty-Eighters had become more conservative; many of them were beginning to admire the policies of Bismarck. Gradually their leadership was passing over to younger men, more recent immigrants from Germany. Nod date can be set, however, for the change of leadership. Some continued prominent for more than a decade following 1880. But the decline of Forty-Eighter leadership undoubtedly began about 1880 with the greatly increased number of younger immigrants at that time.

NOTES

1. Koerner, *Das deutsche Element*, 278.

2. *Chicago und sein Deutschtum* (Cleveland: German-American Biographical Co., 1901–02), 46; *Chicagoer Freie Zeitung* (2 July 1896), the 25th anniversary number; *Illinois Staats-Zeitung* (21 April 1898), 44, 51, the 50th anniversary number; Emil Mannhardt, "Die ersten beglaubigten Deutschen in Chicago," *Deutsch-Amerikanische Geschichtsblätter*, 1:1, 38ff.

3. *Chicago und sein Deutschtum*, 46–47; Mannhardt, op. cit., 38ff.; and by the same author in *Deutsch-Amerikanische Geschichtsblätter*, 1:3, 17, claim that Meyer was the first. The *Chicagoer Freie Presse* (2 July 1896), and the *Illinois Staats-Zeitung* (21 April 1898), claims that Wellmacher was the first.

4. *Chicago und sein Deutschtum*, 46; Mannhardt, "Die ersten beglaubigten Deutschen," 39.

5. According to Mannhardt, op. cit., 39, official records prior to the great fire in 1871 are very rare.

6. Ibid, 39.

7. Ibid, 40–41.

8. The only one listed was German.

9. *Norris's Business Directory* (Chicago: Geer and Wilson, 1846), 30–52.

10. Mannhardt, op. cit., 43.

11. Mannhardt, op. cit., 41; Koerner, *Das deutsche Element*, 248.

12. See 215. According to Koerner, *Das deutsche Element*, 278, he was editor of the *Illinois Staats-Zeitung* for a while, but this is a mistake.

13. *The Bench and Bar of Chicago*, 465ff.; Koerner, *Das deutsche Element*, 248.

14. A. C. Cole, *Era of the Civil War*, 23.

15. See 38–39, *The Biographical Dictionary and Portrait Gallery of Representative Men of Chicago* (Chicago: American Biographical Pub. Co., 1892), 518–22, 646–48.

16. E.g. Dr. Ernst Schmidt. See 43, *Chicago und sein Deutschtum*, 116ff.

17. Cole, *Era*, 23; U.S. Census Office, *Statistical View of the United States . . . Compendium of the Census, 1850, Table III; U.S. Census Report, 1850*, 36–37 (Washington, D.C. Government Printing Office, 1860): 1:104, 613.

18. Cole, *Era*, 23–24; *Chicago Daily Democratic Press* (2 February, 19 June 1854, 5 Nov. 1857); *Free West* (23 February, 18 May 1854) – these papers quoted in Cole, *Era*, 23–24; John M. Peck, *A Gazetteer of Illinois* (Jackonsville: R. Goudy), 1834, 1837 editions John M. Peck, *A New Guide for Immigrants to the West* (Boston: Gould, Kendall, and Lincoln, 1836), 57; *Jahresbericht der Deutschen Gesellschaft von Chicago*, cover page.

19. To be sure a small group of political exiles in the thirties were university men, but they did not settle in Chicago.

20. Paul Selby, "Lincoln and German Patriotism," *Deutsch-Amerikanische Geschichtsblätter*, 12, 510ff.

21. *Biographical Dictionary and Portrait Gallery of Representative Men of Chicago*, 70–73; F. W. Scott, *Newspapers and Periodicals in Chicago*, 61–62; Otto C. Schneider, article in *Deutsch-Amerikanische Geschichtsblätter* 7, no. 2, 65ff.; F. I. Herriott, "Germans of Chicago and Stephen A. Douglas in 1854," *Deutsch-Amerikanische Geschichtsblätter* 12:381ff.; Selby, "Lincoln and German Patriotism," 510ff.; Cole, *Era*, 123ff.; and 143ff.; *Illinois Staats-Zeitung* (8 April 1898), 4ff.

22. Koerner, *Memoirs*, 2:545–47; *Chicago und sein Deutschtum*, 168.

23. In spite of this the chronicler in *Chicago und sein Deutschtum*, 118, he never took a position.

24. See 86.

25. *Chicago und sein Deutschtum*, 116ff. See also, *Deutsch-Amerikanische Geschichtsblätter* 3:1, 12ff. Dr. Otto L. Schmidt is best known of the sons. He is a capable physician and has in addition devoted much time to work in the field of history. He has held many positions of prominence in that connection, e.g. president of the German-American Historical Society of Illinois, president of the Chicago Historical Society, and also president of the Mississippi Historical Association. He was chosen a member of the Board of Education early in 1927.

26. *Illinois Staats-Zeitung* (18 Sept. 1891); *Appleton's Cyclopedia of American Biography*, 1:368.

27. *Illinois Staats-Zeitung* (25 July 1891); *Chicago und sein Deutschtum*, 113–14.

28. *Chicago und sein Deutschtum*, 1143–15; *Deutsch-Amerikanische Geschichtsblätter*, 7, 58–61.

29. *The Biographical Dictionary and Portrait Gallery of Representative Men of Chicago*, 646–48, 518–22; *Chicago und sein Deutschtum*, 124–25, 213.

30. These were not Chicago men. Both men did not subscribe to all of these planks, but to the majority of them.

31. Hassaurek advocated that all salaries be the same.

32. Koerner, *Memoirs*, 1:566–67; Ernest Bruncken, "German Political Refugees, 1815–1860," *Deutsch-Amerikanische Geschichtsblätter*, 3:4, 44ff.

33. *Jahrbuch der Deutschen in Chicago für das Jahr 1915*, 99. The *Vorwärts* chapter was a socialist one founded in a few years.

34. Abolition is, of course, strictly in harmony with socialism.

35. See chap. 3 of Townsend's work.

36. Bruncken, op. cit., 3, no. 4, 48; 4, no. 1, 50.

37. According to Bruncken, , op. cit., 5, no. 1, 39–41.

38. Bruncken, op. cit., 3, no. 4, 44ff.; 5, no. 1, 43ff.

39. *Aus grosser Zeit* (Chicago: Verein der Deutschen Patrioten von 1848–1849 von Chicago und Umgegend, (1900), 100; Carl Schurz, *Reminiscences*, 2:7, 65–67; Koerner, *Memoirs*, 1:598ff.

40. Koerner, *Memoirs*, 2:87.

41. Koerner, *Memoirs*, 2:74–76.

42. See 32.

43. Bruncken, "German Political Refugees" 4, no. 1, 46.

44. *Aus grosser Zeit*, 100.

45. Koerner, *Memoirs*, 2:21–22.

46. See 32–33, 35.

47. The press of the time does not corroborate the holding of this meeting, but is credited by F. I. Herriott on the claim of Vocke. Herriott, "The Germans of Chicago," 384; Cole, *Era*, 123.

48. Otto C. Schneider, "Vortrag," *Deutsch-Amerikanische Geschichtsblätter* 12, 513, 4ff.; Herriott, op. cit., 386–87; Selby, "Lincoln and German Patriotism," 513–144ff.; Cole, op. cit., 123; *Transactions of the Illinois Historical Society* (1912) 156–58; *Transactions of the McLean County Historical Society* III, 53.

49. Op. cit., 511–12.

50. Herriott, op. cit., 588–89; *Documents Relating to the Kansas-Nebraska Act*, 16.

51. See 32.

52. This is according to Selby, op. cit., 516, quoting Schneider.

53. See 32–33.

54. Bruncken, op. cit., 4, no. 1, 46; Koerner, *Memoirs*, 2:21.

55. *Biographical Dictionary and Portrait Gallery of Representative Men of Chicago*, 70–73; Selby, op. cit., 517–18; Schneider, op. cit., 65; Herriott, op. cit., 381ff.; Cole, *Era*, 123ff., 177; *Chicago Daily Democratic Press* (3 March 1856).

56. Frederick F. Schrader, *Germans in the Making of America* (Boston: Stratford Co., 1924), 191.

57. Koerner, *Memoirs*, 2:21–22.

58. Cole, op. cit., 177.

59. Koerner says that with the exception of the Catholics, the Germans in 1856 "almost marched to the polls under the Republican banner." See Koerner, *Memoirs*, 2:21.

60. Cole says that the German vote of Illinois and neighboring states was so powerful in 1860 that without its assistance Lincoln would have been decisively defeated and without its support during the war he could not have carried it through to its logical conclusion. Cole, *Era*, 341–42.

61. Koerner, *Memoirs*, 2:21–22; *Aus grosser Zeit*, 102.

62. *Bench and Bar*, 465 ff.; Cole, *Era*, 190.

63. This estimate was made in the *Rockford Republican* (10 Oct. 1861), quoted in: Cole, *Era*, 281.

64. Koerner, *Memoirs*, 2:150–51; *Chicago Times* (3 May 1864); Cole, *Era*, 281.

65. *Illinois Staats-Zeitung* (16 Sept., 11 Nov. 1862); Cole, *Era*, 342.

66. 19 Sept. 1862. Translation by Townsend.

67. *Illinois Staats-Zeitung*, 1861–62. Passim.

68. 4 Sept. 1861.

69. 4 July 1861.

70. 20 Sept. 1862.

71. 4 Nov. 1862.

72. 15 May 1863 and passim spring 1863.

73. 27 Sept. 1862.

74. *Illinois Staats-Zeitung* (9, 10, 12–13 Jan. 1863).

75. *Chicago Times* (28 March 1864); Cole, Era, 316.

76. *Illinois Staats-Zeitung* (8, 12, 14 Jan., 3 March 1864), the latter quoting the *Harper's Weekly* with approval.

77. E. McPherson, *Political History of the United States during the Rebellion*, 410; Cole, *Era*, 317.

78. 16 Jan., 8 March 1864, and others.

79. *Chicago Times* (6, 8 October 1864).

80. 11 Nov. 1864 (quoted in Cole, 327). According to Cole the German-American voters "marched to the polls almost a solid phalanx for Lincoln." Cole, *Era*, 327.

81. *Illinois Staats-Zeitung* (4 Jan., 27 February 1864).

82. *Illinois Staats-Zeitung* (24, 26–27 February 1866).

83. Ibid., (26 February 1866).

84. Ibid., (2 June 1866).

85. 19 Jan. 1867, 25 February 1868, and passim, 1868.

86. 25 February 1868.

87. E.g. 31 Oct. 1867, though in that issue a premature Grant movement was disapproved of.

88. Schurz, *The Reminiscences of Carl Schurz* (New York: McClure, 1907), 3:338–53; Koerner, *Memoirs*, 2:545, 566ff.; *Chicago Tribune* (3 Sept., 11 Oct. 1872); E. L. Bogart and C. M. Thompson, *The Industrial State, 1870–1893* (Springfield: Illinois Centennial Commission, 1920), 76.

89. *Chicago Tribune* (11 Oct. 1872) evidently quoting from the *Illinois State Register; Illinois Staats-Zeitung* (12, 14 Aug. 1871), and passim, 1872.

90. *Chicago Tribune* (7 April, 20 June, 30 July, 27 Aug., 8 Sept. 1876); *Illinois Staats-Zeitung* (passim, 1876, and 21 April 1898); *National Demokrat* (passim, 1867); e.g. (27 July 1876).

91. *Illinois Staats-Zeitung* (1880 passim, and 21 April 1898), 61.

92. Ibid, (10 June 1871; 12 Jan., 13, 15 February 1872); *Chicago Tribune* (16 February 1872).

93. *Chicago Tribune* (21, 23–25 Oct. 1872).

94. *Illinois Staats-Zeitung* (19, 23, 25, 28 April, 11, 15 Sept. 1873).

95. Ibid., 2, 6, 28 Oct. 1873); *Chicago Tribune* (10, 25, 29–30 Oct., 2 Nov. 1873).

96. *Illinois Staats-Zeitung* (5 Nov. 1873); *Chicago Tribune* (5 Nov. 1873); *Chicagoer Freie Presse* (5 Nov. 1873).

97. *ChicagoTribune* (7 Jan., 21 July 1875); *Chicagoer Freie Presse*, clipped in *Chicago Tribune* (7 Jan. 1875).

98. Bruncken, "Political Activities of the Wisconsin Germans," *Proceedings of the State Historical Society of Wisconsin* (1901), 200.

99. *National Demokrat* (28 Aug. 1876).

100. *Chicago Tribune* (25, 28 June , 23–24 Sept. 1876).

101. *Illinois Staats-Zeitung* (30 March 1864; 12 July 1867).

102. 25 Jan. 1864; 31 March 1866.

103. 31 May 1866.

104. *Illinois Staats-Zeitung* (6 February 1864; 26 April 1867).

105. 18 June 1866.

106. *Illinois Staats-Zeitung* (2, 26 April 1867; 22 July 1870).

107. 30 Oct. 1873; 5 Aug. 1874.

Part Two

———

German-American Leaders

CHAPTER 4

Gustav Koerner

—Evarts B. Greene

IN 1850 THERE WERE IN THE WHOLE UNION ABOUT 573,000 PERSONS who were born in Germany, and of this total nearly one-half were settled in Missouri and the five states of the Old Northwest. The Germans were not evenly distributed over this country, but were massed so as to give them a decisive influence in certain localities, as for instance in Cincinnati and St. Louis.

The ratio of Germans to the total population was not as large in Illinois as in Missouri, Wisconsin, or Ohio, but they stood in a peculiarly interesting relation to the two antagonistic elements in the native American stock. During the first forty years of the nineteenth century, Illinois was more closely related to the border slaveholding states than to those of the northwest. About 1830, however, two nearly contemporary movements brought into the state the Yankees of New England and New York and the first important body of German settlers. For the most part, the Germans went with the New Englanders to the northern counties, but the most strongly German county in the state was St. Clair, on the Mississippi River, opposite St. Louis.

At Belleville, the county seat, there gathered in the thirties as interesting a group of German students and political refugees as could probably be found in any town of its size in the United States. When Henry Villard visited the place, in 1854, he found it an almost exclusively German community in which he rarely heard English spoken.[1]

The first citizen of this German community for some fifty years was Gustav Koerner, the subject of this paper. For a considerable period he was undoubtedly the most influential German-American in the state. In thus calling attention to Koerner's career it is not my purpose primarily to determine his rank among the politicians and publicists of his time, but rather to illustrate through his personal record, the influence of German immigration in an important period of our national history.

Gustav Koerner

Fortunately for this purpose, Koerner was a prolific writer both in English and in German; of his printed books the best known is his *Das Deutsche Element*, dealing primarily with the emigration of the thirties, and in his last years he prepared for the use of his children a manuscript English autobiography of some fourteen hundred pages which has been my principle reliance in the preparation of this paper.[2]

Koerner was born in 1809 at Frankfurt am Main, and came of respectable burgher stock, his father being a bookseller who, in the later years of his life, took up the collection and sale of paintings. In one way

Gustav Koerner House, 200 Abend, Belleville, Illinois.
Illustration from a lithograph by Theodor Schrader preserved at the
Society Museum. Courtesy of the St. Clair County Historical Society,
Belleville, Illinois.

or another elder Koerner was brought into personal relations with some
of the notable figures of his time, including Father Jahn, the apostle or
primitive German manners, Field Marshal Bluecher, and the great
Stein.

He hated Napoleon intensely and threw himself with enthusiasm
into the national uprising of 1813. In the subsequent period of repres-
sion his sympathies were with the liberals against Metternich and his
allies in the Prussian government. Thus the young Koerner grew up in
an atmosphere of intelligence, taste and thoroughgoing liberalism.

To these advantages of his home were added the best educational
opportunities of his time. Beginning at a model school, organized
according to the theories of Froebel, he passed to the gymnasium of
Frankfurt and then to the universities of Jena, Munich, and Heidelberg.

Fifty years later, after he had become a citizen of Illinois, he received from the University of Heidelberg its formal congratulations on the anniversary of his doctorate. During his student days he was an active member of the *Burschenschaft*, then, as in the days of the Wartburg Festival, one of the recognized agencies of the radical propaganda. He was a student at Jena when the July revolution broke out in Paris and followed closely the progress of the movement in Poland and Germany.

In 1832 he was present at the memorable Hambach Festival and recalls his impressions with the following words: "The enthusiasm was unbounded and the feeling that the wrath of kings and princes would be visited upon a great many of us made the event still more exciting. It was enough even to fire the hearts of old and sterner men; how must it have worked upon us young men. I venture to say that no one who witnessed the poplar uprising, no matter how indifferent he might have been, has ever been able to obliterate from his memory the May Festival of the Hambacher Schloss."

Early in 1833 Koerner was formally admitted to practice, but the revolutionary fever was in his veins, and he could not keep out of the agitation which was all about him. In February of that year he was sent by the revolutionary group in Frankfurt to confer with several of the liberal leaders in different parts of Germany, and on the third of April he took a somewhat prominent part in the so-called Frankfurter Attentat.[3] In the street fighting Koerner was slightly wounded, but managed to escape in disguise, and, after some hesitation, decided to emigrate to the United States. He was probably influenced in part by his personal attachment to a young lady whose family embarked on the same ship and to whom he was betrothed during the voyage.

Arriving at New York in the summer of 1833, he proceeded with his friends by way of the Hudson River, the Erie Canal and Lake Erie to Cleveland. From Cleveland they went by canal boat to Portsmouth on the Ohio, where they took the steamboat for St. Louis. The original purpose of the party was to settle in Missouri, but their dislike of slavery as they saw it in Missouri and Kentucky, resulted in their crossing the Mississippi and establishing themselves in St. Clair County, Illinois.

Some of the immigrants took up farming with more or less success, but Koerner found it more uncongenial and determined to continue in his chosen profession of the law. Appreciating, however, the necessity of learning the English language and the American point of view more thoroughly than was possible in such a distinctly German community as Belleville, he took a short course in law in the Transylvania University at

Lexington, Kentucky. He was at first keenly conscious of his isolation. As he says in one of his letters, "They look upon me in this after all provincial town with much curiosity and I cannot very readily make myself understood."

Trying as this was, he faced the situation with courage. "I must enter thoroughly into this American life; for otherwise I have no hopes for the future with this people so much prejudiced for their country and their manners." Nevertheless he met some people of real refinement and social attractiveness. An interesting incident of his short stay at Lexington was a visit to Henry Clay at Ashland, whom he found very complimentary to the Germans on everything except their politics. Koerner was not much impressed by the legal learning of his professors, or the literary standards of his fellow-students, but felt that his Lexington experience was, on the whole, of great advantage to him in later years.

On his return to Belleville, Koerner read law "pretty hard" and spent much of his time attending the sessions of court in his neighborhood. In June 1835, he presented himself for his bar examination before the Supreme Court of the State, at Vandalia. The Chief Justice and one associate justice held the examination in the bedroom of a cheap tavern, and both the examining judges were in their shirtsleeves. The proceedings lasted hardly half an hour and were certainly not exacting. Koerner was much impressed by the contrast between this characteristic frontier scene and the formal dignity of his previous examination at Heidelberg, at which he examiners appeared in full dress and examined him for four hours in the Latin language.

Beginning with a petty case before a justice of the peace in which he defended two his German friends, Koerner soon rose to a leading position at the bar of southern Illinois. His services were especially in demand among the German population, which was becoming more numerous every year. For their benefit he edited and translated into German the revised statues of the State including certain fundamental documents like the Declaration of Independence and the Constitution of the United States.

From the beginning, however, Koerner showed that his interests were by no means limited to his profession. Almost immediately on landing in New York he had formally declared his intention to become a citizen of the United States, and though he desired to maintain, as far as possible the special ideals and intellectual interests of the German people, he strongly opposed the then somewhat popular idea, of forming a distinctly German state.

He took part in various movements for the improvement of the town of Belleville, where he soon married and became a householder. He assisted in the establishment of a library association, which afterwards developed into a public library, and was also active in the founding of a private school of high grade at a time when the state did not provide for the establishment of public high schools. When the occasion arose, he showed himself a courageous champion of law and order as against the summary vengeance of the mob.

Illinois then offered an unusually favorable field for Germans who were interested in the politics of their adopted country. Aliens as well as citizens were allowed to vote after six months' residence in the state, and by 1840 the German vote had to be reckoned with in Illinois politics. Koerner followed with great interest the congressional debates of 1833 and 1834 when the banking question was the center of discussion. In the gradual realignment of parties between the Whigs and Democrats, he definitely placed himself on the democratic side, partly because he felt that the Democratic Party was more distinctly the champion of the masses against the "moneyed interests," and partly because of his belief that the Whigs were more or less tainted with the Native-American spirit. In Illinois it was the Whigs who demanded citizenship as a qualification for voting, while the Democrats favored the simple residence requirement. Under these conditions the Illinois Germans generally became Democrats and, in 1840, it was probably the foreign voters who gave the electoral vote of Illinois to Van Buren as against Harrison. During the campaign of that year Koerner was frequently called upon to take the stump and deliver speeches both in English and German.

In 1842 Koerner's services and those of his countrymen were recognized by his election to the State legislature. The session of 1843 was one of the most important in the history of the State because it had to face a financial crisis arising from the extravagant internal improvement policy of the preceding period. There was some danger of repudiation, but this disgrace was averted by the intelligent and courageous attitude of Governor Thomas Ford. Koerner then, as throughout his career, was an emphatic advocate of sound money and the financial integrity of the State. The election of a German to the legislature was an unusual event which added much to Koerner's prestige, and the session also brought him into useful personal relations with many of the most prominent politicians of the State.

Three years later, when a vacancy occurred in the State Supreme

Court, the appointment was offered to Koerner, and accepted. Thus the political refugee of 1833 had in twelve years won for himself a place in the highest tribunal of the commonwealth. The appointment gave great satisfaction to Germans everywhere, but when the new Constitution of 1848 limited the salaries of the Supreme Court judges to $1,200, Koerner declined reelection on the ground that he could not afford the necessary financial sacrifice.

Meanwhile his sympathies were strongly enlisted by the European revolution of 1848. The Germans at Belleville, as in the country at large, followed closely the political upheavals in the various states of Germany, and the proceedings of the national parliament at Frankfurt. Koerner believed that the ideal government for Germany would be federal republic, modeled closely on that of the United States; and he was soon convinced, through his reading of the German papers and his correspondence with members of his family in Frankfurt, that the effort to establish a federal constitution on a monarchical basis would come to nothing. In January 1849, a large public meeting was held in Belleville at which it was agreed to publish an address to be prepared by Koerner.

In this document, several hundred copies of which were sent to Frankfurt, the German people were urged to work for a republican government as the only true solution of their national problem. For the present they were advised to content themselves with agitation and passive resistance to illegal acts, holding themselves in readiness for more radical action when the time was ripe. The examples of Switzerland and the United States were referred to as evidence that republican government does not necessarily lead to anarchy, but is entirely consistent with a vigorous assertion of law and order.

From time to time the refugees of the German revolution were welcomed to the State, among them Hecker, the leader of the revolutionists in Baden, who bought a farm and settled in the neighborhood of Belleville. In 1851 Kinkel, whose release from a Prussian prison had recently been brought about in a somewhat dramatic fashion by Carl Schurz, also came to Belleville and collected a considerable sum of money for his revolutionary fund.

Unfortunately the newcomers did not always live in harmony with their brothers who were already on the ground. Many of the exiles of 1848 belonged to the extreme left and, on coming to this country, set themselves at once to correct the deficiencies of the American system. One radical reformer, for instance, proposed to abolish the presidency and the federal senate. With these proposals the more conservative, possibly more Philistine, leaders of the '30s were not at all in sympathy, and there arose presently a vigorous controversy between the "Graue" and the Gruene," the "Greys" and the "Greens."

Koerner was one of the chief conservative leaders and was characterized by the opposition journalists as the "Graue Gustav." He had an especially heated discussion with Boernstein, who controlled the *Anzeiger des Westens*, then perhaps the most important German paper in the west. Though Koerner claims for himself a generally temperate manner, he admits that he gave Boernstein a "Roland for his Oliver," and "occasionally castigated" him for his "palpable charlatanism." One important feature of the radical position was the demand that the State should give fuller recognition to the German nationality. They desired, for instance, German teachers in the schools and the establishment of a German university by the State. Koerner believed that these extreme demands were largely responsible for the nativistic movement of the fifties.

In 1852, Koerner was drawn once more into the main current of party politics by his acceptance of the Democratic nomination for lieutenant governor. In this campaign he met with vigorous resistance from certain dissatisfied elements in the democracy of his own county. The Catholic Germans disliked his aggressive championship of Kossuth, and some of the Democratic voters had misgivings about the nomination of a foreign born citizen for so important an office in the state.

This contest brought Koerner into especially close relations with Douglas, then a candidate for reelection to the United States Senate, and the two men traveled together through the towns of northern Illinois, making speeches in English and German. Koerner and the rest of the Democratic ticket were elected large majorities, notwithstanding a considerable loss of votes in his own county.

So far Koerner had been a thorough going Democrat, but it soon became evident that there would be a division in the party on the question of slavery. Koerner himself had taken a strong stand against interference with the rights of the states and regarded the abolitionists as fanatics. Nevertheless he disliked slavery and was opposed to its extension. In 1834 he wrote in his diary, "Negro slavery is the only rope by which the devil holds the American people." In the legislature of 1843 he smothered in committee a bill to exclude free Negroes from the State, and in 1850 he sympathized with those of his fellow Democrats in

Washington who were making a stand against the doctrines of Calhoun and Davis. During the Democratic convention of 1852 he was, he says, so absorbed in the reading of *Uncle Tom's Cabin* that the convention contest was for a time forgotten; but there is nothing to show that the book influenced his thinking.

With the year 1854 Koerner's position become more difficult. The Kansas-Nebraska bill divided the Democratic Party into two hostile groups, and though he was reluctant to break away from Douglas and the other leaders with whom he had been so intimately associated, he finally took his stand with Lyman and Trumbull on the anti-Nebraska side. The German voters were divided, but a large proportion of them followed Koerner's lead, thus contributing largely to the anti-Nebraska victory in the state and congressional elections of 1854 and to the choice of Trumbull as senator in the following winter.

During the next two years Koerner's political attitude was uncertain. He had broken with the Douglas wing of the Democratic Party, but he was still holding the office to which he had been chosen by Democratic votes. Political conditions in Illinois, as in the country, at large were thoroughly chaotic. The Whig Party had disintegrated and there was at first no organized opposition party to take its place. Furthermore, the strong Know-Nothing movement tended to hold the German in the Democratic ranks. Later, when the Know-Nothings divided upon the slavery question, a considerable number of them became Republicans and this fact also caused Koerner some misgivings. It seemed possible, at least, that the new party made up so largely of Know-Nothing and Whig elements, might take a similar attitude toward the foreign-born population.

When, however, the Republican Convention of 1856 took definite ground against the Native-American doctrine and nominated for President John C. Fremont, who was especially popular with the German voters, Koerner identified himself fully with the Republican Party and at once became one of its must trusted leaders. In his opinion, the strongest elements in the new party came from the old Democratic organization, and he thought it important that Republicanism should not be identified in any way with the distinctive tenets of the Whigs.

Two years later Koerner was forced into a more decided antagonism than ever toward his old political friends. When Horace Greeley urged the Republicans of Illinois to give their support to Douglas instead of nominating an independent candidate for the Senate, Koerner published a sharp criticism of Douglas, asserting that his primary motive in 1858, as well as in 1854, was the desire to improve his presidential prospects. This article, though published anonymously, came to be known as Koerner's, and probably led to his being made permanent chairman of the Republican state convention which nominated Lincoln for the Senate.

Shortly before the national contest of 1860, German Republicans were much disturbed by the passage of a constitutional amendment in Massachusetts which disqualified aliens form the suffrage for two years after their naturalization.[4] Many of the Democratic and German-American papers treated this action by a strongly Republican state as evidence of Know-Nothing tendencies in the Republican Party, and it was proposed at one time to frame a German-American manifesto looking to the organization of a new political party. Such representative Germans as Koerner and Schurz discountenanced the plan, however, and the Republican leaders hastened to place themselves on the liberal side of the alien question.

In 1860 Koerner was sent to the Chicago convention as a delegate at large from Illinois, and with his colleagues worked hard to secure Lincoln's nomination. He found, however, that the German delegates, of whom there were a considerable number, were largely supporters of Seward, who seemed to them a more radical anti-slavery man than Lincoln. As a member of the platform committee he was especially interested in the attitude of the party toward naturalized citizens, and with the help of Carl Schurz secured a resolution on this subject, which was entirely satisfactory from the German point of view.

When South Carolina seceded, Koerner took a decided position against the Greeley proposition to let the erring sisters go in peace. He held that, though it might not be possible to coerce the states, individuals in the states could, as citizens of the Union, be punished for treason. After the firing on Fort Sumter he interested himself in the raising of troops for the Union service, and, after serving for some weeks as unofficial adviser to Governor Yates, was assigned by Lincoln to the staff of General Fremont. Though his personal relations were friendly, he thought the General a poor judge of men and his staff a "curiosity." "Fremont," he writes in a contemporary letter, "is always absorbed in thinking, but whether his thoughts are worthy of anything, results will show." When Fremont's insubordination led to his removal by President Lincoln, Koerner used his influence to quiet the prevailing discontent among the Germans, assuring Lincoln that however dissatisfied they might be for the moment, they were thoroughly loyal to the Union.[5]

During the latter part of the war Koerner was withdrawn from active politics in the United States by his appointment as minister to Spain, where he succeeded Carl Schurz. He was not altogether satisfied with the Spanish mission and would have preferred either Berlin or Vienna, but his efforts to effect an exchange were unsuccessful. During the French intervention in Mexico the Spanish Government required careful handling and Koerner seems to have done his work with skill and tact.

He returned to the United States in 1864 and in the first stages of the reconstruction supported the congressional radicals against President Johnson, publishing in the *Chicago Tribune* a number of articles in defense of his party. During Grant's administration, however, he gradually drifted out of sympathy with the Republican Party. He believed that the influences about the president were thoroughly corrupt, and, as a German, was especially annoyed by the sale of arms to the French government during the Franco-Prussian War. Under these circumstances Koerner was naturally drawn into the liberal Republican movement, and, in the unsuccessful campaign of 1872, he was the Liberal-Republican and Democratic candidate for governor. Four years later, in the Hayes-Tilden campaign, he definitely resumed his membership in the Democratic Party, taking sharp issue at this point with Carl Schurz.

The last years of Koerner's life are of less interest to the student of national history, though he took a keen interest in current issues. His principal achievement during this period was the publication of his *Das Deutsche Element*, one of the most important contributions to the literature of this subject.

Throughout his long career Koerner sought to mediate between his German and American friends. During his early life in America he frequently contributed to the press of Germany articles which were intended to give the German public more adequate views of American life and institutions. He was equally anxious that his American neighbors should appreciate the real character and ideals of the German people. His own conception of the German element in its relation to American life is perhaps best stated in the following passage form an address delivered in 1873 to a society of German pioneers:

> When I speak of the German element, I do not mean a living together and acting together exclusive of other nationalities in this country. What I mean is solely that we should not abandon

our German views, our German manners as far as they are worthy to be kept up, but to instill them into the American life. I mean that we should let our German spirit pour itself into the burning floods, which are still welling up and out of which in the course of time a national type will be cast. That when the time comes, a good part of German honesty, German industry, German geniality, and, above all, love of art and the sciences, may be discernible in that national type, let us all and you, German pioneers, above all, contribute with all our might.[6]

NOTES

1. Henry Villard, *Memoirs of Henry Villard, Journalist and Finacier, 1835–1900* (Boston: Houghton, Mifflin and Co., 1904), 1:34–35; cf. Koerner, *Das Deutsche Element*, 12.

2. I desire to acknowledge my obligation to his daughter, Mrs. Engelmann, of Cleveland, Ohio, for her great kindness in allowing me to make use of this autobiography. The manuscript has also been used by Rattermann in his interesting sketch entitled: *Gustav Koerner: Deutsch-Amerkanischer Jurist, Staatsmann, Diplomat und Geschichtsschreiber, Ein Lebensbild, nach seiner unveröffentlichten Autobiographie, seinen Schriften und Briefen bearbeitet und dem andenken des verstorbenen Freundes in dankbarer Erinnerung gewidmet* (Chicago: Deutsch-Amerikanische Geschichtsblätter, 1903).

Editor's note: Koerner's autobiography was, of course, published subsequent to the publication of this article, and is cited throughout this work. See the selective bibliography at the end of this work for the full citation. Rattermann's biography was also based on Koerner's autobiography and other writings, and the fact that the two were long-standing friends. For Koerner's golden wedding anniversary Rattermann wrote a play that actually was performed for the Koerners in Belleville. See H. A. Rattermann, *Zur Feier der Goldenen Hochzeit von Gustav und Sophie Koerner (17. Juni 1886)* (Cincinnati: S. Rosenthal & Co., 1886). Koerner describes his golden wedding anniversary in his autobiography as follows: "I must say that we were surprised by the tasteful and really splendid reception given us by our fellow-citizens, which took place at the large hall of our city park, which was decorated with the German and American flags and with such an abundance of flowers and evergreens as to convert the hall into a floral bower. Musical performances, the singing of beautiful songs by the different singing societies, a too flattering address by a member of the legal profession, an ode, read by my friend H. A. Rattermann, and a dramatic poem arranged by him with great care and with great taste and performed by four of the most beautiful ladies of Belleville representing the genius of life and the three sisters of fate, Clotho, Lachesis, and Atropos, made of the evening of entertainment." See Koerner, *Memoirs*, 2:746.

It is remarkable that Rattermann's biography, which is the most extensive study available on Koerner, has never been translated. Rattermann's dramatic poem might also be translated and published as a bilingual English-German edition, which would be important, as literary works never can really be fully translated, and the original German would be important to retain together with the translation. Given the importance of Koerner, such translations, especially of Rattermann's biography, would be a significant contribution and would accord Koerner the rightful place he deserves in American history in general, and German-American history in particular.

3. For an account of this uprising, in which Koerner is mentioned, see Karl Fischer, *Die Nation und der Bundestag: Ein Beitrag zur deutschen Geschichte* (Leipzig: Fues's Verlag, 1880), 388 et seq.

4. Article XXIII, ratified 1859.

5. In a confidential letter to General Halleck, Lincoln gives this interesting estimate of Koerner: "Without knowledge of its contents, Governor Koerner, of Illinois, will hand you this letter. He is an educated and talented German gentleman, as true a man as lives. With his assistance you can set everything right with the Germans. I write this without his knowledge, asking him at the same time, by letter, to deliver it. My clear judgement is that, with reference to the German element in your command, you should have Governor Koerner with you; and if agreeable to you and him, I will make him a brigadier-general, so that he can afford to so give his time. He does not wish to command in the field, though he has more military knowledge than many who do. If he goes into the place, he will simply be an efficient, zealous and unselfish assistant to you. I say all this upon intimate personal acquaintance with Governor Koerner." See Abraham Lincoln, *Abraham Lincoln: Complete Works, Comprising His Speeches, Letters, State Papers, and Miscellaneous Writings*, eds. John G. Nicolay and John Hay (New York: The Century Co., 1894), 1:34–35.

6. Taken from the English version in Koerner's manuscript autobiography. See n. 2 regarding the autobiography.

CHAPTER 5

———

Friedrich Hecker

—Alice Reynolds

THE ROLE OF "TRIBUNE OF THE PEOPLE" STRIKES THE DOMINANT NOTE in the life song of Friedrich Karl Franz Hecker, the German revolutionist. Hecker was born 28 September 1811. He died on 24 March 1881. The credo of Friedrich Hecker's whole life revolved around a deep love of humanity and an unshakable faith in a government by the people. The thirty-nine year span of Hecker's efforts in public life spells a fearless and ceaseless championship of human freedom on two continents.[1]

In Germany, within seven short years, the young advocate of Mannheim had become entrenched as "the idol of the people." He himself had mapped the course of his activities early in his life. With every reason to expect the rewards of a successful and lucrative career in his chosen profession, nevertheless, "in the case of the people versus its oppressors, he entered his appearance for the plaintiff." Neither the glamour of repeated offers of high public positions nor the lure of material gain ever diverted him into a betrayal of the trust to which he had voluntarily dedicated himself. And because he remained true to his convictions, the people remained true to him throughout his lifetime and to his memory long years after he was gone.

Friedrich Hecker was well adapted by nature to become a popular hero. Added to a striking appearance, highlighted by wavy light red hair and full beard, and personal magnetism, was extraordinary mental equipment. He had an insatiable lust for knowledge and was an assiduous student of history. This erudition was at once his most potent weapon against the wiles and hypocrisy of his enemies and the secret of his hold upon the common people. His utterances rang with such sincerity of conviction that he invariably swept his hearers along with him and inoculated them with his beliefs. He was endowed with a rare gift of oratory, poetical in approach, incisive in its eloquence, teeming with telling wit, capable of inflaming the hearts of the masses. He spoke from

Friedrich Hecker

the heart, to the heart, as man to man, in language, which the people could understand.

Naturally, he had his less attractive side, expressed in occasional displays of roughness. He was apt to be explosive. His impetuosity appears on both sides of the ledger, some regarding it as a liability, which contributed to the failure of the revolution; others placed it in the column of assets, maintaining that it was an essential quality to the execution of his mission.[2]

Hecker's appointment as advocate and procurator of the Supreme Court of Mannheim in 1838 served to bring his talents to public notice. His profound knowledge of jurisprudence and his brilliant performance in the art of pleading soon gained him wide recognition.

As a child and as a youth, Friedrich Hecker had felt the impact of the liberal forces which had been gathering and gaining momentum since the betrayal of the Germanic people by their rulers after the close of the Napoleonic wars. The imagination of his receptive mind became fired and inflamed with visions of a free and united Fatherland and a republican Europe. Life at the universities added fuel. Liberal doctrines flourished the teaching of the professors by virtue of academic freedom, and the *Burschenschaften* furthered the philosophy. Thus the roots of Hecker's convictions ran deep. Small wonder, then, that we find him after his election to the Second Chamber of Baden in 1842, straightway allying himself with the "extreme left" wing, dauntlessly and eloquently voicing his republican views.

Hecker and the courageous editor Gustav Struve entered the political scene when popular indignation was at white heat.[3] Vacillating policies of the grand duke in Baden had heaped coals of fire upon the liberal movement, which had been increasing in popularity. Concessions granted in alarm only to be later revoked, and to crown it all the foisting upon the people of a minister who was the blind tool of the hated Metternich, arch enemy of all democratic efforts.[4]

Hecker immediately made demands, principally popular representation at the reactionary Diet and the convocation of a German parliament. His reputation spread. The people felt that he was their man. They came from miles around to listen for hours to his inspiring speeches. Some would bring their young sons and lifting the latter to their shoulders whisper, "That is Hecker!" And the youngsters would boast to their classmates, "We have seen Hecker." Hecker beards became the vogue. In fact, so generally had his name become identified with the cause of the people that in 1845, stopping at Berlin en route to Stettin, in company with the elder, also democratically minded Itzstein, he and his company were expelled from all Prussian states by the authorities. The incident only served to enhance the fame of the youthful deputy.

But just as the sun of success was rising over the people's horizon, it was suddenly eclipsed by the proverbial technique of appeasement. Someone had put a clever bee in the bonnet of the panicky grand duke. He chose a minister form the ranks of the "moderate" opposition. Overtures were made and concessions granted. Some of Hecker's supporters had been flirting with the government and now succumbed to its advances. The opposition evaporated. Hecker's convictions were not built on quicksand, and his piercing blue eyes penetrated the veil of trickery, hypocrisy and pseudo reforms. Disgusted with so spineless a political set-up, he resigned his seat and sought diversion and consolation in the adventure by a trip through the wilds of southern France and Algiers.

During Hecker's absence the intrepid Struve kept the fires of agitation burning through the columns of his newspaper. He inveighed against censorship. The darts of his arrows struck their mark through the land.

After a few months the "champion of liberty" returned, refreshed by his communion with nature, and his thoughts clarified by sober contemplation. He was importuned from all sides to resume his seat in the Second Chamber. Accepting the challenge, once more he entered the lists in the people's crusade with grimmer determination and renewed zeal.

The course of events between the meeting of 12 September 1847, and the collapse of the revolution on 18 April 1848, makes exciting reading. The story is recorded in the annals of history.[5] The demands formulated at the Offenburg meeting savor of a "Bill of Rights." Hecker's "Proclamation" to his fellow countrymen, on the eve of the battle, as he planted the banner of the German Republic, could be read with profit today. It is a masterpiece of exhortation to a people to free itself from its age-old bondage to autocratic rule, and an impassioned defense of the republican form of government as exemplified by the United States of America.

Hecker fled to Switzerland, and was enthusiastically received. Here, with Carl Schnauffer, he edited a "radical" newspaper, which was smuggled into all corners of Germany.[6] The loyalty and devotion of the German people spoke eloquently through his reelection to the Second Chamber. The government with a verdict of high treason, refused him admission.

He sailed to America. Upon his arrival in New York 8 October 1848, he found himself welcomed with all the marks usually according "a conquering hero." Philadelphia, Baltimore, Louisville, and Cincinnati duplicated the demonstrations.[7] The ovations of St. Louis climaxed all previous ones, and from here he issued an impassioned appeal for moral and financial support of revolutionary movements in his native land. His plea met with tremendous success. Meanwhile in Germany, the seed, which he had sown, were not allowed to die. Hecker *Lieder* sprang up everywhere and were sung in defiance of the police.[8] The ferment culminated in another revolutionary eruption in early spring 1849. Hecker was sent for. The message was delayed. He arrived too late. The Prussian war machine had again triumphed.

Completely disillusioned, he returned to the homestead which had had purchased near Belleville, Illinois, and fully expected to withdraw from political entanglements and to settle down to a peaceful existence on the farm. Fate decreed otherwise. Within a few years a signal of distress sounded in the land "which received the exile in its motherly arms." Gratefully he responded to her call. He was an indefatigable crusader for the emancipation of the black race as he had been for the political liberation of his native country.

He was one of the founders of the Republican Party. His name and that of Abraham Lincoln headed the first Republican ballot in 1856 as the two presidential electors from Illinois and he was vigorous supporter of Honest Abe. Two regiments headed by him as colonels acquitted themselves with distinction in the Civil War, but a severe wound suffered at Chancellorsville eventually forced his retirement.[9]

After the war years we detect a certain rhythm in the life of the crusader. Periods of retirement, when in plowing his fields he found refreshment from his mental labors, alternated with periods of emergence into the limelight as lecturer, orator, and publicist in the columns of the newspapers here and abroad. Whenever the fate of liberty hung in the balance, with all the fire and brilliance of the young lawyer at Mannheim, the older man appeared to defend them. The peroration of his festival speech on 4 July 1871, at Trenton, Illinois, appears in *The World's Best Oratory* by Brewer, who makes an interesting prophecy in his introductory paragraph.[10]

When Hecker departed from Strassburg in 1849, he received a mandate from the people of Germany. Throngs of his countrymen, including women and children, came from across the Rhine to bid him Godspeed and to beg him not to desert them and the cause of German freedom. He never forgot. A visitor from Germany writes:

> I called especial attention to how Hecker's intellectual participation in Germany's political life had been a great influence through his fiery letters since 1866; how a greater split in the liberal party had been prevented through the fact that he had taken a definite national stand and how through his speech for liberty which was published in all German newspapers, he captivated the hearts of the people again.

Hecker's quiet reply holds timely significance:

I was the Mephisto of the monarchy and wish to remain so. Beware, over there, you emotional politicians, that a reaction does not again cause you to lose much. In the Prussian still lurks a damnable aristocratic clique, which, hand in hand with the priests, is capable of anything. Be on your guard and don't trust too much.

The glory of Bismarck's regime failed to dim the perception of the indomitable warrior in the battle for human rights. It was not glory, which he wanted for his German people but economic and political freedom.

In 1873 he visited his Fatherland. The people received him in triumph; his tremendous popularity had not decreased with the years. Neither had the animosity of the authorities. Although he was under a strict surveillance, his utterances were an uncompromising declaration of republican faith. In Prussian controlled Frankfurt the police broke up a torchlight procession gathering in his honor. A delegation sent to his headquarters begged him to speak to the populace. "No speeches can be made here," thundered the snarling voice of authority. "Now I know your Reich thoroughly," he said to a friend, "I only wonder how you stand it," and at Hamburg as he was leaving, he exclaimed, "I rejoice that I soon breathe free air again. Three more days in Prussia and I would suffocate."

A Study of the Bismarckian constitution brought from him the warning that it contained no "Bill of Rights."[11]

At the dedication of the Hecker Monument in St. Louis in 1882, a speaker said:

It is an historic monument of universal liberty erected to the memory of the two greatest struggles for freedom in this century—1848 and 1861—in honor of that champion, Friedrich Hecker, who, by the part he acted in both, has become a representative of them and has linked them together. It is a monument to that same inseparable freedom that binds together nations, continents to one another—a monument of international, intercontinental, of the Atlantic freedom, as it were. . . . The life of Friedrich Hecker, whose name and features this monument bears, exemplifies the qualities of great citizenship and staunch republicanism, truthfulness and incorruptibility, simplicity and loyalty, devotion to a cause and willingness to sacrifice, love of freedom and hatred of all things servile.[12]

NOTES

1. Since the publication of this article, much work has been done on the Forty-Eighters, especially for the 150th anniversary of the revolution of 1848 in 1998. For two works dealing with Hecker, see the comprehensive biography of Hecker by Sabine Freitag, *Friedrich Hecker: Biographie eines Republikaners* (Stuttgart: Franz Steiner Verlag, 1998); and a work that traces the continued interest in Hecker in Germany and America, Alfred Frei, ed., *Friedrich Hecker in den USA: Eine deutsch-amerikanische Spurensicherung* (Konstanz: Stadler Verlagsgesellschaft mbH, 1993).

2. Lawrence S. Thompson and Frank X. Braun describe Hecker as "a democrat, but above all he was a man who lived for action, no matter whether we see him as 'half a hero and half a highwayman,' or as the 'scholar and gentleman who exemplified all the social graces of his native Baden.'" See Zucker, *The Forty-Eighters*, 117.

3. Gustav Struve (1805–70) worked for German republic and "was elected to the *Vorparlament*, but considering it too weak left this 'debating society' to raise an armed band to cooperate with Hecker. He was defeated and exiled, but returned to become a leader in the establishment of the ephemeral republic in Baden. After its collapse, Struve was condemned to five years of penal servitude, but was freed by a mob. After spending some time in Switzerland and England, he came to the U.S. in 1851. . . . His thesis was that tyranny is detrimental to economic and cultural progress. He was an ardent Republican, supported Lincoln, volunteered as a private in the Civil War, and advanced to the rank of captain, but left the service when an aristocrat was appointed his superior officer." See Zucker, *The Forty-Eighters*, 346.

4. Regarding Prince Metternich, see Justine Davis Randers-Pehrson, *Germans and the Revolution of 1848–1849*, New German-American Studies (New York: Peter Lang Pub. Co., 1999), 18:245–57.

5. Regarding the revolution of 1848, see Randers-Pehrson, *Germans and the Revolution of 1849–1849*.

6. Schnauffer (1823–54), a Forty-Eighter, was "very much influenced by his association with Hecker and Struve" and fled to Switzerland after the Revolution, later to England, and arrived in Baltimore in 1851, where he edited a newspaper, the *Wecker*, an "antislavery paper which stood for freedom, popular education, and general enlightenment." However, his

legacy continued on, as his wife maintained publication of the paper after his death. Also, Schnauffer, who was devoted to the Turner movement, was widely considered one of the best Turner poets. See Zucker, *The Forty-Eighters*, 339.

7. Shortly after his arrival in Cincinnati on 18 October 1848, Hecker helped establish the first Turner society in America. See Zucker, *The Forty-Eighters*, 92ff.

8. For an example of a popular Hecker song, see Zucker, *The Forty-Eighters*, 90.

9. Kaufmann notes regarding Hecker's Civil War service that "At the outbreak of the Civil War, he first enlisted as a private in the 3rd Missouri Regiment, then organized the German 24th Illinois Regiment, but due to conflict with his officers he resigned and formed a second Hecker Regiment, the 82nd Illinois, which became one of the best in the Western army." See Kaufmann, *Germans in the American Civil War*, 295.

10. See D. J. Brewer, ed., *The World's Best Orations: From the Earliest Period to the Present Time* (St. Louis: F. P. Kaiser, 1899). Kaufmann writes of Hecker's oratory: "Hecker was one of the most prominent leaders of the German people in America; he was an outstanding orator, able to bring the masses to true enthusiasm." See Kaufmann, *Germans in the American Civil War*, 295.

11. It might be noted that most Forty-Eighters enthusiastically celebrated German unity under the leadership of Bismarck. Carl Wittke notes that "with few exceptions, they joined the great majority of German-Americans in blessing the German army and the new Germany under Prussia, Bismarck, and the Hohenzollerns. They had envisaged the unification of the German states along quite different lines, but their disappointment was largely forgotten in the universal rejoicing that hailed the final achievement of a united fatherland." One of the few critical voices among the Forty-Eighters was Hecker. Although he celebrated German unity, he "expressed the fervent hope that the fatherland might become 'strong in the liberties of the citizen,' and like the United States, a symbol of freedom for the world." During his trip to Germany, he "spoke in praise of the American bill of rights, freedom of the press, and jury trial, and frankly stated that German immigrants had made a wise decision when they left their native land for the free republic across the Atlantic." It might also be noted that Hecker took great pride in being a German-American, and in emphasizing his German heritage, as well as American citizenship. As early as 1849, he had stated in an address in St. Louis "that 'the German fatherland now lives in the Far West,' rather than in

Europe, and that genuine republicanism could expect support henceforth only from America." See Wittke, *Refugees of Revolution*, 362–63.

12. The St. Louis monument was not the only one honoring Hecker. After his death, the National Hecker Monument Society collected the necessary funds and in 1883 dedicated the Hecker Monument in Cincinnati, which is located in Washington Park in the Over-the-Rhine district. See Don Heinrich Tolzmann, *German Heritage Guide to the Greater Cincinnati Area* (Milford, Ohio: Little Miami Pub. Co., 2003), 73.

CHAPTER 6

Francis A. Hoffmann

–D. I. Nelke

FRANCIS ARNOLD HOFFMANN WAS BORN AT HERFORD, PROVINCE OF Westphalia, in the kingdom of Prussia, 5 June 1822, and was the son of Friedrich Wilhelm and Wilhelmine (nee Groppe) Hoffmann. His father was the proprietor of a bookstore and bindery. The son received his elementary education at the parochial school. At the age of twelve years he was sent to the Friedrich gymnasium, a classical institution of learning in his native town. A remarkable degree of devotion to horticulture and agriculture was already inherent in the lad. He always had his little patch in his father's garden, on which fruit trees were raised, grafted and budded. The vacations were spent by the young student, whenever possible, at the house of some relative where his thirst for country life could be satisfied.

He left his native country in 1840, being then but eighteen years of age, and reached New York penniless.[1] Having borrowed eight dollars from a friend in that city, he started for Chicago, which was then beginning to be a considerable village. After a long, tedious journey in freight boats on the Hudson River and Erie Canal, and a small schooner on the lakes, he arrived at Chicago in September of that year. Money-less and friendless, and unable to speak the English language, he found a poor prospect for "getting a start in the world."

Rather than do nothing, he accepted the position of bootblack at the Lake House, which at that time was the first-class hotel of that city. A month subsequently he accepted an offer to teach at a small German school at Dunkley's Grove in DuPage County, at the extraordinary salary of fifty dollars per annum, with the privilege of boarding around among the parents of the pupils. His next step was into the pulpit, being ordained as a minister by the Lutheran Synod of Michigan. The district of his services embraced Chicago and other points in Cook County, as well as the counties of DuPage and Will in Illinois and the county of Lake in Indiana. While engaged in this work as a minister he took an

Franz A. Hoffmann

active part in all public affairs. He represented his county in the famous river and harbor convention held at Chicago in 1847. Here he formed the personal acquaintance of Horace Greeley and many other prominent men.

During the earlier part of the 1840s a German weekly was established at Chicago, and Hoffmann wrote the editorials at this log cabin in DuPage County, one of the proprietors of the paper walking a distance of fifteen miles every week for copy, bringing along a bundle of exchanges, which was received by the parson as payment in full for his editorial labors![2]

A few years later Hoffmann became the owner of forty acres of prairie about twenty-five miles west of Chicago. Now his greatest earthly desires were realized. He erected a small frame house on the premises, built wire fences, which would keep the cattle neither in nor out, planted forest and fruit trees and at scientific farming, such as then in vogue. He became a frequent contributor to the columns of the *Prairie Farmer*, published by John S. Wright at Chicago.

In 1852, on account of failing health, Hoffmann quit the ministry and removed to Chicago, where he read law. After he was admitted to the bar he established himself in the real-estate business, in which he was very successful. In 1853 he was elected a member of the City Council. From 1854 to 1861 he was engaged in banking, and then engaged in insurance business, and was elected president of the Chicago Board of Underwriters. He was appointed consul for the United States at Chicago by a number of German governments. For four years he was also commissioner of the Illinois Central Railroad Company, in which capacity he was instrumental in inducing thousands of German families to settle in the central part of the state, by which means that section had its agricultural resources rapidly developed.

In 1856 the anti-slavery conventions of Illinois nominated Hoffmann for lieutenant governor, by acclamation, against his earnest protest; but it was subsequently learned that he was disqualified by his not having been a citizen fourteen years, as required by the Constitution.[3] Four years afterward, the Republican state convention at Decatur again nominated him, still against his will, for lieutenant governor, by acclamation, on the ticket with "Dick" Yates for governor. At this convention John Hanks, of Macon County, presented two of the rails made by Abraham Lincoln the first year after he came to the state. Lincoln, who headed the national ticket for that campaign, was not in the hall, but was sent for, and in a short time made his appearance, the delegates rising to cheer him as he entered.

When quiet was restored, Richard J. Oglesby arose and addressing the presiding officer, said: "An old citizen of Macon County wishes to make a presentation to the convention." On announcement two old fence-rails were borne forward to the stand, inscribed: "Abraham Lincoln, the rail-splitters' candidate for the presidency in 1860: two rails from a lot of three thousand made in 1830 by Thomas Hanks and Abraham Lincoln, whose father was the first pioneer of Macon County."

After the cheering had subsided Lincoln related in his happiest manner the circumstances attending the making of the rails used in fencing a field and building a cabin for his father, the first work he did in Illinois. The national convention to nominate a candidate for the presidency was held at Chicago a few days later. The ticket was triumphantly elected, and Hoffmann filled the office of lieutenant governor during four of the most stirring and eventful years of our nation's history, from 14 January 1861 to 1865. He was a most earnest and efficient co-worker with Governor Yates in the military preparations and other public services of those momentous years of war and peril. We venture the assertion that a more popular gentleman than Lieutenant Governor Hoffmann never presided over the Senate of the State of Illinois. When Lincoln was nominated for re-election for the presidency in 1863, Hoffmann was nominated for presidential elector of the state at large. He probably traveled more miles and made more speeches than all the other candidates for the electorship combined.

In all positions Hoffmann was faithful and efficient, bringing to the discharge of his duties the highest and best qualities of his nature. He has always been most popular among the common people, and, like Lincoln, loved to appeal to their broad sense of justice and right. He was the trusted and faithful friend of Lincoln, Governor Yates and General Grant, and was also very intimately acquainted with Stephen A. Douglas, whose political opponent he was. They had in him a most implicit confidence for all the obligations of war and peace; and, while he was a strong partisan, his political opponents gave him the credit of having, in the highest degree, the two cardinal virtues of a public servant—honesty and capability. He was among the last of a race of public men who have given glory to the state and grandeur to the nation. With him closes an era in politics which, for importance in the history of nations, in the development of liberty in the achievements of men, has no parallel in the annals of time.

During his political and business career Hoffmann resided on a farm near Chicago, spending much of his time in horticultural and agricultural pursuits. It is, however, as a practical horticulturist and as an agricultural writer and editor that "Hans Buschbauer" has won his brightest laurels. In this capacity he has not only won an enduring reputation, but has also been the guide, philosopher and friend of thousands of his countrymen who have made (America) their home, bringing to it the industry, the capacity for patient toil—for the confidence in a friend which, once given, is never withdrawn, that distinguish the children of the Fatherland. Nor is he one of those editorial writers, alas, too common, who if they are honest, might well say:

We farm (on foolscap) with complete success,
And till large farms with paper, pen and ink;
And, sitting indoors, at a regular price,
Give large amounts of good outdoor advice.

Since 1875 Hoffmann has lived at Riverside farm, near Jefferson.[4] In almost a quarter of a century since he has made Riverside his home and the expression of his thoughts in matters agricultural and horticultural, he has delighted his friends, whether of the Fatherland or of the land of his adoption (whom he has in so many ways served so well) by his writings in the Milwaukee *Germania*, a weekly, which enjoys a large circulation.

In addition to this, he is the agricultural editor the *Chicago Warte* and the *Buffalo Volksfreund*.[5] He has also been a voluminous author on agricultural subjects, writing in the German language, and very large editions of his works have been issue—among them Buschbauer's handbook on the culture of grasses and fodder plants, and his works on poultry breeding, bee culture and horticulture.[6]

On 22 February 1844, occurred the most interesting event in Governor Hoffmann's life, namely his marriage to Miss Cynthia Gilbert. She was an American lady, and a daughter of a well-to-do farmer, a most noble woman, devoted wife and mother and wise counselor. They are the parents of four sons, namely: Francia A., Jr., a prominent lawyer of Chicago; Dr. Julius Hoffmann, a resident of Jefferson; Dr. Adolph Hoffmann, now located in Colorado; and Gilbert, who has charge of the Riverside farm, the home of the Governor. On 22 February 1894, the fiftieth anniversary of the marriage of the honored couple took place. Surrounded by some two score of children, grandchildren and intimate friends, Francis A. Hoffmann and his faithful helpmate stood in the parlor of their beautiful home at Riverside, and heard the clergyman repeat the words which fifty years before had joined their hearts and labors. The couple, whose golden wedding was thus celebrated, is known from Maine to California and from the lakes to the gulf among German agriculturists and humble tillers of the soil as "Hans and Grethe."

For sixteen years Hoffmann has been the agricultural editor of the *Milwaukee Germania*, and his wife the editor of the household department of that widely circulated publication.[7] They have conducted their editorial labors in the study of their lovely farm home, which is situated about a mile from Jefferson Junction. It is here that their relatives and friends joined them in their celebration of the fiftieth anniversary of their marriage. The mails and wires carried also the congratulations of more than five hundred friends, in all sections of the country. Many congratulations came from people who were the Governor's scholars more than fifty years ago.

In the parlor of the Riverside farmhouse, at one o'clock P.M., the company assembled. The room was lavishly decorated with floral offerings from all quarters, forming a perfect arbor of roses, violets and lilacs, and garlands. To make the occasion happier, if possible, the congratulatory conversation was punctuated with the crowing of a newly arrived baby boy, in the morning presented to Gilbert Hoffmann by his wife, and adding a grandson to the family of the veteran editor. At one o'clock the happy couple clasped hands, and the Rev. Henry Vogel, of Jefferson, repeated the wedding ceremony. At its conclusion Georg Brumder, publisher of the *Germania*, made a speech of congratulation on behalf of his employees, and Chris. Koerner, of the editorial staff, presented the couple with a handsome French rococo clock and two golden candelabra.[8] The presents were numerous and varied. A charming incident was the presentation, by Professor Rosenstengel, of the State University of the following letter from the faculty of the Agricultural College:

Madison, Wisconsin, 17 February

Dear Governor Hoffmann: By the bearer of this, Professor Rosenstengel, we, the members of the College of Agriculture of the University of Wisconsin, send to you and your beloved wife our cordial greetings. Through your untiring efforts among the German-American farmers for the upbuilding of agriculture, and for a higher intellectual development on the farm, you have won a position without a counterpart in this whole great country. It is scarcely an exaggeration to say that "Hans Buschbauer" is known, loved and quoted in every German-American home in America. Realizing all this, how can we but rejoice with you on this happy anniversary day which comes to you and your family with all its happiness, finding you surrounded by your personal friends and knowing that tens of thousands scattered over America are saying, "This is Hans' golden wedding day." May many happy days yet come to you and your good wife, is the heartfelt wish and prayer of all of us at the Agricultural College, who are in a position to measure, in some small degree, the great good done for American agriculture.

H. A. Henry, Dean of College of Agriculture
S. M. Babcock, Professor of Agricultural Chemistry
E. L. Goff, Professor Horticulture
E. A. Holl, Assistant Professor of Agricultural Chemistry
F. H. King, Professor Agricultural Physics
John A. Craig, Professor of Animal Husbandry
H. L. Russell, Professor of Bacteriology

Professor Rosenstengel also read the following letter from Professor Adams:

University of Wisconsin, 21 February

Dear Professor Rosenstengel: It gives me great pleasure to learn that you are tomorrow to go to Jefferson for the purpose of being present at the golden wedding of the Honorable Francis A. Hoffmann. It was my purpose to send a letter by mail; but I shall now be gratified if you will present it for me in person. I wish, on behalf of the university, not only to express my congratulations on the occasion of this auspicious event, but also to thank Mr. Hoffmann very sincerely and heartily for the numerous and valuable contributions he has made to science on which so many of the people of this and other states very largely depend for their welfare and comfort. Mr. Hoffmann, by the use of his pen and example, has become known in all parts of the land; and it is a matter of sincerest congratulations that his health and vigor have enabled him to continue his usefulness in full measure to the present time. In behalf of the university I beg to express the hope that his health and happiness, and that of his wife, many continue in undiminished measure for many years to come.

Have the kindness to present this message from the university, and believe me,

Very truly yours,
C. K. Adams, President

Such in brief is the life of one of the founders of the great Republican Party. He has passed the Psalmist's span of time, of three score years and ten, with his mental and physical qualities unimpaired by participation and active interest in all the events of the day; he has seen the nation grow from twenty million people to nearly seventy million; he has seen slavery abolished and the republic tried by the greatest civil war that history records and emerge from it stronger and more firmly rooted in the hearts of the people than ever before; he has also felt himself grow into the affections of the great host to whom he weekly preaches the doctrine of industry and usefulness through his agricultural papers; he is widely known and loved for his simplicity and kindness, and in this respect resembles his great preceptor, Abraham Lincoln.[9]

The labors of "Hans Buschbauer" are probably better known to the farmers of the Northwest, and particularly of the German element, than those of any other man who has ever appeared in its history; and, though he has never become the possessor of great wealth, he and his beloved wife feel themselves rich beyond expression in the evidences of love and esteem which surround their useful life.[10] He has been honored by public confidence and held many and most important offices; but his literary labors under the *nom de plume* of "Hans Buschbauer," are the crowns of a well-spent life, and its influence will forever be felt in the well-tilled and fruitful farms of the Northwest.

NOTES

1. According to J. H. Lacher, Hoffmann (June 5, 1822–Jan. 23, 1903), "fled to America to escape conscription." See J. H. A. Lacher, "Francis Arnold Hoffmann." Dictionary of American Biography Base Set. American Council of Learned Societies, 1928–1936, Reproduced in Biography Resource Center (Farmington Hills, Mich.: The Gale Group. 2004) <http://galenet.galegroup.com/servlet/BioRC>.

2. The paper was the *Chicagoer Volksfreund*, which Hoffmann edited from 1845 to 1846. See Arndt and Olson, *The German Language Press*, 1:85.

3. Lacher notes: "When Douglas' Kansas-Nebraska Bill made the extension of slavery the dominant issue in politics, Hoffmann and his countrymen, theretofore Democrats, immediately protested. This was followed by an immense demonstration, Feb. 8, 1854, at which he took the leading part, his sensational speech predicting the defection of the Germans should the measure pass. When the bill became a law, he proved a strong factor in winning an Anti-Nebraska majority in the legislature, which elected Lyman Trumbull to the United States Senate in 1855. A friend of Lincoln, he was one of the organizers of the Republican Party

in Illinois and in 1856 was unanimously nominated for lieutenant governor, but he proved ineligible because not yet of constitutional age. He
spoke and wrote effectively, both in English and German, in 1856, 1858,
and in 1860, when he was again nominated for lieutenant-governor and
duly elected, serving with credit for four years." See Lacher, "Francis
Arnold Hoffmann."

4. According to Lacher, due to failing health "Hoffmann retired in 1875 to
his estate on Rock River near Jefferson, Wis. He had been an assiduous
student of agriculture and horticulture since boyhood, and he devoted
the rest of his life to the instruction of his countrymen in farm economy.
He became editor of *Der Haus- und Bauernfreund,* an agricultural supplement to *Die Germania* of Milwaukee; *Die Deutsche Warte* of Chicago; and
the *Deutsches Volksblatt* of Buffalo. He assumed the pen name of Hans
Buschbauer for these papers and for the books he wrote on agricultural
subjects. Attaining great popularity and influence in his new field, he
was urged to reenter politics but declined, continuing his literary activities and idyllic life at his home, 'Tusculum,' until his death." See Lacher,
"Francis Arnold Hoffmann."

5. For further information about the *Germania* and the *Volksfreund,* see
Arndt and Olson, *The German Language Press,* 1:329–30, 681–82.

6. Buschbauer's handbook appeared as *Populäres Handbuch des Grasbaus,
Futterpflanzen und der Milchwirtschaft* (Milwaukee: Verlag von Geo. Brumder, 1873). Hoffmann's library, the Francis Hoffmann Collection, is
located at the Martin Luther College Library in New Ulm, Minnesota,
and consists of more than one hundred titles.

7. As agricultural editor Hoffmann edited the weekly supplement, *Der
Haus- und Bauernfreund,* for the newspapers published by the Germania
Publishing Co. Altogether, it appeared from 1873 to 1939, and was
exceptionally popular with German-American families, and probably
could best be described as the German-American prairie home compan-
ion journal. See Arndt and Olson, *The German Language Press,* 683.

8. Regarding Brumder, see Gerhardt Becker, *A Bibliography and List of
Library Holdings of Milwaukee Publisher George Brumder (1839–1910)* (Milwaukee: University of Wisconsin-Milwaukee, Gold Meier Library, 2000).

9. For references by Lincoln about Hoffmann, see Abraham Lincoln, *The
Collected Works of Abraham Lincoln,* ed. Ray P. Basler, et al. (Washington:
Lincoln Sesquicentenial Commission, 1959), 2:345; 7:315. For Lincoln's references to Germans, see 2:345, 380, 475, 523n, 524; 3:328–29,
377n, 380; 4:166, 201–03, 367–68, 388, 418n, 476n, 479, 563n; 5:100–
01, 106, 419n; 8:83.

10. According to Victor R. Greene, Buschbauer enjoyed a "a huge reader-ship of 150,000" by means of his writings in the German-American press. See Victor R. Greene, *American Immigrant Leaders*, 56.

Part Three

———

CONCLUSION

CHAPTER 7

Illinois' German Heritage

–Don Heinrich Tolzmann

German-American Immigration History

IN 1869, FRIEDRICH MUENCH, A WELL-KNOWN MISSOURI GERMAN author, published an article in the German-American historical journal, *Der Deutsche Pionier*, describing German immigration in the nineteenth century. He divided it into three time periods: First, there were those who came before the revolution of 1848; second, were those who came after 1848; and, finally, those who came after the American Civil War. Albert B. Faust summarized Muench's analysis in his history, *The German Element in the United States (1909)*, as follows:

> Immigration No. 1, This period of German immigration attracted by such books as Duden's, turned to Missouri and other Western states, and devoted themselves to agriculture. Laborers and peasants, without any high standard of life and accustomed to hard work, found the situation to their satisfaction and gradually but steadily became prosperous. The better educated, sometimes even in spite of strenuous efforts, frequently died in the struggle. The adventurers of this group also met disappointment, and, although frequently useful as border fighters on the advance guard of civilization, did not achieve permanent success. There was also a group of refugees of 1817-18, and it was their office to elevate the tone of the other German immigrants. The Germans were commonly all Jeffersonian Democrats in their politics, as distinct from the aristocratic Whigs, and they were opposed to slavery. After the Mexican War and the discovery of gold in California, conditions in the West grew better and the German farmers became more prosperous.

> The Immigration No. 2, This period of German immigration

was heartily welcomed by the first, but the former were not well satisfied with their countrymen in America. They did not like the backwoods conditions of the earlier immigration, and only a few of them, as did Hecker, became farmers. Most of them went into the cities as merchants, manufacturers, or brain-workers of various kinds. A very frequent occupation for them was journalism, and in their newspapers they declared that we older men had not remained German enough, nor had we asserted our influence sufficiently. A war of words frequently occurred between the representatives of the two immigrations, the older receiving the nickname, "*die Grauen*," and the younger "*die Grünen.*"

The Grays had passed through an experience of twenty years of toil under primitive American frontier conditions, and had lost much of their youthful ardor for impracticable ideas. When the younger element, the Greens, arrived, they set themselves up as instructors or dictators, but the Grays were not disposed to listen to them. A better understanding came about when the new Republican Party arose and the Lincoln campaign began. Then the Germans united against slavery as one man, and the old wounds which the Grays and the Greens had inflicted in their newspaper campaigns were entirely forgotten. The Greens were useful in quickening the minds of the older generation; the latter, forming a conservative element, restrained the new arrivals in their fantastic dreams. Without the first immigration, the second would have had a much more difficult position. It would not have gained influence and would have made many a false step. Without the support of the first immigration, the second might have been quickly absorbed without leaving a trace behind. The second played an important part in American history.

Immigration No. 3, The third immigration came after the period of 1866. They were mostly of the working class, with far better schooling than the same class of thirty years before. In comparison with the earlier immigrations they were overbearing, dissatisfied with conditions as they found them in the new country, and too well impressed with those they left at home. As a rule they would not do the work of an inferior class, and as a result frequently found all desirable positions occupied. . . . Even these as a rule prosper well. Conditions are so much better here than they were thirty or forty years ago, and though the immigrants come in hundreds of thousands, they will find a place after paying for their necessary experience. I have no fear for the green or even the greenest (*die Grünen und Allergrünsten*). . . .[1]

The Nineteenth Century

The German immigrations described by Muench brought ever-increasing numbers of Germans to Illinois that resulted in their becoming the largest single ethnic element in the state. Clear patterns of settlement emerged, with Germans early on focusing on southern Illinois, especially St. Clair and surrounding counties. After the Civil War, Belleville was even referred to as the "German Athens of Illinois" due to the Latin Settlement there. By the 1840s, German immigrants began to settle rather evenly across the state, with German immigrants concentrating, however, in the north in Cook County, especially in Chicago, which from then on became the major German-American center of the state. The growth and development of the German element was reflected by a marked increase of sociopolitical influence.

German-American community leaders played an important role in the founding of the Republican Party in the 1850s–60s. Interest in obtaining German-American votes no doubt caused Lincoln to secretly acquire ownership of the *Illinois Staats-Anzeiger*, published in Springfield, which thereafter functioned "as a faithful Republican mouthpiece and organ."[2] And, when it came to the election of 1861, German-Americans were, of course, actively involved in the campaign for Lincoln.

When the Civil War broke out, Germans-Americans enthusiastically responded to the call to arms, with 130,804 of them volunteering for military service, placing them behind only three other states in terms of the number of German-Americans in service (New York, Ohio, and Pennsylvania). Hecker himself organized two Illinois Regiments, the Twenty-fourth and the Eighty-second, and Koerner the Forty-third. Other German regiments were the Ninth, Twenty-seventh, Thirty-sixth, Forty-third, Forty-fifth, Fifty-seventh, and the Fifty-eighth. Other German units were the Twelfth, Thirteenth and Sixteenth Illinois Cavalry Regiments, and the artillery batteries of Stollemann, D'Osband, and Gumbert.[3]

After the Civil War, German-Americans could point not only to their recent achievements in the War Between the States, but also to their percentage of the population. In 1870, the German-speaking population was estimated at 400,000 out of a total population of 2.5 million in Illinois. Of the German-speaking element, 211,000 were German-born and 9,000 were Swiss-born. Of the foreign-born, slightly more than half, or 102,111, were located in five counties: Cook—65,883; St. Clair—12,328; Adams—8,957; Madison—8,924; and Will—6,019. Most likely half of the state's German-speaking population could be found in these counties as well, while the rest of the German element was settled throughout the state's various counties. In terms of urban areas German-Americans were especially strong in Belleville, Bloomington, Blue Island, Cairo, Carlinville, Chicago, Decatur, Galena, Havana, Joliet, Pekin, Peoria, Peru, and, Rock Island, and Springfield. German-Americans in the state were mainly engaged in agriculture, but were also involved in every field of business and industry, with the major concentrations of business and industry in Chicago.[4]

Religious institutions developed throughout the state to serve the growing German-American population. By 1870, the "German Catholics were served by 120 priests, the Lutherans by 205 ministers, the Reformed Church by 12. The German Baptists had 11 congregations with 12 Sunday schools and 84 teachers. The Evangelical Church had 70 ministers and 105 Sunday schools. There were 18 German Methodist churches, 10 German Presbyterian, 33 'Unierte Kirchen,' 1 free Protestant and 2 Herrnhuter congregations." There were also a wide variety of German societies and lodges across the state, many of them with their own clubhouses. Especially impressive was the Germania Club of Chicago, as well as the sixteen Turnvereine across the state. These religious and secular institutions provided the foundations and organizational structure of German-American community life throughout Illinois.[5]

German instruction was available in Illinois at public, private and parochial schools throughout the state, although there was no state law regarding it, and German-Americans, especially members of the Turnvereine, promoted the introduction of physical education into the public schools. After the founding of the German library in Belleville, German-Americans established several private libraries across the state and got involved with and supported public libraries so that they also acquired German books, newspapers, and journals. The *Illinois Staats-Zeitung* often stressed with great pride that the director of the Chicago Public Library was Frederick Hild, a German who served as head librarian,

1887–1909, and whose name is perpetuated in a branch library at 4536 North Lincoln Ave. in Chicago. One of the most ambitious undertakings was that of the Germania Club of Chicago, which established a library to collect works by German-American authors, and which culminated in the publication of an anthology of German-American literature in 1893, edited by Dr. G. A. Zimmermann, a member of the Club's library board.[6]

German-American authors published a wide variety of works, many of which were published in Chicago. However, they could also turn to other publishers in nearby St. Louis and Milwaukee, as well as to the presses of German-American newspapers in Illinois. Rudolf Hofmeister compiled a list of fifty-three German-American authors active in Chicago alone, noting that although incomplete, his list provides "an inkling of the large number of German-American authors active in Chicago at one time." Although active in business and public affairs, Caspar Butz, a Forty-Eighter, for example, published numerous poems on a wide variety of topics, and brought out a work now considered a classic in German-American literature: *Gedichte eines Deutsch-Amerikaners* (1879).[7]

German theaters thrived in Chicago, while German-Americans in southern Illinois had access to those in nearby St. Louis. German theaters produced works by German, as well as German-American authors. For example, in 1889, several performances of Schiller's plays were held at German theaters in Chicago in honor of the German author's 130th birthday. And, in 1892, at the Schiller Theater in Chicago *Die Pioniere*, a play by the German-American author Julius Gugler, was performed that dealt with the German-American experience. German-Americans were also actively involved in various fields of the arts, architecture, and music, with the major activities and contributions taking place in Chicago.[8]

The three immigrations described by Muench contributed to the growth and development of the German element in Illinois, but it was the arrival of the Forty-Eighters that proved to be crucial in terms of establishing the German element as a group that had to be reckoned with. The Forty-Eighters assumed the role of German-American community leaders and spokesmen, and formulated and promoted an agenda designed to advance German-American interests. As Muench observed, many of them gravitated to the German-American press, by means of which the German element came to exert socio-political influence across the state.

In 1870, there were twenty-seven German newspapers, of which six were dailies: three in Chicago, and one each in Belleville, Peoria, and Quincy. Weeklies appeared in the following cities: Alton, Aurora, Belleville, Bloomington, Chicago, Edwardsville, Freeport, Galena, Highland, Nauvoo, Ottawa, Peoria, Quincy, Springfield, and Warsaw. Altogether, seventy towns and cities in Illinois have a history of publishing German-American newspapers and journals. The top six, with the number of publications per place, were Chicago, 273; Belleville, 20; Quincy, 19; Peoria, 18; Springfield, 14; and Bloomington, 13. Together these six places formed the major German-American press centers in the state of Illinois.[9]

The growth and development of the German element was reflected, of course, by increased political influence. The following were elected to the office of representative in the state legislature: John Stuntz, 1832; Gustav Koerner, 1842; Peter Lott, 1844; G. M. Kretzinger and F. Remann, 1846; Edmund Abend, 1848; D. Wolf, 1852; A. H. Trapp, 1854; A. F. C. Mueller, 1856; John Scheel, Wm. Engle, and Caspar Butz, 1858; Peter Kiefer, 1860; R. Roessler and John Kistler, 1862; Geo. H. Metz, 1867; Geo. Gundlach and H. B.Miller, 1869; G. A.Koerner, Th. Miller, Edw. Roessler, Aug. Reise, Joseph Reinhard, Wm. Massenberg, Wm. Vocke, and H. C. Senne, 1871. Note that the first German-American was elected as early as 1832, but that it was only after the election of Koerner in 1842 that German-Americans were elected with regularity and in increasing numbers.[10]

German-Americans also were elected to some of the highest state offices, beginning with Koerner, who was elected lieutenant governor, 1853–57, and was then followed several years later by Hoffmann, 1861–

Masthead of the *Eintracht*, a German-American newspaper published since 1922 in Skokie, Illinois.

65. Other German-Americans elected to state office were E. Rummel, secretary of state, 1869–73, and H. Dilger, adjutant general, 1869–73. At the local and county level German-Americans were also elected to a wide variety of offices. Koerner, Hecker, and Hoffmann were no doubt the major German-American political leaders of their time. Other important leaders of their generation were (in alphabetical order): Lorenz Brentano, Caspar Butz, Georg Hillgaertner, E. Rummel, Georg Schneider, and S. J. Stibold.[11]

Several public policy issues were of concern to German-Americans in the late nineteenth century. In general the Illinois Germans supported the Republican Party and protectionism, but like Carl Schurz, they could also be politically independent, basing their vote on principal rather than party. Many, therefore, shifted to the Democrats in 1884 and 1892 when Grover Cleveland ran for president, but then became disenchanted with his policies, especially those relating to the issue of free silver. The German-American press supported the Spanish-American War, but avoided the jingoistic journalism that characterized the non-German press. German-Americans strongly supported and defended German bilingual education in the public schools, and elected representatives to the school boards to maintain German programs throughout the state. Also, due to their connections with the Old Country, they took an avid interest in news relating to European affairs, usually "with leanings toward the Germanic view and times with a definite Anglophobia."[12]

In 1892, John Peter Altgeld, a German immigrant, was elected governor, the first German-American elected to the state's highest office. His family had immigrated to Richland County, Ohio, where Altgeld grew up. After brief service in an Ohio volunteer regiment in 1864, he moved west, studied law, and was elected state's attorney for Andrew County, Missouri in 1874. He then moved to Chicago, and was elected to the superior court of Cook County in 1886. When he resigned from the bench in 1891, he was chief justice of the court. In 1884, he published a book, *Our Penal Machinery and its Victims*, a controversial work that advocated prison reform.[13] His election to office in 1892 was part of the wave of success that had swept Cleveland back into the presidency for a second term in 1890. His German heritage no doubt stood him in good stead at the polls as well.

After taking office, Altgeld acted on an appeal for clemency from some of the anarchists, who had been convicted for complicity in the murders during the 1886 Haymarket Riot in Chicago; four of their associates had already been executed in 1887. After reviewing the case, Altgeld pardoned three of the anarchists who had been sentenced to life imprisonment. It might be noted that eight of the ten men indicted and six of the eight convicted were German, and two of the three pardoned by Altgeld were German. However, most German-Americans were conservative and had supported their conviction, and the executions. Moreover, "the *Illinois Staats-Zeitung* was as violent as any in its denunciation of the German-American anarchists; it claimed that the rage was just as great among the body of the German-Americans as among others, and bitterly resented the bad name that such action tended to give to the Germans of the country." It also vigorously supported the executions of 1887.[14]

His decision to issue the pardons as well as the guilt or innocence of the anarchists is still debated today. However, what is not debatable was that his decision was controversial. The general public clearly and overwhelmingly supported the convictions of the anarchists and their executions, as did German-Americans, who went out of their way to demonstrate that they harbored no support whatsoever for political extremists who just happened to be German-American. Altgeld's pardon brought forth a tremendous storm of protest, and the governor was widely ridiculed as John "Pardon" Altgeld. In 1894, a militant strike against the Pullman factories took place, and President Cleveland called in federal troops to restore order in respond to the call from the Illinois Attorney General, although Altgeld strongly protested the action as a violation of state's rights. In 1896, he was re-nominated for office, but defeated in the election, and his political career was over.

The Haymarket pardons adversely affected German-American affairs in several ways. First, nativists claimed that the evils of socialism and anarchism had been brought to America by German immigrants and were now being fomented by German-Americans. Second, this was further exacerbated by the fact that the imprisoned individuals had been pardoned by a German-American governor. This nativist reaction translated into increased support for the control and restriction of immigration, and also no doubt aroused some anti-German sentiment. Finally, for German-Americans it meant the loss of an elected official they had helped elect to office, and one who might have become another Koerner or Hoffmann, and even had been mentioned as a possible presidential candidate.

Nevertheless, German-Americans could take heart in the words of wisdom expressed by none other than the foremost German-American of the time: Carl Schurz.

On 15 June 1893, he spoke at the German Day celebration, which was held in Chicago in conjunction with the World's Fair, and called on German-Americans to look beyond the transitory issues of the day, and focus on the enduring foundation of German-American identity. What does it mean to be a German-American? What is the role of the German element in American society, and what are the duties and responsibilities of German-Americans? In addressing such basic questions, Schurz explained and defined German-American identity.

Schurz began by stressing American citizenship, stating that "We are proud of the mighty and noble nation of which we feel ourselves a part, proud of the glorious Stars and Stripes, the symbol of dearly-won national unity, the emblem of a great past and a still greater future. - of all these we are as proud as the proudest." He also emphasized contributions made by German-Americans, noting that "On the roll of heroes and martyrs of the Republic, German names have never been wanting. In the domain of thought and in the workshop, the German mind and the German hand have toiled with diligence, and with abundant results; and we may say that the soil of America has been enriched by the sacrifice of German blood and labor." And, he maintained that the role played by German-Americans in American society was widely recognized: "Ask the true patriot and he will tell you that he confidently relies upon the sane and fair sense and the patriotic inspiration of the German-American citizen."[15]

With regard to the German ancestral homeland, he observed that German-Americans should be "proud to be the offspring of a great nation," and compares the Old and the New World to one's mother and spouse, stating, "he who does not revere his old mother will not truly love his bride." German heritage and American citizenship, therefore, blended harmoniously together. Moreover, German-Americans "can accomplish great things for the development of the great composite nation of the New World," if in their works and deeds they combine and meld "the best that is in the German character with the best that is in the American." In so doing, German-Americans would honor their American citizenship, as well as their German heritage.[16] German-Americanism had now been defined by the foremost German-American of the time.

The Twentieth Century

Schurz's 1893 German Day address at the World's Fair in Chicago typi-
fied the growing sense of pride in German-American identity that characterized German-Americans by the turn of the century. This was no
doubt best expressed in vast array of German-American organizations
they had created to preserve and advance the German heritage, including, social, cultural, musical, historical, trade, and professional organizations. These organizations offered a wide variety of programs, activities,
functions, and festivals promoting the German heritage, and many had
their own clubhouses that served as German heritage cultural centers.

In 1871, the celebration of German unity across the United States
led to discussion of the need for German-American unity, and it was
suggested that a national association of German-American societies be
established to promote the preservation of German heritage and German-American relations. This idea was evolved further on 6 October
1883 when the two hundredth anniversary of the founding of the first
permanent German settlement in America at Germantown, Pennsylvania, was celebrated as the German-American Bicentennial.

The 1883 German-American Bicentennial was also celebrated in
Illinois, and of special note was the celebration that took place at
Belleville. It was held at the city park and included musical presenta-
tions by the Philharmonic Society and the Liederkranz, which were followed by the main address delivered by Gustav Koerner. He spoke of the
significance of the event, as well as of the contributions German-American had made to the United States, and emphasized the fact that the
first protest against the institution of slavery in America had been issued
by German-Americans at Germantown in 1688. He concluded his
address by saying that German-Americans should fulfill their civic duties
and responsibilities as American citizens, but also reminded the not to
forget: "that we are descendants of a great and noble people, in whose
destiny we take the warmest interest, and for whom our hearts beat with
unfading love." Koerner also noted: "Since that time, this day, called the
'German Day,' has been more or less celebrated by the German population, and in some of the larger cities, particularly in St. Louis, the festival has led to demonstrations of such vast proportions as to surpass the
expectations of the naturalized as well as the native citizens."[17]

After 1883, German-American organizations came to sponsor German Day, and in 1899 a federation of them in Pennsylvania founded the

German-American Central Alliance of Pennsylvania. This Alliance called for a national meeting on the 6 of the October 1901 in Philadelphia, at which time the National German-American Alliance was formed. The National German-American Alliance consisted of state chapters, which in turn consisted of federations at the city, or town level in urban areas, or at the county level in rural areas. By the time of the First World War, the Alliance claimed more than two million members nationally, and had become the largest ethnic organization in American history. The German-American Alliance of Illinois had a total membership of thirty thousand. By way of comparison, the Wisconsin Alliance had thirty-seven thousand members, while the Missouri Alliance had more than twenty thousand. Altogether, the Alliance had branches in forty states.[18]

The German-American Alliance of Illinois came into being by evolution. In June 1904, the German-American Alliance of Missouri and Southern Illinois had been formed, and one of its first projects was participation in the celebration of German Day that was held in conjunction with the Louisiana Purchase Exposition in St. Louis. German-Americans took great pride that the main address at the 1904 German Day was presented by Carl Schurz, who had so successfully expressed and epitomized what it meant to be German-American. Two years later, in 1906, the German-American Alliance of Chicago was formed, and became one of the largest local branches of the Alliances in the country. Thereafter, other Alliances were formed across Illinois.[19]

At the national convention of the Alliance in New York in 1907, the Illinois Alliance reported that eighty-one German-American societies with a total of nine thousand members had joined the Alliance, so that there appeared to be enough members to form a state Alliance. Therefore, in 1908, the southern Illinois Alliances split off from the Missouri Alliance to join the Alliance of Chicago and other Illinois Alliances to form the German-American Alliance of Illinois. The state Alliance promoted and sponsored statewide celebrations of German Day, which was also sponsored in towns and cities throughout Illinois. By the time of World War I, there were close to seven hundred German-American organizations in Illinois, and most were affiliated with the state Alliance. Annual conventions were held at various places in the state, and usually in early September.[20]

The National Alliance published a journal entitled *Mitteilungen*, and also took over publication of a journal that carried its reports, *German-*

American Annals. It also claimed every German-American newspaper as its organ and worked closely with the press for the publications of its news releases and reports. The Alliance's platform stated that it aimed to awaken and strengthen a sense of unity among German-Americans:

> ... for the mutual energetic protection of such legitimate desires and interests not inconsistent with the common good of the country and the rights and duties of good citizens; to check nativist encroachments; to maintain and safeguard the good relations existing between America and the old German father-land.[21]

With regard to German-American contributions, the Alliance asked for the "full and honest recognition of these merits and opposed every attempt to belittle them."[22] It stated that the best way of obtaining these goals was to join the Alliance, and invited all to join it, and if there were no local branches to establish one. The Alliance also claimed it had the right and obligation to enter the political arena at any time to defend its principles and that it would inaugurate and support all legislation for the common good of the country. What did the Alliance stand for? Its goals and purposes were to:

1. Increase the feeling of unity in the German element in the U.S.
2. Promote good citizenship.
3. Oppose nativist influences.
4. Cultivate relations between America and Germany.
5. Further the study of German-American history.
6. Recommend German instruction in schools.
7. Recommend physical education in schools.
8. Encourage the naturalization of immigrants and the exercise of voting rights.
9. Oppose immigration restriction.
10. Recommended the repeal of Sunday laws and oppose prohibition as violations of personal liberty.

In short, the basic goal of the Alliance was "to preserve and unite what is best in German culture and character, and devote it to the best interests of the U.S."[23] This essentially was paraphrasing what Carl Schurz had said in his 1893 German Day address in Chicago, and demonstrates the national impact this he exerted and the degree to which German-Americans identified with his exposition of German-American identity.

In 1907, the Alliance was incorporated by an act of Congress with the assistance of Congressman Richard Bartholdt of Missouri. One of its first activities was to collect funds for the creation of Founders Monument at Germantown, Pennsylvania in honor of the first German settlers there. It also erected monuments elsewhere, and supported various philanthropic and cultural programs and projects. At the state level, the state chapters of the Alliance actively worked to defeat all attempts at anything that smacked of prohibition, and at the local level reviewed and endorsed candidates in accordance with its platform. There is no question that the German-American Alliance had acquired considerable influence across the state of Illinois, with its largest local chapter being located in Chicago.

One of the organizations that affiliated with the Illinois Alliance was a recent creation, and a valuable one for the German heritage, the German-American Historical Society of Illinois. Its mere creation reflected the growing sense of German-American identity and pride. It was established in April 1900 in Chicago, and its distinguished membership included Dr. Otto L. Schmidt, Emil Mannhardt, Dr. G.A. Zimmermann, and Wilhelm Vocke.[24] In 1901, the Society commenced publication of a quarterly journal of German-American history, but switched to a yearbook in 1912, when Julius Goebel, Chair of the German Department at the University of Illinois-Urbana, became its editor.[25] Under his direction, the yearbook acquired a national reputation as an outstanding German-American historical journal, and its focus expanded from coverage of Illinois German-American to topics covering German-American historical topics elsewhere as well. It also issued special supplements, including one focusing on Gustav Koerner.[26]

Julius Goebel, born in Frankfurt am Main in 1857, had studied at the Universities of Leipzig and Tübingen and had taught at Johns Hopkins University, Stanford University, and Harvard before coming to Urbana. Goebel published several books dealing with German-American history, as well as German literature and culture, and spoke frequently at German-American programs throughout the state. A student reporter described a meeting with Goebel as follows: "A genial gentleman with a perfect Van Dyke beard, opened the door for me and invited me to come in and make myself comfortable. He reminded me of a German aristocrat with an American heart—an industrious scholar with plenty of time for hospitality with a stranger—a writer of past events with the dreaminess of the future in his deep-set eyes."[27] Another reporter described one of his lecture series as follows: "The lecturer's mastery of his subject and the grace and elegance of his delivery have greatly endeared him to his audience, and the wish of hearing him soon again in a similar course was expressed last evening on all sides."[28]

Goebel was especially interested in the German author, Goethe, and edited volumes of his poetry, as well as an edition of *Faust*. He wrote of Goethe: "No poet before him, neither Shakespeare, nor Sophocles, has disclosed to us as he has done the depths of the human heart and has shown us the deep abysses of man's nature."[29] He felt that because Goethe "understood man so thoroughly he has also been able to show more clearly than anyone before him man's power and man's duty. Not in glittering idealizations in which no one believes and which no one can realize, but in forms true to life and immortal which are of our flesh, in high demands which set in activity the best that is in us. . . . To Goethe, then, we must turn if we would seek that which is holy, eternal and inviolable in the human breast that which science can give nor explain, nor take form us—to Goethe, who knew life most profoundly, who interpreted it most clearly."[30]

Goebel focused particularly on advancing an appreciation and understanding of the role played by German-Americans in American history. "With characteristic energy and a devotion utterly unselfish. Julius Goebel threw himself into the endeavor of bringing about a realization of his ideals. No organization of his countrymen was too modest, no publication too fugitive for him to give lavishly of his time in speaking and writing. It is impossible to list the scores of addresses he made for a cause that seemed to him nothing less than holy, or the countless articles that appeared in magazines and newspapers both obscure and widely read."[31]

In January 1914, Goebel completed a collection of his essays, expressing the hope that German-American aspirations would stay on track and continue to bear fruit. Little did he realize that war clouds were on the horizon "and that conditions were being created which would shatter the realization of these dreams, if not forever, at least for many years. . . . There can be no doubt that the World War was the major catastrophe of Julius Goebel's life—and it will be to his credit that, in spite of his pronounced view firmly maintained, which might all too easily be misconstrued in a time of such national hysteria, his loyalty to his adopted country was never assailed."[32]

When the war broke out in 1914, German-Americans were as naturally pro-German as were Anglo-Americans pro-England. They soon felt that the American press in general was more favorably disposed towards England and her allies than Germany and Austro-Hungary. And, in spite of his declarations of neutrality, Wilson was felt to be definitely pro-England in word and deed. By means of the Alliance and the German-American press, German-Americans, therefore, sought to maintain American neutrality and clarify the actual facts with regard to the war. Already in August 1914, the Illinois Alliance complained to the White House that although the British cable was allowed by freely send its news to the United States, the radio stations that provided news from Germany were being censored by the U.S. Navy.[33]

The Chicago *Abendpost* and the *Illinois Staats-Zeitung* both maintained that England, rather than Germany was ultimately the chief culprit responsible for the outbreak of the war, as it had the most to gain from a victory of the Triple Entente.[34] The German-Ameican press also claimed that if anything the war would bring about greater unity among German-Americans as a group, which in fact was true as membership in German-American societies and readership of German-American newspapers actually did increase. On 1 December 1914, the publisher of the *Illinois Staats-Zeitung* presided over a mass meeting in Chicago to call attention to the munitions trade that was supplying arms to England and its allies, and to request an arms embargo. German-Americans protested the British blockade of Germany, and the *Illinois Staats-Zeitung* even suggested that Wilson be impeached for his lack of neutrality in foreign affairs. After Wilson approved loans to the Allies by American bankers, German-Americans understandably protested that this violated American neutrality. And, in September 1915, the Illinois Alliance sent a telegram to Wilson calling such loans crimes against humanity. It claimed that it was "a great injustice to take away from the American nation so large a sum of money, which could be used for the development of its own industry and commerce."[35] Moreover, at the annual convention of the German-American Alliance in Peru, Illinois that year, the group threatened to boycott any bank involved in such loans.

In February 1916, a meeting of fifty German-American newspaper editors was held in Chicago. It was led by Horace L. Brand of the *Illinois Staats-Zeitung* and Paul Mueller of the *Chicago Abendpost*. Plans were formulated to organize a national association of German-American newspaper publishers that would enable the German-American press to obtain news from the Central Powers and provide a more accurate coverage of the war. Mueller was elected president and visited Wilson in March of that year, and reported to him that most German-Americans opposed his foreign policy. As the 1916 presidential election approached, the *Illinois Staats-Zeitung* increasingly considered Hughes, a Republican, the best candidate for president, and the secretary of the German-American Alliance of Illinois announced that it had long since been in favor of Hughes.

In March 1916, the Illinois Alliance held a special meeting to make plans for the fall election and adopted the slogan of "Everyone against Roosevelt and Wilson." It also informed all the branches of the Illinois Alliance that the German-American vote held the balance of power in the state and that it should make its presence known. The Alliance also claimed that it was working together with other German-American organizations against the re-election of Wilson, and that it now represented a total of seventy-five thousand votes. At the September 1916 convention of the Illinois Alliance, the mere mention of the name of Hughes brought a round of applause. And, when it came to the fall of 1916, many papers, including the influential *Illinois Staats-Zeitung*, not surprisingly endorsed the Republican candidate. The reelection of Wilson was, of course, a major disappointment for German-Americans who had supported Hughes, and given Wilson's record, it was almost a foregone conclusion that war was inevitable.

In his history of the Chicago Germans, Andrew Jacke Townsend summarized the German-American position with regard to the war: "The German view as to the causes of the war was accepted. England was especially blamed. Chicago Germans refused to believe the alleged atrocities in Belgium; news came from English sources and was unreliable. They thought Germany had the right to engage in submarine warfare," and were "justifiable weapons against allied violations of international law." German-Americans were especially hostile towards England:, which "was blamed for starting the war, her violations of neutral rights were cited frequently, England was regarded as chiefly responsible for the Lusitania episode, and the English were said to be engaged in propaganda for their cause." German-Americans were particularly enraged at England's blockade of Germany, and "the starving of the Germans was bitterly condemned." They were "overwhelmingly against embroiling the United States in the war" and "the events leading to our entry into the war were viewed with sadness," but after the declaration

German-Americans were ready to do their duty. The First World War had a great impact on German-Americans: "From 1914 to April 1917, it caused them to stand solidly together for the propagation of their views. Even after 1917 the feeling of solidarity was strong to the feeling that they were being persecuted." German-Americans obviously suffered from the ensuring anti-German hysteria and sentiment, and "were frequently looked on with suspicion and were forced to adopt an attitude of defense. The use of German, the German press, and the teaching of German in the schools were all frowned upon."[36]

Across the United States, German-Americans not only enlisted in great numbers, but also invested heavily in the Liberty Loan drives as ways to demonstrate their patriotism. Nonetheless, they were swept up in the winds of war that engendered an anti-German hysteria and sentiment. German-Americans did their duty, but most likely felt like future Senator Everett Dirksen, who was born in a German-speaking family. In his autobiography he wrote of his mother's concern of his forthcoming service in the U.S. Army, noting that "My mother was quite upset. There were many quiet hours when we sat together mostly in silence thinking of where my military duty would take me and whether or not I would ever return from the conflict if I were assigned to overseas service. I tried as best I could to console her. I hoped she would find comfort in the fact that a service star in the front window of our home would be a loud and clear announcement to the neighborhood and to the world that one member of the family was in military service, for we had to remember that we were of German extraction, and there was a certain prejudice about us."[37]

During his visit, Dirksen noticed "the glossy photo of Kaiser Wilhelm and his entire family which was prominently displayed on the wall of our living room. In our town they were still publishing a German language newspaper, and this photograph had come to Mother a few years before as a premium for a year's subscription when paid in advance." Dirksen then said: "Mother, I believe it would be the wise and discreet thing to remove that photograph from the wall. I would wrap it securely in heavy paper and put away until this very unpleasant business is over." He noted: "That was the principal reason why she had come to this country from Germany only a decade or more after the Civil War. She pointed out that there was no law to compel her to remove this picture. She thought the Kaiser was a good family man and not to be blamed for what the politicians had done."

Dirksen responded: "But Mother," I persisted, "there will be not only neighbors but strangers in and out of our house while I am gone. You know how the war generates deep feelings and even deeper hates as the war spirit rises. Sentiment against the Kaiser may grow to cyclonic proportions; someone will complain about you and that never fails to develop a wretched and embarrassing situation." Nonetheless, Dirksen's mother stood her ground, and Dirksen wrote: "so as I boarded a train for Camp Custer, Michigan, to be sworn into the army as a private first class, the photograph of the Kaiser and his family still hung on our living room wall."

In his address at the 1933 German Day celebration in Chicago, Georg Seibel summarized the wrongs and injustices German-Americans had endured throughout the First World War. He spoke of "great suffering during the bitter war years." German-Americans across the country had been "interned, beaten, ruined in business because they were German. German books were burned, and 'patriotic' women avowed never to buy German goods again. We were called barbarians and Huns; we were the 'scum of humanity' because we were German. The world had gone mad with war hysteria." The German-Americanism that Koerner and Schurz had so ably represented and which had become not only a source of pride to German-Americans, but the very foundation of the definition of German-American identity now stood under direct assault during the First World War. Two events exemplifying the anti-German hysteria were the dissolution of the German-American Alliance of Illinois. and the lynching of Robert P. Prager at Collinsville, Illinois.

The National German-American Alliance came under increasing pressure as the country was swept up into the anti-German hysteria of the time. In January 1918, Sen. William King of Utah introduced a bill in Congress to repeal the 1907 charter of the Alliance. "This became the national signal not only for concerted action against the Alliance across the country, but against German-Americans in general as well. Moreover, it signified that the anti-German hysteria was going to receive official support and backing from the U.S. Congress."[38] Senate hearings were then held from February through April 1918, and in July, the U.S. Congress repealed the charter. Fortunately, however, the Alliance had already seen the handwriting on the wall, and had officially dissolved itself on 11 April 1918. It issued a final statement, indicating that:

As American Citizens of German blood, whole-heartedly and without reservation, we say to our fellow citizens that together with them we shall ever stand ready to defend this government and this country against all foes, internal and external, to the end that the liberty and freedom guaranteed by the Constitution shall forever prevail.[39]

The same day the Executive Committee of the German-American Alliance of Illinois met at the Bismarck Hotel in Chicago, and voted the same way, thereby destroying the central organization representing the numerous German-American societies across the state of Illinois.

On 4 April 1918, Robert P. Prager, a German-American coal miner, was taken by a mob and lynched in Collinsville, although he was guilty of no crime, or offense, but had only been accused of being "pro-German." The *New York Times* carried an article the next day entitled "German is Lynched by an Illinois Mob." Newspapers also reported that no "concrete instances of disloyalty by Prager" could be found. Due to his membership in a St. Louis lodge, he was buried in St. Louis, and in accordance with "a request said to have been made by the dying man, an American flag was draped over his coffin." The inscription on his gravestone reads simply: "Robert P. Prager, born Feb. 28, 1888 at Dresden, Saxony–Died Apr. 5, 1918 in Collinsville, Ill. The Victim of a Mob." Eleven men were then placed on trial for lynching Prager, but in a gross miscarriage of justice, were acquitted in a jury trial. Gov. Lowden issued the following statement:

Of course, I was much disappointed in the Prager case. Prager was hanged because of a suspicion of his disloyalty to the government. Patriotism was the guise worn by the perpetrators of this crime. The jury seemed to think that it could best show its own loyalty by condoning this crime of those who claimed to act in the name of loyalty. The result was a lamentable failure of justice. . . . Democracy is on trial. Every activity of a mob is an assault upon the very principal of democracy. Every man who join the mob is answerable, morally and legally, for everything the mob does. A true patriot in this crisis is he who not only helps his country to win battles abroad, but who also helps his country to preserve order at home.[40]

Although German-Americans found it advisable to remain silent publicly on the topic of Prager's lynching, many were angry and bitter about the lynching and the acquittal of the members of the lynch mob. Otto Butz, son of Caspar Butz and president of a pro-war group, the

Friends of German Democracy, protested the matter in a letter to President Wilson. The President responded that his administration would "cooperate with every effort to see to it that the loyal residents of the United States of German birth or descent are given genuine proof of the sincerity of our constitutions." "However, by now many German-Americans "were beginning to doubt whether the Constitution really protected them." They had "tried to demonstrate their loyalty with apparently little influence on public opinion." One commentator wrote that German-Americans were bewildered by what had happened, feeling the pain of "a deep sense of unfairness." One German-American wrote to Sen. James Hamilton Lewis about the "war of injustice and hatred" being waged against German-Americans. He claimed that it was a "war of destruction," and that:

> Annihilation is its aim . . . the German language is to be tabooed, every man and woman of German stock and name is to be made a despised pariah, and left to the tender mercies of any bloodthirsty mob, or any scoundrel, who uses the Stars and Stripes to hide behind, so as to be enabled to safely carry out his plans of private vengeance or greed or mere ordinary cussedness.[41]

The demise of the Alliance and the lynching of Prager reflected the mean spirit of the time and demonstrate the extent to which German-Americans suffered as a result of their German heritage during the First World War. After the war, German-Americans generally supported the Republican Party as a consequence of the way Woodrow Wilson had handled the war, as well as the following peace negotiations. They now looked forward to Warren G. Harding's call for a return to "normalcy." This by and large was the path taken by German-Americans nationally in the 1920s. In the 1920 presidential election, Harding won a smashing victory at the polls, and German-Americans continued to support the Republican ticket throughout the decade, although LaFollette did attract some in 1924. As elsewhere, German-Americans opposed the League of Nations, as well as the World Court, reflecting their aversion to becoming entangled in international organizations.

German-American community life also began to re-assert itself after the war, and German Day celebrations returned to Chicago. In 1925, the *Chicago Abendpost* reported that "the German oak tree is still alive despite some devastating storms."[42] Still reeling from the blows of the

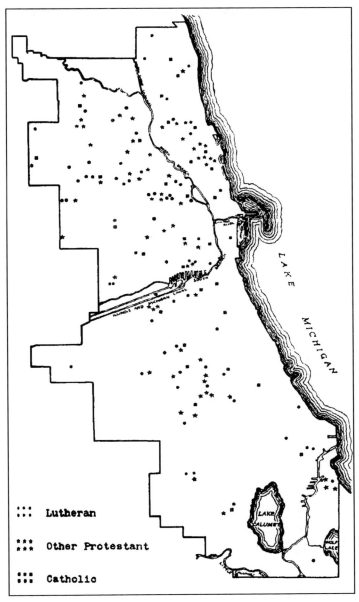

German Churches in Chicago in 1923.

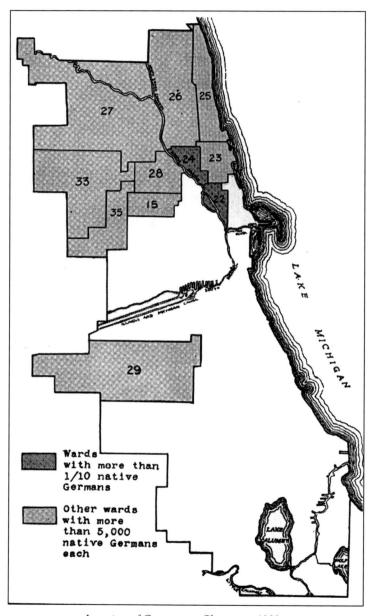

Location of Germans in Chicago in 1929

war, German-Americans now faced an internal problem posed by the emergence of the pro-Nazi German-American Bund. The German-American press warned against joining, or having anything to do with the Bund, reflecting the widespread opposition of German-Americans to the organization. Moreover, the Bund was excluded from the annual German Day celebrations in Chicago, when the Bund's swastika flag was banned from display. The Bund then collapsed after its national leader, Fritz Kuhn, was convicted in 1939 for embezzling the organization. While successfully addressing the question of the Bund, German-Americans were still at work striving to overcome the blows they had endured during the war.

Speaking at Lincoln's Birthday Party at the Germania Club in Chicago in February 1940, Major A. F. W. Siebel stated that German-Americans have "no animosity for any class of persons," and that:

> We admire that which is noble in all nationalities and detest the man who would minimize the significance of contributions made by any people. We shall insist upon bestowing credit where credit is due, whether that be upon men of German descent or otherwise. Germania stands for pure Americanism but we shall not be bludgeoned into a wholesale hatred of the land where our fathers died without exercising our own judgement and without analyzing the suspicious evidence presented. We shall admire the good in all nations and abhor the evil and we are not parading under the assumption that we have a monopoly of all that's good.[43]

Siebel also noted that German-Americans were in need of leadership, and called them to recall Carl Schurz and all that he stood for:

> Not since the days of Carl Schurz have we had a leader who could correctly lead. Oh for a man who can restore our element to its proper position in the American social structure. A man uninfluenced by ulterior motives. A man devoid of ambitions for himself who will strive on only in the unselfish desire to help others. A man who will rise without aspirations of his own but by the impetus of those around him rising by virtue of his unselfish assistance. A man of independent action whose course is not shaped by alluring promises benefiting him alone. A man who is unfettered by his own inability to steer an independent course. A man emancipated entirely from the strings

of political control for he who has ambitions of his own cannot properly serve the interests of others. A man who will remain undaunted when facing impenetrable propaganda against his cause and continue to fight for the righteousness of man. He must revere the virtues of his ancestors for without that he has no pride of ancestry and without that he has no pride with which to face the world.[44]

Siebel noted that "a man of rectitude and ability that measures up to these specifications if the only one that can preserve the culture that your ancestors have contributed to Americanism, and the search for and development of such a man is the objective of the Germania Club." He also called on the assistance of all to develop such leadership among German-Americans so that "we may again attain the position once occupied in the councils of our country. May pride of ancestry envelop our aspirations to attain the perfect American and thereby keep step with the music of the flag that flutters in the breeze and carries the spirit of justice and liberty to the heart of America."[45]

Writing for the the Germania yearbook, published in 1940, William F. Bieber, Manager of the Germania Club, noted the importance of the society, stating that "present day influences seek to rend asunder all the achievements of our ancestors that might reflect a background to our people of German descent, that might enable them to travel onward and upward with equal strides of other nationals...Unfortunate as it may be, the world wide conditions make it imperative that we join somewhere to insist upon a position in our American civilization commensurate with the quality of our contributions."[46]

No doubt sensing that war clouds loomed on the horizon, Bieber commented on the responsibilities of German-Americans, should there be another world war. He observed that "ours is the noble and solemn obligation to keep our heads cool in the midst of bedlam," and that German-American "must preserve the priceless, spiritual inheritance" of those "who came before us to a land which at their time knew naught of international hate. We can cultivate the soil of society for the greater peace to come, seeking refuge with the great poets of our race in the temple of art, beauty, the realm of truth. We can travel the highway of our national destiny by cultivating that highest expression of all human art and emotion which knows no political or economical feuds, we can march on and sing our song."[47]

Bieber's words of wisdom were well-spoken and good advice as another world war followed the next year. Having hardly recovered from World War One, German-Americans faced a world war for the second time. Commenting on the German-American experience, Ernst Ott noted that:

> . . . the disastrous consequences of two world wars left the German-American community in a rather fragmented state, particularly at the end of World War II. As a result of strong anti-German sentiments, German language teaching in schools was dropped, German institutions closed down, and many German societies dissolved. American citizens of German descent, suspected of pro-German sympathies were, often without due process, interned and kept interned up to 3 years after the war ended. By then even German POWs were already released and shipped back home.[48]

When the Second World War came, German-Americans served as staunchly as they had in the preceding war, solidly demonstrating their Americanism. Like everyone, German-Americans faced the turmoil of two world wars, as well as Prohibition and the Great Depression, but they were much harder for them. The wars involved their ancestral homeland, and Prohibition and the Depression affected one of their great areas of industrial strength: the brewing industry, as well as all those related to it. Therefore, it would be well into the post-war era before a true period of "normalcy" began to return for them, and when issues and interests relating to the German heritage would again emerge.

German immigration also increased before and after the war. Many migrated before the war due to opposition to the Third Reich, and during and after the war many had lost their homelands, and were also forced to immigrate. These immigrations both contributed immensely to the state of Illinois in general, but also to the German element and heritage in particular. No doubt the most prominent of the pre-war immigrants were those who had been associated with the Bauhaus in Dessau, which had been dissolved in 1933. In 1937, the New Bauhaus was moved to Chicago, where Laszlo Moholy-Nagy, a Hungarian-born German-educated member of the Bauhaus, directed it.

In 1939, the New Bauhaus was renamed the School of Design, and later on became a college known as the Institute of Design. In 1949, it became part of the Illinois Institute of Technology. In 1938, Ludwig Mies van der Rohe, also a member of the Bauhaus in Germany, became head of the Illinois Institute of Technology, originally the Armour Institute. The Institute, as well as the campus he built became internationally well known. Mies van der Rohe, who was called a "poet of steel and glass is credited with having revolutionized the world or architecture in the United States, and was chosen by President Kennedy to receive the first U.S. Medal of Freedom. His major building projects include the Lake Shore Apartments in Chicago, as well as the Seagram's Building on New York's Park Avenue.[49]

News of the ethnic cleansing of Germans throughout southeastern Europe caused leaders of the Donauschwaben of Chicago to form the American Aid Society of German Descendants in 1944. It provided aid to refugees in Germany and Austria, and sponsored seventeen thousand immigrants. The Society now operates a heritage museum in Lake Villa, Illinois that also includes a library. In the 1960s, the Society dedicated the Nick Pesch Monument, which honors the victims of the Second World War. Further reflecting the immigration of people "displaced" from their homelands was the founding of the Society of Danube Swabians in 1953. The Society offers a weekend school and a museum at its cultural center in Des Plaines, Illinois.[50]

Many immigrants "often started from scratch, bringing with them only their ingenuity and willingness to work hard."[51] The pre- and postwar immigrations were followed by continued immigration into the 1950s and 1960s, providing a valuable contribution to the state of Illinois, as well as to its German heritage, which was rejuvenated by this fresh infusion from the Old Country. They were one of the factors contributing to the German heritage revival of the post-war period. Other factors involved were those affecting German-Americans elsewhere across the country, and which worked to bring about pride and recognition of the German heritage for the first time since before the world wars.

In the postwar era, Germany emerged as a powerful NATO ally of the United States, and German-American organizations again began to celebrate the German heritage. An additional boost to ethnic identification came in the 1970s with the increased interest nationally in "roots," which helped generate the widespread acceptance and recognition of ethnicity as a permanent and vital factor in American life. The celebration of the American Bicentennial in 1976 proved to be a major turning point in German-American history, as it served to illuminate the role German-Americans had played in the building of the nation for the first time since before the period of the world wars. Conferences, symposia, exhibits, publications, etc. contributed to the resurgence of interest in the German heritage. In 1980, the U.S. Census announced that German-Americans were the nation's largest ethnic group in the country, and also in the state of Illinois. Soon thereafter, the German-American Tricentennial (1983) commemorated the founding of the first permanent German settlement at Germantown, Pennsylvania. The Tricentennial centered on the 6th of October, the date on which Germantown had been founded in 1683. As a result of a national campaign, the 6th of October was declared as German-American Day in 1987 by President Reagan, and has been celebrated ever since across the country. In 1989, the fall of the Berlin Wall and the eventual unification of Germany were celebrated across the U.S., and especially by German-Americans. All of these events contributed to a nationwide rebirth of interest in German heritage since the 1970s, and recent German-American history needs to be viewed in this context.

Although German-Americans live across the state of Illinois, and German-American societies, festivities, restaurants, etc. can also be found throughout the state, the main population centers remain essentially the same as those in the nineteenth century, with Chicago as the major center of German-American life in Illinois. After the German-American Alliance disbanded in 1918 at the national, state, and local levels, other organizations emerged to take its place. Two years after the German-American Alliance of Chicago dissolved, the United German American Societies of Greater Chicago was formed, thereby filling the void left by the Alliance. According to its president, Erich Himmel, it is "the umbrella organization of seventy-eight active German clubs and societies with an estimated membership of ninety-six hundred men, women, and children." UGAS coordinates the annual calendar of events, the Steuben Parade, and the celebration of German-American Day on the 6th of October. It also "maintains close relations to the German Consulate in Chicago, the Chicago City Government, the Chicagoland and German-American Chamber of Commerce, the press, and broadcast media, as well as with German-American clubs and societies in the Midwest and from coast to coast." In short, the German-American organizational world of the Chicago area weathered the storms of the heritage.[52]

In 1921, the German-American Citizens League was formed in Chicago to replace the National German-American Alliance that had just been dissolved. The GACL had been formed as the result of two national German-American conferences that had been held in Chicago in 1920–21, and had been attended by delegates from twenty states. The leadership for the new organization came mainly from leaders of the Chicago Alliance, as well as the state Alliance. The GACL official organ was a weekly newspaper, the *Deutsch-Amerikanische Bürger-Zeitung*, which commenced publication in 1920. Like its predecessor, the GACL did not survive another world war, but the newspaper did and appeared until 1955. Three years after its demise a new organization was formed in Chicago, the German-American National Congress, or D.A.N.K. (Deutsch-Amerikanischer National Kongress).

The German-American National Congress may be viewed as the successor organization to the GACL, as well as its predecessor, the National German-American Alliance. As the largest German-American national organization, it has some thirty chapters and numerous associate member societies from coast to coast. With headquarters at the D.A.N.K.-Haus, 4740 N. Western Ave., the organization is especially strong in the state of Illinois with branches throughout the state, and although it is a national organization, at the state level it basically has replaced its predecessor, the German-American Alliance of Illinois. Its headquarters really serves as the central German cultural center of the city, and also houses a library of more than four thousand volumes. D.A.N.K. also publishes a newspaper, the *German-American Journal*, edited by Ernst Ott, who has also served as national president of the organization. The goals of the organization are to

1. Represent as a nationwide organization all German-Americans on a national level.
2. Foster friendship between the United States and Germany.
3. Preserve the German language, customs, and culture.
4. Educate children and adults in German culture, language and history.
5. Instruct members in the principles of American citizenship and encourage a general interest in American politics.
6. Encourage pride in all German-Americans and interested supporters of the German heritage.[53]

A recently published guide of German-, Austrian-, and Swiss-American societies of the area lists numerous organizations throughout the state of Illinois. They sponsor a wide range of programs, events, and activities.[54] German sites can be found throughout Chicago, but the area in and around Lincoln Avenue is where many German shops, businesses, and restaurants, among other things, are located. At the Lincoln Square Mall there is a mural conceived by the artist Lothar Speer that depicts German scenes, including such well-known landmarks as the Brandenburg Gate in Berlin and a house in the Black Forest. Also located there is a German-style Maypole, and adds a German motif to the area that is the site of various German-American festivities, including Mayfest and Oktoberfest. Among the shops of interest in the area are the Delicatessen Meyer and the Merz Apothecary. Some places even have signs indicating that "Wir sprechen deutsch." A well-known restaurant in the area is certainly the Brauhaus. A tradition recently begun in Chicago is the now annual *Weihnachtsmarkt*, or Christmas Market, sponsored by the German-American Chamber of Commerce in cooperation with the city of Chicago. Also, reference must be made to the Goethe-Institut Chicago, whose cultural programs enrich the German cultural heritage of the area.[55]

In Illinois there are a variety of German-American radio programs offered, and several German-American newspapers as well, not to mention the numerous newsletters published by the various German-American societies throughout the state. Two German cultural centers in Iowa and Missouri also serve the territory in Illinois adjacent to them. The first is the German-American Heritage Center in Davenport, which embraces the Quad City area that includes Rock Island and Moline, Illinois. And, in St. Louis, the German Cultural Center at the University of Missouri–St. Louis also provides programming that relates to southern Illinois.[56]

Southern Illinois remains a German heritage center, and is, of course, centered at Belleville. A most promising project underway there revolves around the Gustav Koerner House. According to the St. Clair Historical Society, plans call for a complete restoration of the Koerner's home, which will then serve as an interpretative center. On behalf of the project, a German lecture series has been sponsored. Given the importance of Belleville in general and Koerner in particular, the project provides but another indication that the historic German heritage centers continue to lead the way in terms of cultural leadership in Illinois. According to Diane Walsh, the Gustave Koerner House Committee had raised the necessary funds by November 2004, clearing the way to begin the skilled historical inventory and expert architectural assessments of the house. She noted that:

Ideas for use of the home include that of a museum to educate the public about Gustave Koerner's life and accomplishments, and those of his wife Sophie. Interpretive themes receiving consideration involve Koerner's rise to prominence through elected office; relationship with Lincoln and the Republican Party; appointment as U.S. Minister to Spain; prolific writings and publications; influence in raising the 43rd Regiment during the Civil War; and Gustave and Sophie Koerner's involvement in a host of other civic and educational activities in the Belleville community.[57]

The Continuum

An element as large as that formed by German-Americans no doubt will continue to play an important role in the social, cultural, economic, and political life of the state of Illinois. Insight as to its future role might be ascertained by considering the role German-Americans have played in the past. The German-American political tradition in Illinois reaches, of course, back to well before the Civil War, but no doubt its foremost spokesmen in the nineteenth century were Koerner, Hecker, and Hoffmann. Of the three, it was Koerner who best articulated a philosophy of German-American civic identity. He placed this within the general context of his views on the role of the American people in having establishing a republican form of government and their duties and responsibilities. He claimed that it was the people and the institutions a country creates that make it great:

> Ancient Greece, with all its colonies, was much smaller than some of our states, and yet it was the greatest country in antiquity, and the civilized nations of today, consciously are still living under the influence it exercised through its statesmen, orators, philosophers, poets and artists. What makes our own country great, what makes our breasts swell with pride when the word, 'Our Country' is sounded, are the men and the women who dwell in it and the frame of government which they have given themselves . . . we are really an upright, brace, generous, naturally kind and even amiable people.[58]

Koerner noted that America is a multi-ethnic country bound

together by "our Republican institutions, securing us political and religious liberty, giving every man an equal chance to get along in the world . . . while still allowing for individual and even national differences in non-essentials. To love our country, native or adopted, before any other; to obey the laws which we have given to ourselves; to reform them if we do not like them, is all that we are required to do under our constitution."[59]

He also described the American people in general as "a sober, practical, reflective and with all its democratic instincts, in the main, a conservative people." He also felt that America was on the road to becoming a great power and that "no people can be great that does not combine realism with idealism."[60] Within the framework of these views on the American people and the republican form of government it has established, he then says with regard to the duties of German-Americans:

> Let it be your aim to fulfill the duties of American citizens, to whom the world's history has assigned so high a task, in full measure and with pleasure; to make ourselves conscious, that we, an important part of the most progressive nation, have in consequence assumed a great responsibility before the present time and before posterity. At the same time, however, do not let us ever forget that we are descendants of a great and noble people, in whose destiny we take the warmest interest, and for whom our hearts beat with unfading love.[61]

In short, Koerner stressed the republican form of government and the liberties it provides as that which unites the various elements that make up the American people. He emphasized that German-Americans have the same civic duties and responsibilities as other citizens, but at the same have a duty and responsibility to maintain their German heritage. Koerner, therefore, provided a basic philosophy of civic and ethnic identity for German-Americans that could inform their involvement in public affairs.

However, as has been seen, it was exactly this philosophy of German-American identity that came under attack during the First World War, causing German-Americans to have to re-define and re-invent themselves. This caused German-Americans to de-emphasize their heritage and confine their expressions of German heritage to the social, cultural, and religious realms. When it came to the political realm,

German-Americans expressed themselves at the ballot box and through the German-American press, rather than by means of their organizations. And, when German-Americans engaged in politics thereafter, they more often than not did so as individuals of German heritage, rather than as ethnic politicians.

At the ballot box German-Americans supported the Republican Party when it came to presidential elections after World War I. Illinois also followed this general national trend, but during the Depression and World War II switched to support for the Democratic ticket. Thereafter, Illinois returned to the Republican camp and remained there through the Reagan years except for the 1960s, when it voted for JFK and LBJ. After the Reagan administration, it again swung over to the Democrats. We can, therefore, only conclude that this may somewhat roughly approximate how German-Americans have voted in the presidential elections since the First World War.

Another way to explore German-American involvement in public affairs is to examine the career of Everett M. Dirksen (1896–1969), who was considered the most powerful and influential Republican in Congress in his time. Although a German-American, Dirksen did not play ethnic politics, but based his career on principle and pragmatism. He did not play on his German heritage, although it no doubt assisted him in getting elected in Illinois, as everyone knew his background. In 1932, he was elected to the U.S. House of Representatives, and although he supported the New Deal, was isolationist in terms of foreign policy, and thus opposed to Roosevelt. Later on, he supported Truman's foreign policies, but opposed his Fair Deal programs. After election to the Senate in 1950, Dirksen continued to espouse an isolationist position, and was not only well known as a conservative, but supported Sen. Joseph McCarthy of Wisconsin. He fought against the programs of the Democrats, and in the 1950s became a strong supporter of Eisenhower.

The high point of his career was during the Kennedy and Johnson administrations, and worked with both of them on a number of measures, including the Civil Rights Acts of the 1960s. An astute politician, Dirksen was known for his methods that "included rational persuasion, consensus-building, calling in personal favors, and assiduous logrolling. He displayed in his office the motto, 'The oil can is mightier than the sword.' Typically working a sixteen-hour day despite precarious health, he achieved master over both the tactics of political maneuver and the substance of major legislation." Well liked by the general public, Dirksen was known for his warmth, good humor, and eloquence in public speaking. He once said that: "I am a man of principle, and one of my basic principles is flexibility." Dirksen's flexibility is indicative of the flexibility German-Americans utilized in re-inventing and re-defining themselves in the post-World War I era.[62]

The role played by German-Americans in public affairs in Illinois seems to suggest that German-Americans are basically conservative, and more often than not vote Republican when it comes to presidential elections. However, they also appear to be independent-minded, and consider the candidate, as well as the party platform of the candidate, and make their judgements accordingly. They also come out of a tradition that stands for fiscal responsibility at home, and for the avoidance of entanglements abroad. Like Senator Dirksen, they take a pragmatic, rather than ideological approach to the issues, and one that is no doubt grounded on a political tradition that evolved from Koerner, Hecker, and Hoffmann.

Since World War I, German-Americans have maintained their German heritage by means of their secular and religious institutions and organizations, as well as by means of their press and media. Politics by and large has been left to individual expression as well as to the German-American press and media. This lowered public profile "contrasts with that of other ethnic groups" that are more active in public affairs by means of their organizations.[63] Nonetheless, German-Americans continue to exert great influence not only because of their percentage of the population, but due to the great social, cultural, and economic influence they exert in the state. If there are any guideposts for them to follow in the future they certainly can be found in the examples set by such outstanding German-Americans as Koerner, Hecker, and Hoffmann. By word and deed they defined and exemplified what it means to be German-American, with pride in one's citizenship, as well as one's heritage.

Summing up the German impact on Illinois, it might be noted that German immigration has had a deep and lasting influence on the social, cultural, economic, religious, and political landscape of the state. The story of German immigration, settlement, and the German-American experience is one that reaches back to the early nineteenth century, and is an important dimension in the history of Illinois that continues on to the present time, winding its way through the years surveyed here. It is a story that needs to be told if you want to understand Illinois.

The D.A.N.K.-Spatzen Children's Choir,
directed by Alexandra Pradella-Ott.

The Annual Steuben Day Parade in Chicago.

NOTES

1. Albert B. Faust, *The German Element in the United States* (New York: The Steuben Society of America, 1927), 1:588–89.

2. See Arndt and Olson, *The German Language Press*, 1:107.

3. For information on the Illinois German regiments, see Kaufmann, *Germans in the American Civil War*, 107.

4. Schem, *Lexikon*, 5:503.

5. Arndt and Olson, *The German Language Press*, 1:46.

6. Hofmeister, *The Germans of Chicago*, 191.

7. Ibid, 228.

8. For further information on these areas, see Hofmeister, *The Germans of Chicago*, esp. chaps. 12–14.

9. Arndt and Olson, *The German Language Press*, 46–110

10. Schem, *Lexikon*, 5:503.

11. Ibid.

12. Townsend, *The Germans of Chicago*, 170.

13. John Peter Altgeld, *Our Penal Machinery and Its Victims* (Chicago: A.C. McClurg, 1886).

14. Townsend, *The Germans of Chicago*, 56.

15. Carl Schurz, *Speeches, Correspondence and Political Papers of Carl Schurz*. Selected and ed. by Frederic Bancroft (New York: G. P. Putnam's Sons, 1913), 5:181–82, 190.

16. Ibid.

17. See Koerner, *Memoirs*, 2:725.

18. Information on the state branches of the Alliance is drawn from Clifton J. Child, *The German-Americans in Politics*, and: Albert Godsho, *Chronological History of the National German-American Alliance of the United States* (Philadelphia: National German-American Alliance, 1911).

19. Regarding the Chicago Alliance, see National German-American Alliance, Zweigverband Chicago, *Festschrift zum Deutschen Tage in Chicago gefeiert am 6. Oktober 1907* (Chicago: Hermann Loesicke, 1907).

20. See, for example, the program of the annual meeting of the Illinois Alliance at Peoria, Illinois: National German-American Alliance, Staatsverband, Illinois, *Zweite jährliche Konvention, Peoria, Ill., 11. und 12. September 1909* (n.p.:1909).

21. Tolzmann, *The German-American Experience*, 262.

22. Ibid.

23. Godsho, *Chronological History*, 37.

24. For further information on the members of the Society mentioned here, see Hofmeister, *The Germans in Chicago*, 228.

25. The journal, *Deutsch-Amerikanische Geschichtsblätter*, was published from 1901 to 1937.

26. Another valuable supplement was George W. Spindler, *The Life of Carl Follen: A Study in German-American Cultural Relations*, Historical Mono-graphs Published under the Auspices of the German-American-American Historical Society Illinois, ed. Julius Goebel (Chicago: University of Chicago Press, 1917).

27. Mary Goebel Kimball, "Julius Goebel," *Deutsch-Amerikanische Geschichts-blätter*, 530. The papers of Goebel (1857–1931) are located at the Archives of the University of Illinois at Urbana Champaign Library.

28. Ibid, 535.

29. Ibid, 541–42.

30. Ibid, 542.

31. Ibid, 547.

32. Ibid., 551.

33. Child, *The German-Americans*, 32.

34. Carl Wittke, *German-Americans and the World War* (Columbus: Ohio State Archaeological and Historical Society, 1936), 7. The following information about the German-American press of Illinois is drawn from Wittke's valuable study.

35. Child, *The German-Americans*, 61.

36. Townsend, *The Germans of Chicago*, 97.

37. Everett McKinley Dirksen, *The Education of a Senator*. Foreword by Howard H. Baker, Jr., Introduction by Frank H. Mackaman (Urbana: University of Illinois Press, 1998), 22.

38. Don Heinrich Tolzmann, ed., *German-Americans in the World Wars* (München: K.G. Saur, 1995), 2:1071.

39. Ibid, 2:1073.

40. Ibid, 1:300.

41. Leslie Vincent Tischauser, "The Burden of Ethnicity: The German Question in Chicago, 1914–1941," (Ph.D, Diss., University of Illinois at Chicago Circle, 1981), 47.

42. Hofmeister, *The Germans of Chicago*, 79.

43. *Germania Club Yearbook and Historical Review*, 1940–41. (Chicago: Germa-nia Club, 1940), 95.

44. Ibid.

45. Ibid.

46. Ibid, 79.

47. Ibid, 90.

48. Bert Lachner and Ernst Ott, *Heimat North America* (Chicago: Bert Lachner, Landmark Books, 1997), 32.

49. Regarding the New Bauhaus, see Peter Hahn and Lloyd C. Engelbrecht, eds., *50 Jahre new Bauhaus: Bauhausnachfolge in Chicago* (Berlin: Bauhaus-Archiv, 1987).

50. See Lachner and Ott, *Heimat*, 48–53.

51. Ibid, 32.

52. Lachner and Ott, *Heimat*, 40.

53. Ibid, 37.

54. See *Spurensuche: German-speaking Communities in Chicago and in the Midwest* (Chicago: German-American National Congress, German-American Education Fund, and The American Aid Society of German Descendents, 2003).

55. See the virtual tour of the Goethe-Institut Chicago at http://www.goethe.de/uk/chi/vtour/index2b.htm.

56. For information on the Davenport center, see www.gahc.org. And for information regarding the St. Louis center, see http://www.germanculturecenter.org/.

57. E-mail message from Diane Walsh (18 November 2004). For further information, see http://www.compu-type.net/rengen/stclair/koerner.htm.

58. Koerner, *Memoirs*, 2:730.

59. Ibid, 728.

60. Ibid, 728.

61. Ibid, 725.

62. See the Dirksen site: http://www.dirksencenter.org print_collections_dirksen.htm.

63. *Spurensuche*, 9.

Guide to Sources

—Don Heinrich Tolzmann

REFERENCE WORKS:

Arndt, Karl J. R. and May E. Olson, *The German Language Press of the Americas*. (München: K.G. Saur, 1976–80).

Hoffmann, John. *A Guide to the History of Illinois*. (New York: Greenwood Press, 1991).

Pochmann, Henry. *Bibliography of German Culture in America to 1940*. Rev. and corrected ed. Arthur R. Schultz. (Millwood, N.Y.: Kraus, 1982).

Schultz, Arthur R. *German-American Relations and German Culture in America: A Subject Bibliography, 1941–1980*. (Millwood, N.Y.: Kraus, 1984).

Tolzmann, Don Heinrich. *German-Americana: A Bibliography*. (Metuchen, New Jersey: Scarecrow, 1975).

——. *Catalog of the German-Americana Collection, University of Cincinnati*. (München: K.G. Saur, 1990).

Whitney, Ellen M., Janice A. Petterchak, and Sandra M. Stark. *Illinois History: An Annotated Bibliography*. (Westport, Conn.: Greenwood Press, 1995.

GENERAL WORKS:

Bergquist, James M. "The Political Attitudes of the German Immigrant in Illinois, 1848–1860," (Ph.D., Diss.: Northwestern University, 1966).

Bess, F. B. *Eine populäre Geschichte der Stadt Peoria*. (Peoria, Ill.: W.H. Wagner and Sons, 1906).

Blanke, Lore. *Franz Arnold Hoffmann (1822–1903): Politiker auf deutschamerikanischem Kurs = Francis A. Hoffmann (1822–1903): German-American Opinion Leader*. (Stuttgart: Verlag H.-D. Heinz, 1993).

Bornmann, Heinrich J. *Bornmann's Sketches of Germans in Quincy and Adams County.* Translated by Lester Holtschlag and Lenore Kimbrough. (Quincy, Ill.: Great River Genealogical Society, 1999).

Cogggeshall, John M. "Ethnic Persistence with Modification: The German-Americans of Southwestern Illinois," (Ph.D., Diss.:Southern Illinois University at Carbondale, 1984).

Dietzsch, Emil. *Geschichte derDeutsch-Amerikaner in Chicago (von der Gründung der Stadt an bis auf die neueste Zeit).* (Chicago: M. Stern, 1881).

Dietzsch, Emil, and Max Stern and Fred Kressmann. *Chicago's Deutsche Männer: Erinnerungs-Blätter zu Chicago's Fünfzigjährigem Jubiläum. Geschichte der Stadt Chicago, mit besonderer Berücksichtigung des Einflusses der Deutsch-Amerikaner auf ihre Entwickelung.* (Chicago: M. Stern & Co., 1885).

Fiedler, Timothy John. "Ethnic Identity in Later Generations: The Case of German-Americans in Waterloo, Illinois: A Preliminary Investigation," (Ph.D., Diss.: Southern Illinois University–Carbondale, 1980).

Germania Club Year Book and Historical Review. (Chicago: The Club, 1940).

Goethe-Feier der Deutschen von Chicago zu Johann Wolfgang von Goethe's 150-jährigem Geburtstag, Sonntag, den 3. September 1899, Sunny Side Park. (Chicago: Press of Max Stern, 1899).

Harzig, Christine. *Familie, Arbeit und weibliche Öffentlichkeit in einer Einwanderungsstadt: Deutschamerikanerinnen in Chicago um die Jahrhundertwende.* (St. Katharinen: Scripta Mercaturae Verlag, 1991).

Hoefer, H. *Lebensbild von Simon Kuhlenhölter, von 1860 bis 1882, Pastor der Evang. Salems-Gemeinde in Quincy, Ills.* (St. Louis: Aug. Wiebusch & Son Printing Co., 1886).

Hofmeister, Rudolf. *The Germans of Chicago.* (Champaign, Ill.: Stipes, 1976).

Keil, Hartmut and John B. Jentz, eds. with the Assistance of Klaus Ensslen, et al, *German Works in Chicago: A Documentary History of Working-Class Culture from 1850 to World War I.* (Urbana: University of Illinois Press, 1988).

———. *German Workers in Industrial Chicago, 1850–1910: A Comparative Perspective.* (DeKalb, Ill.: Northern Illinois University Press, 1983).

Kircher, Henry A. *A German in the Yankee Fatherland; The Civil War Letters of Henry A. Kircher.* Edited by Earl J. Hess. (Kent, Ohio: Kent State University Press, 1983).

Koerner, Gustav. *Das deutsche Element in den Vereinigten Staaten von Nordamerika, 1818–1848.* (Cincinnati: A. E. Wilde & Co., 1880).

——. *Memoirs of Gustave Koerner, 1809–1896, Life-Sketches Written at the Suggestion of His Children.* Edited by Thomas J. McCormack. (Cedar Rapids, Iowa: The Torch Press, 1909).

Lachner, Bert. *Chicagoland: A World Class Metropolis: A German-American Perspective = Chicagoland: eine Klasse-Stadt von Weltruf: eine deutsch-amerikanische Perspektive.* (Glen Ellyn, Ill.: B. Lachner & Associates, 1994).

Lachner, Bert and Ernst Ott. *Heimat North America: English and German.* (Glen Ellyn, Ill.: Landmark Books Unlimited, 1997).

Mannhardt, Emil. *Deutsche und deutsche Nachkommen in Illinois und den östlichen Nord-Central-Staaten.* (Chicago: Die Deutsch-Amerikanische Historische Gesellschaft, 1907).

Roskoten, Oliver J. *Die Existenzberechtigung deutsch-englischer Schulen in Amerika.* (Peoria, Illinois: Deutscher Schulverein, 1904).

St. Francis Church, Teutopolis, Illinois. *Beiträge zur Geschichte von Teutopolis und Umgegend: Unter besonderer Berücksichtigung des Wirkens der dortigen Franziskaner.* (St. Louis: In der Office der "America," 1902).

Schade, Gerhard. *Reflections on Some of the People and Issues in the Early Days of the German Evangelical Synod of North America.* (Chicago, n.p., 1977).

Schmidt, Axel W.-O. *Der rote Doktor von Chicago, ein deutsch-amerikanisches Auswandererschicksal: Biographie des Dr. Ernst Schmidt, 1830–1900, Artzt und Sozialrevolutionär.* (Frankfurt a.M.: Peter Lang, 2003).

Seeger, Eugen. *Chicago: Entwickelung, Zerstörung und Wiederaufbau der Wunderstadt.* (Chicago: M Stern, 1872).

Skilnik, Bob. *The History of Beer and Brewing in Chicago, 1833–1978.* (St. Paul, Minnesota: Pogo Press, 1999).

Spurensuche: German-speaking Communities in Chicago and in the Midwest. (Chicago: German-American National Congress, German-American Education fund, and the American Aid Society of German Descendents, 2003).

Tischauser, Leslie. "The Burden of Ethnicity: The German Question in Chicago, 1914–1941," (Ph.D., Diss.: University of Chicago at Chicago Circle, 1981).

Tolzmann, Don Heinrich. *The German-American Experience* (Amherst. N.Y.: Prometheus Books, 2000).

Townsend, Andrew Jacke. *The Germans of Chicago*. (Chicago: Deutsch-Amerikanische Historische Gesellschaft von Illinois, 1932).

Tucker, Marlin Timothy. "Political Leadership in the Illinois-Missouri German Community, 1836-1872," (Ph.D., Diss.: University of Illinois at Urbana-Champaign, 1968).

JOURNALS

Deutsch-Amerikanische Geschichtsblätter (1901-37): Published in Chicago by the German-American Historical Society of Illinois, this journal of German-American history is a veritable "gold mine" of information on the German heritage of Illinois, and was edited for many years by Julius Goebel.

Deutsch-Amerikanische Monatshefte für Politik, Wissenschaft und Literatur (1864-67): Published in Chicago, this journal was considered a German-American version of the *Atlantic Monthly*, and is a valuable source of information for the time period during and after the Civil War.

Der Deutsche Kulturträger (1913-14): A journal of German-American culture that was published in Chicago, and contains articles, essays, and reviews on all aspects of German-American culture.

German-American Journal (1959-to date): Published in Chicago by the German-American National Congress, this journal has been edited for some time by Ernst Ott, and contains news, articles, and information of interest to German-Americans.

Die Glocke (1906-08): Published in Chicago, this journal focused on German-Americana literature and the arts, and contains numerous illustrations.

Jahrbuch der Deutschen in Chicago (1916-18): Published in Chicago, and edited by Michael Singer, this historical journal focused on the Chicago Germans, and is of special value for the period of the First World War.

Die Neue Zeit (1919-32): Published in Chicago, this German-English weekly was edited by Michael Singer, and covered politics, the arts, and literature.

ARCHIVES, LIBRARIES, AND SPECIAL COLLECTIONS

A. Archives

For a guide to archival and manuscript collections relating to the history of Illinois, see Hofmann, *A Guide to the History of Illinois*, 205–309. This consists of bibliographical essays covering the following institutions: the Illinois State Historical Library, the Illinois State Archives, the Chicago Historical Society, the University of Illinois at Chicago, the University of Chicago, the Newberry Library, other Chicago-Area Repositories, the University of Illinois at Urbana-Champaign, the Southern Illinois University, the Northern Illinois University, other downstate repositories, the Library of Congress, and the National Archives.

B. Internet Guide to Libraries

Academic libraries in Illinois:
<http://sunsite.berkeley.edu/Libweb/Academic_IL.html>.

Libraries with genealogy collections:
<http://www.outfitters.com/illinois/history/family/specific.html>.

Public libraries in Illinois:
<http://sunsite.berkeley.edu/Libweb/Public_IL.html>.

C. Special Collections

The D.A.N.K. Library: The German-American National Congress, Deutsch-Amerikanischer Kongress (D.A.N.K.) maintains a library of more than 4,000 volumes in Chicago. See <http://www.dank.org/>.

The German Library Society of Belleville: The Belleville Public Library holds the original collection of the German Library Society discussed in chapter one. Although there is no updated catalog of this valuable collection, there is an older published catalog available: *Classified Catalogue of the Belleville Public Library, Belleville, Illinois: With Dictionary Catalogue, or Index of Authors, Titles and Subjects*. (Belleville, Ill.: Post and Zeitung Publishing Co., 1900). See also, <http://library.wustl.edu/units/spec/archives/aslaa/directory/belleville-public-library.html>.

The German-Americana Collection: The German-Americana Collection at the University of Cincinnati holds a wealth of materials on German-American history, literature, and culture, including the private library of Julius Goebel, professor German at the University of Illinois at Urbana–Champaign. The catalog to the Collection also indexes the yearbooks of the German-American Historical Society of Illinois. See Don Heinrich Tolzmann, *Catalog of the German-Americana Collection*, esp. 1:255-70. Also, consult the Collection's Web site <http://www.libraries.uc.edu/libraries/arb/ger_americana/>.

The Max Kade Institute for German-American Studies: The Institute, located at the University of Wisconsin–Madison, maintains a collection of German-Americana that may be accessed by means of its Web site at <http://csumc.wisc.edu/mki/>.

The Rattermann Collection: Shortly before the First World War, Julius Goebel facilitated the acquisition of the private library of Heinrich A. Rattermann, the well-known German-American historian of Cincinnati, Ohio, for the Library of the University of Illinois at Urbana–Champaign. Consisting of more than eight thousand volumes, it was no doubt one of the largest German-Americana collections in the country. Although there is no published catalog to the Rattermann's book collection, there is a manuscript catalog of it available at the University of Illinois Library at Urbana–Champaign. Also, there is a guide to the manuscript part of Rattermann's library. See Donna-Christine Sell and Dennis Francis Walle, eds., *Guide to the Heinrich A. Rattermann Collection of German-American Manuscripts*. (Urbana: University of Illinois Library, 1979). Rattermann's manuscript collection contains several items of interest, including Rattermann's correspondence with Koerner. See < http://www.library.uiuc.edu/ihx/>.

For the history of the Rattermann library, see Mary Edmund Spanheimer, *The German Pioneer Legacy: The Life and Work of Heinrich A. Rattermann by Sister Mary Edmund Spanheimer*. 2nd Edition. Edited by Don Heinrich Tolzmann. (Oxford: Peter Lang, 2004), 135-40.

Index

A

Aargau, Switzerland 6, 50
Abend, Edmund 134
Abend, Eduard 5, 17, 34, 40
Abend, Heinrich 16, 36
Abend, Jos. 40
abolition 87
Abraham Lincoln: Complete Works, Comprising His Speeches, Letters, State Papers, and Miscellaneous Writings (Lincoln) 105
Academy of Arts and Sciences (Boston) 26
Ackermann 39
Adams Co., Ill. 53, 54, 132
Adams, C. K. 123
Adams, Professor 123
Adler des Westens (newspaper) 53
African-American regiment 13
Aggemann, J. H. 40
Alexian Brothers Hospital 70
Altgeld, John Peter 135, 136
Alton, Ill. 43, 50, 51, 134
Ameiss, David 40
American Aid Society of German Descendants 154
American Bicentennial 154
American Immigrant Leaders (Greene) 63, 126
American Institute, The 25
American Journal of Science 28
American Philosophical Society of Philadelphia 26
Amrein, Anton 40
Andrew Co., Mo. 135
Ann Arbor, Michigan 28
Annalen der Rechstspflege in Rheinbaiern 21
Anneke 73

anti-Douglas meeting 61
anti-Nebraska victory 101
anti-Nebraska views 75
Anzeiger des Westens 10, 100
Appleton's Cyclopedia of American Biography 87
Arenz, Franz 43, 52
Arenz, J. A. 43, 53
Arenzville, Ill. 52
Arkansas 13
Army of the Tennessee 58
ARNDT, KARL J. R. 34, 35, 57, 60, 61, 124, 125, 164, 167
Arnzten, Bernard 76
Aschaffenburg, Germany 13
Ashland, Ky. 97
Ashley bill 79
Atlanta, Ga. 45, 58
Augsburg, Germany 29
Augsburg, Ill. 63
Aul, Friedrich 40
Aurora, Ill. 134
Aus grosser Zeit 88
Austria 12
Austrian refugees 154
Austro-Prussian War 84

B

Babcock, S. M. 123
Bacharach, Germany 7
Bache, Alexander Dallas 25, 26, 37
Baden, Germany 58, 67, 99, 113
Bald Hill 58
Baltimore, Md. 5, 110
Bandeliers 49
Banks, Gen. 13
Barnsbach, Julius A. 43, 47, 48
Barth, Karl 40
Bartholdt, Richard 141

Basler, Ray P. 125
battle of Buena Vista 47
battle of Idstedt 12
battle of Lookout Mountain 45
battle of Missionary Ridge 45
battle of Missunde 12
battle of Pea Ridge 45
battle of Ringgold 57
Battle of Shiloh 13, 47
Bauhaus 153
Baum, Philipp 40
Baumann family 6
Baumeister, Mr. 54
Baumgarten, Moritz 65
Bautiers 49
Bavaria, Germany 21, 68
Bavarian government 22
Bavarian revolutionary movement 68
Beardstown, Ill. 43, 51, 52, 53
Becker, Gerhardt 125
Beelman, Conrad 40
*Beiträge zur Geschichte von
    Teutopolis und Umgegend: Unter
    besonderer Berücksichtigung des
    Wirkens der dortigen Franziskaner*
    (St. Francis Church) 169
Belleville German library 132
Belleville Latin Settlement 35
Belleville Savings Bank 17
Belleville, Ill. 6, 10, 11, 17, 21, 22,
    23, 24, 29, 31, 33, 37, 44, 45, 46,
    47, 48, 52, 58, 65, 66, 67, 75, 93,
    96, 97, 98, 99, 105, 111, 132, 134,
    138
Belleviller Beobachter 10, 36, 44
Belleviller Zeitung (newspaper) 44
Bello, Captain 27
Bench and Bar of Chicago 86
Benton 15
Beobachter 34
Berchelmann, Dr. Adolph 5, 16, 30,
    36, 40
Berg Academy (Freiberg, Saxony) 26
Berg, Anton 65
Bergkotter, Heinrich 40
Bergquist, James M. 167
Berkley 28
Berlin Wall 155

Berlin, Germany 11, 19, 29, 44, 52,
    58
*Berühmte deutsche Vorkämpfer für
    Fortschritt, Freiheit und Friede in
    Nord-Amerika: Von 1626 bis 1898:
    Einhundertundfünfzig Biographien,
    mit sechzehn Portraits*
    (Ruetenik) 33
Bess, F. B. 167
*Bibliography and List of Library
    Holdings of Milwaukee Publisher
    George Brumder (1839–1910)*
    (Becker) 125
*Bibliography of German Culture in
    America to 1940* (Pochmann) 167
Bieber, William F. 152
Biermann, Jos. 40
*Biographical Dictionary and Portrait
    Gallery of Representative Men of
    Chicago* 87, 88
*Biographical Dictionary and Portrait
    Gallery of Representative Men of
    Chicago, The* 86, 87
Bismarck Hotel in Chicago 147
Bismarck, Otto von 84, 85, 114
Blanke, Lore 62, 167
Blankenburg, Köln, Germany 52
*Blätter fuer literarische
    Unterhaltung* 30
Bloomington, Ill. 132, 134
Blue Island, Ill. 132
Bluecher, 95
Board of Penitentiary Commissioners
    (Joliet, Ill.) 69
Boernstein, 100
Bogart, E. L. 90
Bopp, Adam 39
Bornmann, Conrad 39, 40
Bornmann, Heinrich J. 168
*Bornmann's Sketches of Germans in
    Quincy and Adams County*
    (Bornmann) 168
Bossle, Michel 40
Boyer, Valentin A. 54
Brand, Horace L. 143
Braun, Frank X. 113
Breck, James 74
Brehl, Mr. 54
Bremer, Georg 40

Brentano 55
Brentano, Lorenz 62, 71, 72, 78, 79, 80, 135
BREWER, D. J. 114
Briesacher, Georg 40
Briesacher, Jos. 40
Brockhaus 30
Brown, John 70
Brumder, Georg 122
Buena Vista 11
Buff, Heinrich 40
Buffalo Volksfreund 121
Buffalo, N.Y. 55
Bund 151
Bunsen 37
Bunsen family 19, 37
Bunsen School 21
Bunsen, Dr. Gustav 5, 16, 36
Bunsen, Georg C. 5, 18, 30, 36, 40
Bunsen, Josias 19
Bunsen, Robert Wilhelm 19
Bureau of Coastal Surveys 25
BURNETT, ROBYN 167
Burschenschaft 16, 29, 37, 96
Busch, Georg 40
Buschbauer, Hans 120, 122, 124, 125
Busse 39
Butz, Caspar 69, 74, 75, 76, 78, 79, 80, 85, 133, 134, 135, 147
Butz, Otto 147

C
Cairo, Ill. 132
Calhoun, 15, 101
California 28
Cameron, Simon 77
campaign journal 44
canal 54, 55
Carlinville, Ill. 132
CARRIER, LOIS 57
Cass County, Ill. 43, 52
Catalog of the German-Americana Collection, University of Cincinnati (Tolzmann) 32, 167, 172
Catholics. *See also,* German Catholics 89
Central Railroad of Illinois 56
Centreville, Ill. 33
Chancellorsville (battle) 111

Charlottenburg, Germany 19
Chicago Abendpost 143, 148
Chicago Board of Underwriters 119
Chicago Daily Democratic Pres 86
Chicago Democrat (journal) 55
Chicago German Meetings, 1843–44 43
Chicago Germans 76
Chicago Historical Society 87
Chicago Jaeger 76
Chicago Public Library 132
Chicago Tribune 79, 80, 81, 83, 90, 103
Chicago und sein Deutschtum (Schmidt) 86, 87
Chicago Volksfreund 54, 66
Chicago Warte 121
Chicago Whiskey Ring scandal 83
Chicago, German population in 54
Chicago, Ill. 5, 32, 43, 51, 65, 66, 67, 69, 70, 71, 73, 74, 75, 76, 117, 131, 132, 134, 138
Chicago's Deutsche Männer: Erinnerungs-Blätter zu Chicago's Fünfzigjährigem Jubiläum. Geschichte der Stadt Chicago, mit besonderer Berücksichtigung des Einflusses der Deutsch-Amerikaner auf ihre Entwickelung 168
Chicagoer Freie Presse 82, 86, 90
Chicagoer Freie Zeitung 86
Chicagoer Volksfreund 124
Chicagoland: A World Class Metropolis: A German-American Perspective = Chicagoland: eine Klasse-Stadt von Weltruf: eine deutsch-amerikanische Perspektive (Lachner) 169
Chillicothe, Ohio 51
Christmas tree 39
Chronicle, The (newspaper) 52
Cincinnati, Ohio 5, 32, 51, 110
convention of 1872 69
Circleville, Ohio 51
Cire, J. L. 51
Civil Service Reform 69
Civil War 45, 47, 111
Civil War, German-American regiments in the 131, 132

Claussenius, Henry 67, 72
Clay 15
Clay, Henry 52, 60, 97
Clayton Amendment 75
Cleveland, Grover 135, 136
Cleveland, Ohio 45, 96, 104
Clinton Co., Ill. 63
Clinton County, Ill. 44
Coahuila 11
Coerper, Karl 51
COGGGESHALL, JOHN M. 168
Cohen, Peter 65
Colberg 29
COLE, A. C. 86
Collected Works of Abraham Lincoln, The (Lincoln) 125
Collinsville, Ill. 146, 147
Cologne 29
Colorado 121
Columbus, Ohio 51
Colvin 82
Concordia Turnverein Library (Moline, Ill.) 38
Conradi, August 40
Constants 49
Constitution of 1848 99
Constitution of the United States (translated) 97
Cook Co., Ill. 55, 117, 131, 132, 135
Cotta 26, 30
Craig, John A. 123

D
D'Osband, 131
Davis, doctrine of 101
Decatur, Ill. 132
Decker, Ernst W. 40
Declaration of Independence (translated) 97
Delsch, Christian 40
Democratic Party 53, 73, 98, 101
Democrats 66, 73, 74, 75
Denmark 11
Des Plaines, Ill. 154
Deschner, Joh. 40
Dessau 153
Deutsch-Amerikaner 74

Deutsch-Amerikanische Geschichtsblätter 32, 33, 58, 86, 87, 170
Deutsch-Amerikanische Monatshefte für Politik, Wissenschaft und Literatur 69, 170
Deutsche Element, Das (Koerner) 86, 94, 103
Deutsche Kulturträger, Der 170
Deutsche Pionier, Der 32, 58
Deutsche und deutsche Nachkommen in Illinois und den östlichen Nord-Central-Staaten (Mannhardt) 60, 169
Deutsche Warte, Die 125
Deutsches Volksblatt 59, 125
Die Feueranbeter (Moore) 23
Diehl, Peter 40
Dietsch 85
DIETZSCH, EMIL 168
Dilg, August 29
Dilger, H. 135
Dingworth, Bernh. 40
Dirksen, Everett 145, 146
Documents Relating to the Kansas-Nebraska Act 88
Donauschwaben of Chicago 154
Dönnewald, Albert W. 40
Douglas Democrats 78
Douglas, Stephen A. 73, 74, 100, 101, 120
Dover 47
Dresden, Saxony, Germany 29, 147
Duden, Gottfried 6, 34
Dulon, Dr. 58
Dunkley's Grove, Ill. 55, 66, 117
DuPage Co., Ill. 55, 62, 117, 118
Dutch Hill 6

E
Eastern Virginia 79
Eckert, Georg 40
Eckert, J. G. 40
Eckert, J. Wendel 40
Eckert, Philipp 40
Edwardsville, Ill. 48, 51, 134
Effingham 63
Effingham, Ill. 63
Eidmann, Heinrich 40

Eighty-second Illinois Regiment 114, 131
Eine Stimme aus Amerika, über verfassungsmässige Monarchie und Republik (Hilgard, Sr.) 23
election of 1840 98
election of a German to the legislature 98
elections in 1836 and 1840 43
Electoral College of Illinois 15
Elkhorn Pass (Pea Ridge) 57
Engelbach, Dr. Georg 43, 51
Engelmann 13
Engelmann family 15, 16, 34, 37
Engelmann, Adolph 11, 13
Engelmann, Dr. Georg 29
Engelmann, Friedrich Theodor 5, 7, 9, 21, 29, 30, 34, 40, 45
ENGELMANN, G. E. 32
Engelmann, Gretchen 33
Engelmann, Ludwig 40
Engelmann, Mrs. 104
Engelmann, Sophie 15
Engelmann, Theodor 10, 44
England 67
England, Sigel's exile to 58
Engle, Wm. 134
ENSSLEN, KLAUS 168
Era of the Civil War (Cole) 86
Erie Canal 96, 117
Ernst, Ferdinand 5, 6, 16, 32
Essai sur le droit au travail et les questions qui s'y attachement (Hilgard, Sr.) 23
European revolution of 1848 99
Ewers, Aloysius 40
exiles of 1848 99
Existenzberechtigung deutsch-englischer Schulen in Amerika, Die (Roskoten) 169

F

Familie, Arbeit und weibliche Öffentlichkeit in einer Einwanderungsstadt: Deutschamerikanerinnen in Chicago um die Jahrhundertwende (Harzig) 168
Faust 142

Faust, Albert B. 129
FAUST, ALBERT B. 164
Fein, G. P. 40
Fichte 19
FIEDLER, TIMOTHY JOHN 168
Fields and Leslie 11
Fifty-eighth Illinois Regiment 131
Fifty-seventh Illinois Regiment 131
Finklang, Matthias 40
Finstingen, Lothringen, Germany 51
first geological map of Louisiana 28
first German newspaper 44
first mayor of Beardstown 53
first national meeting of German-American community leaders and representatives 38
first newspaper in Illinois west of Springfield 52
first schoolhouse in Beardstown 52
Fischer, Georg 39, 40
FISCHER, KARL 105
Flick, Michael 40
flour mill, first in Arenzville 52
Follenius 37
Ford, Thomas 98
Forrest's cavalry 13
Fort Henry 13
Fort Sumter 102
Forty-Eighters 67, 68, 72, 75, 85
Forty-Eighters, The (Zucker) 114
Forty-Eighters: Political Refugees of the German Revolution of 1848 (Zucker) 58, 59, 61, 62, 113
Forty-fifth Illinois Regiment 131
Forty-fourth Illinois Regiment 57
Forty-third Illinois Regiment 12, 15, 35, 47, 76, 131
Forty-third Wisconsin Regiment 13
Founders Monument at Germantown, Penn. 141
Fourth Volunteer Infantry Battalion 11
France 27, 67, 68
Franco-Prussian War 84, 103
Frankfurt am Main, Germany 11, 15, 16, 17, 19, 50, 94, 95, 96, 99, 112, 141
Frankfurt Revolt 10, 16, 50
Frankfurter Gymnasium 17

Frankfurter Voluntary Infantry 19

Franklin, Benjamin 21, 25

Franz Arnold Hoffmann (1822–1933): Politiker auf deutschamerikanischem Kurs = Francis A. Hoffmann (1822–1903): German-American Opinion Leader (Blanke) 62, 167

Freedom, Ill. 22

Freeport, Ill. 134

Free-Soilers 73

FREI, ALFRED 113

Freiberg, Saxony, Germany 26

Freie Presse 83

Freiheitsbote für Illinois, Der (newspaper) 44, 57

FREITAG, SABINE 113

Freivogel, Jos. 40

Fremont, John C. 15, 69, 76, 77, 78, 79, 101, 102

French intervention in Mexico 103

French Revolution 22

French Switzerland 49

Friedrich gymnasium 117

Friedrich Hecker in den USA: Eine deutsch-amerikanische Spurensicherung (Frei) 113

Friedrich Hecker: Biographie eines Republianers (Freitag) 113

Friedrich, Ferdinand 40

Friedrich, Heinrich 40

Friedrich, Karl 16

Friedrichstadt 12

Friends of German Democracy 148

Fritz, Adam 40

Froebel, 95

Fulda, Kurhessen, Germany 52

Funk 39

Funk, Georg 40

Funk, Martin 40

Funk, Michael 40

G

Galena, Ill. 132, 134

Garfield 81

Garfield, James A. 69

Gasconade County, Mo. 38

Gazetteer of Illinois, A (Peck) 86

Gedichte eines Deutsch-Amerikaners (Butz) 133

Gehler, Anton 65

Geiger, Joh. 40

Geological and Agricultural Survey (Mississippi) 27

Gerke, Dr. H. Ch. 43, 49

Gerke, Philip 49

German Aid Society of Chicago 67

German Athens of Illinois 131

German Catholics 74, 75, 76

German Christmas customs 38

German Day celebrations 137, 146, 148

German Element in St. Louis: A Translation from German of Ernst D. Kargau's St. Louis in Former Years: A Commemorative History of the German Element, The (Kargau) 32

German Element in the United States, The (Faust) 164

German farmers, the condition of 129

German Farmers' Club Library (Spring Bay, Ill.) 38

German General Beneficial Society 53

German Heritage Guide to the Greater Cincinnati Area (Tolzmann) 32, 115

German heritage, means of maintaining 161

German in the Yankee Fatherland; The Civil War Letters of Henry A. Kircher (Kircher) 168

German instruction 132

German libraries 132

German Library Society 5, 30

German Library Society (Peoria, Ill.) 38

German Library Society (Peru, Ill.) 38

German Newspaper, 1844 43

German newspapers 43, 134

German refugees 154

German Relief and Aid Society 72

German schools, private 31

German societies and lodges 132

German Society for the Protection of Immigrants 69

German theaters 133
German Workers in Industrial Chicago, 1850–1910: A Comparative Perspective (Keil) 168
German Works in Chicago: A Documentary History of Working-Class Culture from 1850 to World War I (Keil, et al.) 168
German-American Alliance in Peru, Ill. 143
German-American Alliance of Chicago 155
German-American Alliance of Illinois 139, 144, 146, 147
German-American Alliance of Missouri and Southern Illinois 139
German-American Annals 139
German-American authors 133
German-American Bicentennial 138
German-American Central Alliance of Pennsylvania 139
German-American educational institution, establishment of 38
German-American Experience, The (Tolzmann) 2, 57, 60, 164
German-American Forty-Eighters, 1848–1998, The (Tolzmann) 59
German-American Historical Society of Illinois 87, 141, 172
German-American Journal 170
German-American newspapers 133
German-American organizations in Illinois 139
German-American regiment 13
German-American Relations and German Culture in America: A Subject Bibliography, 1941–1980 (Schultz) 167
German-American Studies: Selected Essays (Tolzmann) 2
German-American urban centers 31, 32
German-Americana: A Bibliography (Tolzmann) 32, 167
German-born population 93
Germania Club of Chicago 132, 133
Germania Club Year Book and Historical Review 168

Germania Publishing Co. 125
Germania Society 72
Germania, Die 125
Germann, Friedrich 39, 40
Germans and the Revolution of 1848–1849 (Randers-Pehrson) 113
Germans in the American Civil War (Kaufmann) 58, 114, 164
Germans in the Making of America (Schrader) 88
Germans of Chicago, The (Hofmeister) 168
Germans of Chicago, The (Townsend) 170
Germans to Illinois 131
Germans-Americans in the Civil War 131
Germantown, Ill. 63
Germantown, Pa. 138, 141
Germany 24, 27, 67
Giessen Immigration Society 19, 51
Gilbert, Cynthia 121
Girard College 25
Glaser, Friedrich 40
Glocke, Die 170
Goebel, Julius 141, 142
Goedeking (father of Heinrich) 52
Goedeking, Heinrich 43, 51, 52
Goethe 142
Goethe-Feier der Deutschen von Chicago zu Johann Wolfgang von Goethe's 150-jährigem Geburtstag, Sonntag, den 3. September 1899, Sunny Side Park 168
Goff, E. L. 123
Göppingen, Württemberg, Germany 35, 46
Göttingen, Germany 21
Grant's San Domingo policy 80
Grant, Ulysses S. 13, 47, 51, 80, 103, 120
Graü versus Grüne (Greys versus Greens) 100
Grauen, die 130
Great Depression 153
Greeley, Horace 80, 101, 102, 118
GREENE, EVARTS B. 93
GREENE, VICTOR R. 63
Greens. *See also,* Grünen 100

Greys. *See also,* Graü 100
Groppe, Wilhelmine (Mrs. Francis
    Hoffmann) 117
Grossmann, Karl 40
Grünen, die 130
Grünerwald, Christian 40
Grünstadt, Germany 21
Gugler, Julius 133
Guide to the History of Illinois, A
    (Hoffmann) 167
Guide to the History of Illinois, A
    (Hofmann) 171
Gumbert, 131
Gundlach, Geo. 134
Gustav Koerner: Deutsch-
    Amerkanischer Jurist, Staatsmann,
    Diplomat und Geschichtsschreiber,
    Ein Lebensbild . . .
    (Rattermann) 104
Gustave Koerner House
    Committee 157

H
Haas, Adam 40
Halle 17, 29
Halleck, Henry W. 15, 105
Hambach Festival 96
Hamburg, Germany 47, 112
Hanks, John 119
Hanks, Thomas 119
Hannover, Germany 29
Hardi family 6
Harding, Warren G. 148
Hardy, Jakob 39
Haren, Eduard 16
Harper's Weekly 89
Harrison, Carter H. 71
Harrison, William Henry 98
Harvard University 141
Harwarth, Heinrich 40
Harwarth, Wilhelm 40
HARZIG, CHRISTINE 168
Hasel, F. A. M. 40
Hassaurek, Friedrich 72, 87
Hassel, August 29
Hauck, Bartholomaeus 53
Haus- und Bauernfreund, Der 125
Havana, Ill. 132
Haxthausen, Heinrich von 29

Haxthausen, Herman von 29
HAY, JOHN 105
Hayes 80
Hayes-Tilden campaign 103
Haymarket Riot 71, 136
Heberer, Georg 40
Heberer, Johann G. 40
Heberer, Thomas 39
Hecker Monument Society,
    National 115
Hecker, Friedrich Karl Franz 11, 37,
    67, 99, 107, 109, 110, 111, 112,
    113, 114, 115, 130, 131, 135, 161
Hecker's First Illinois Regiment 76
Hecker's Second Illinois Regiment 76
Hehr, Georg 40
Hehret, Georg 39
Heidelberg, Germany 6, 10, 21, 23,
    26, 70, 97
Heidelberg, University of 95
Heimat North America: English and
    German (Lachner and Ott) 169
Heimberger, Gustav 6, 40
Heinzen, Karl 72
Henckler, Georg 40
Hennig, Cornelius 40
Henry, H. A. 123
Herford, Germany 55, 117
HERRIOTT, F. I. 87, 88
Hertel, Nikol. 40
Hesing, 79
Hesing, Anton C. 71, 82, 83
Hessen-Darmstadt, Germany 6
Highland 43, 49, 50
Highland, Ill. 49, 134
Hild, Frederick 132
Hild, Michael 40
Hildenbrandt, J. L. 30
Hildesheim, Germany 6
Hilgard
    Theodor Erasmus 36
Hilgard family 7, 16, 37
Hilgard farm 19
Hilgard, Eduard 6, 30, 40
Hilgard, Eugen Woldemar 5, 24, 26,
    27, 28, 37
Hilgard, Fritz 30
Hilgard, Julius C. 5
Hilgard, Julius E. 22, 24, 25, 36

Hilgard, Otto 30
Hilgard, Theodor E., Jr. 6, 21, 26
Hilgard, Theodor E., Sr. 5, 21, 22, 23, 24, 26, 30, 40
Hilgard, Theodor Erasmus 33, 40
Hillgaertner, Georg 55, 74, 135
History of Beer and Brewing in Chicago, 1833–1978, The (Skilnik) 169
History of the Germans of Alton (lecture) 51
Hock, Jos. 40
HOEFER, H. 168
Hoeffgen 68
Hoff, Philipp 41
Hoffman, Gilbert 122
Hoffmann 136, 161
Hoffmann Library 125
Hoffmann, 134
Hoffmann, Adam 41
Hoffmann, Dr. Adolph 121
Hoffmann, Dr. Julius 121
Hoffmann, Francis A., Jr. 121
Hoffmann, Francis Arnold 43, 55, 56, 64, 66, 74, 76, 85, 117, 118, 120, 121, 123, 124
Hoffmann, Francis, Collection 125
Hoffmann, Gilbert 121, 122
HOFFMANN, JOHN 167
Hoffmann, Th. A. 51
Hoffmann, Wilhelmine (nee Groppe) 117
Höfken 54
HOFMANN, JOHN A. 171
Hofmeister, Rudolf 133
HOFMEISTER, RUDOLF 168
Hohenheim, Germany 6
Hohenzollerns 114
Holl, E. A. 123
Holstein 29
HOLTSCHLAG, LESTER 168
Holtz, Samuel 39
Holzappel, August 41
Homann, 51
Homestead Acts 75
Höreth, J. L. 40
Horst, Peter 41
Huber, Jacob 41
Hudson and the Erie Canal 55

Hudson River 96, 117
Hughes 144
Humbert, Dr. Friedrich 43, 50
Humboldt, Wilhelm 10

I

Illinois 26, 67
Illinois Alliance at Peoria, Ill. 164
Illinois and Michigan Canal 54
Illinois Central Railroad Company 119
Illinois German regiments 164
Illinois History: An Annotated Bibliography (Whitney, et al.) 167
Illinois Institute of Technology 153
Illinois Staats-Anzeiger 131
Illinois Staats-Zeitung 55, 61, 67, 68, 69, 71, 72, 74, 75, 76, 77, 78, 80, 81, 84, 85, 86, 87, 89, 132, 136, 143
Illinois State Convention (Bloomington) 62
Illinois State Register 90
Illinois: Crossroads of a Continent (Carrier) 57
Immigration No. 1 (pre-1848) 129
Immigration No. 2 (post-1848) 129
Immigration No. 3 (post Civil War) 130
Imperial Supreme Court at Trier 21
Industrial State, The (Bogart & Thompson) 90
Institute of Design 153
International Bank of Chicago 56
Irish 73, 74

J

Jackson, Tennessee 13
Jaeger, J. H. 43
Jaeger, John H. 51
Jahn, Father 95
Jahrbuch der Deutschen in Chicago 87, 170
Jahresbericht der Deutschen Gesellschaft von Chicago 86
Jeckel, Philipp 41
Jefferson, Ill. 121, 122
Jefferson, Thomas 30
Jeffersonian Democrats 129
Jena, Germany 10, 17, 29

Jena, University of 95
JENTZ, JOHN B. 168
Johns Hopkins University 141
Johnson, Andrew 79, 103
Johnson, Richard M. 15
Johnson's Encyclopedia 28
Joliet, Ill. 54, 69, 132
Juncker, Rev. Heinrich Damian 43, 51
Junger, Michael 41
Just, Samuel 41

K

Kaiserslautern, Germany 10
Kalbfleisch, Peter 41
Kane, Judge 25
Kansas-Nebraska Bill 61, 74, 75, 101, 124
KARGAU, ERNST D. 32
Karlsruhe, Germany 58
Kaskaskia, Ill. 5
KAUFMANN, WILHELM 57, 58
Kaysing, Christian 41
Kaysing, Heinrich 41
Kaysing, Jacob 41
Keck, Jos. 41
Kehrer, Joh. 41
KEIL, HARTMUT 168
Kennedy, John F. 154
Kentucky 47, 96
Kettler, C. H. 41
Kiefer, Joseph 43
Kiefer, Peter 134
KIMBROUGH, LENORE 168
King Lear 23
King, F. H. 123
King, William 146
Kinkel 99
Kircher, Heinrich 45
KIRCHER, HENRY A. 168
Kircher, Joseph A. 45, 51, 52
Kistler, John 134
Kleinschmidt, Michael 41
KLOSS, HEINZ 38
Knöbel, Friedrich 41
Knöbel, Heinrich 41
Knöbel, Jakob 41
Knöbel, Karl 41
Knobloch, Balthasar 39
Knobloch, John 39

Knobloch, John Wendelin 39, 41
Knobloch, Thomas 39
Knötz, Franz 41
Know-Nothings 68, 74, 83, 101, 102
Koblenz, Germany 21
Koepfli family 43, 49
Koepfli, Dr. Kaspar 49
Koepfli, Salomon 49, 50, 52
Koerner family 37
Koerner House 157
Koerner, Chris. 122
Koerner, G. A. 134
Koerner, Gustav 5, 15, 30, 31, 32, 33, 34, 35, 37, 38, 41, 60, 61, 65, 66, 75, 76, 80, 93, 94, 96, 97, 98, 99, 100, 101, 102, 103, 104, 105, 131, 134, 135, 136, 138, 141, 146, 157, 158, 159, 161, 172
KOERNER, GUSTAV 33, 43, 57, 59, 60, 85, 86, 87, 88, 89, 90, 104, 105, 164, 166, 169
Koerner, Sophie 158
Konradi, Dr. August 29
Kopp, Jos. 41
Kossuth, 100
Kracht, W. 41
Krafft, Friedrich 48
Krafft, Theodor J. 6, 41, 48
Kratsch, J. G. 41
Kress, Friedrich 41
KRESSMANN, FRED 168
Kretzinger, G. M. 134
Krick, J. Adam 41
Krick, Joh. 41
Kriechbaum, Georg 41
Kriege, Hermann 55, 61
Kuhn, Fritz 151
Kulm, Germany 44
Kumm, Jacob 41
Kuntz, Georg 41
Kurtz, Kaspar J. 41

L

Lacher, J. H. A. 64
LACHER,, J. H. A. 124
LACHNER, BERT 169
LaFollette 148
Lake Co., Ind. 55, 117
Lake Erie 96

Lake House 117
Lake Shore Apartments
   (Chicago) 154
Lake Villa, Ill. 154
Lake, Bernhard 41
Lassalle, Ill. 54
Latin farmers 30, 52
Latin Settlement 5, 30, 31, 37, 45, 131
Läuffert, Jakob 41
Lauter School (Charlottenburg,
   Germany) 19
League of Nations 148
Lebanon, Ill. 45
*Lebensbild von Simon Kuhlenhölter,
   von 1860 bis 1882, Pastor der
   Evang. Salems-Gemeinde in
   Quincy, Ills* (Hoefer) 168
Ledergerber 59
Ledergerber, Fritz 45
Ledergerber, Joseph 30, 41, 45
LeHavre, France 10
Leipzig, Germany 16
Lewis, James Hamilton 148
Lexington, Ky. 15, 97
Liberal Republican movement 69, 85
Liberal Republicans 80
Liebig, Conrad 41
Lieder 110
*Life of Carl Follen: A Study in
   German-American Cultural
   Relations, The* (Spindler) 165
Lincoln Rifles 76
Lincoln's Birthday Party 151
Lincoln, Abraham 15, 21, 62, 68, 69,
   76, 77, 78, 79, 89, 102, 105, 111,
   119, 124, 125, 131
LINCOLN, ABRAHAM 125
Lintz, Heinrich 41
Literatur-Blatt 30
Little Rock, capture of 13
London 29, 69
London, England 70
Lookout Mountain 57
Lott, Peter 134
Louisiana 28, 79
Louisville, Ky. 110
Lowden, Gov. 147
Lusitania episode 144
Lutheran Synod of Michigan 117

Luzern, Switzerland 49
Lyceum (Metz, Germany) 21
Lyman 101
Lyon, France 58

M

Macon Co., Ill. 119
Madison Co., Ill. 43, 44, 47, 48, 49,
   51, 132
Madison, Ill. 5
Malaga, Spain 26, 27
Malzacher, Louis 65
Mannhardt, Emil 141
MANNHARDT, EMIL 32, 33, 58, 59, 60,
   62, 86, 169
Mannheim, Germany 16, 21, 58, 107,
   111
Marbach, Joseph 65
Marburg, Germany 52
Marine Settlement 49
Marion Co., Ill. 63
Marseilles, France 26
Martin Luther College Library (New
   Ulm, Minn.) 125
Marx, Karl 72
Mascoutah, Ill. 33
Massachusetts 73
Massenberg, Wm. 134
Massmann, Joh. 41
Massow, Ewald von 29
Mattern, Friedrich 65
Mattoon, Ill. 63
Maus, Johann 41
May Festival of the Hambacher
   Schloss 96
mayor of Belleville 17
mayor, first of Beardstown 53
McClellan, George B. 79
MCCORMACK, THOMAS J. 169
MCPHERSON, E. 89
McPherson, General 58
Mecklenburg, Germany 44, 57
Medical Society of St. Clair
   County 17
Medill, Mayor 81
Meiningen, Germany 16
*Memoirs of Gustave Koerner, 1809–
   1896, Life-Sketches Written at the
   Suggestion of His Children*

(Koerner) 35, 36, 37, 38, 39, 59, 60, 87, 88, 89, 90, 105, 164, 166, 169

Memoirs of Henry Villard, Journalist and Finacier, 1835–1900 (Villard) 104

Merger, Georg 39

Merkel 39

Merker, Philipp 39

Meser, Georg 39

Metamorphosen (Ovid) 23

Methods and Results: Formulae and Factors for the Computation of Geodetic Latitudes, Longitudes, and Azimuths (Hilgard, J.) 36

Metropolitan Hall 78

Metternich 95

Metz, Geo. H. 134

Metz, Germany 21

Metzler, Christian 41

Metzler, Valentin 41

Mexican War 13, 35

Meyer, Mathias 65, 86

Michael Reese Hospital 70

Michaelis, Richard 80

Michel, Jacob W. 41

Michigan 55

military enlistment, German 76

mill in St. Clair County 47

Miller, H. B. 134

Miller, Th. 134

Milwaukee Germania 121

Milwaukee, Wis. 133

Mirus 16

Missionary Ridge 57

Missionsbote (religious monthly) 55

Mississippi 27

Mississippi Historical Association 87

Mississippi River 28, 37, 53, 96

Missouri 31, 48, 78, 93, 96

Missouri's German Heritage (Tolzmann) 32, 34, 35, 36

Mitteilungen 139

Mittelstadter, Georg 41

Moholy-Nagy, Laszlo 153

Mohr, Jakob 39

Monroe Co., Ill. 5, 22, 44

Morgan Co., Ill. 51

Morgenblatt 30

Morrill fund 28

Möser, Heinrich 41

Mueller, A. F. C. 134

Mueller, Paul 143

Muench family 37

Muench, Friedrich 23, 36, 37, 129, 131, 133

Müller, Balthasar 39, 41

Müller, Conrad 41

Müller, Jakob 39

Müller, Michael 41

München, Germany 6, 10, 11, 52, 70

Munich, University of 95

N

Nahler, J. J. 65

Napoleon 84, 95

Nation und der Bundestag: Ein Beitrag zur deutschen Geschichte, Die (Fischer) 105

National Academy of Science 25, 26, 28

National Bank of Illinois 69

National Demokrat 80, 90

National German-American Alliance 139, 146

National German-American Alliance, Staatsverband, Ill. 164

National Medical College 27

Native-American doctrine 101

Native-American spirit 98

nativist movement 54, 100

NATO 154

Nauvoo, Ill. 134

NELKE, D. I. 117

Nette, Dr. 29

Neubarth, J. G. 41

Neue Zeit, Die 61, 170

Neuhoff, Georg 5, 16, 41

New Bauhaus 153

New England 93

New Guide for Immigrants to the West, A 86

New Hope Church 58

New Orleans Academy of Science 28

New Orleans, La. 11

New Switzerland 43

New York 5, 26, 58, 93, 97, 131

New York Times 147

Newspapers and Periodicals in Chicago (Scott) 87
Nibelungen 23
Nick Pesch Monument 154
NICOLAY, JOHN G. 105
Ninth Illinois Regiment 131
Nordamerikanische Rathgeber, Der 49
Norris Company 25
Norris's Business Directory 86
North Market Hall 76
Northern Europe 69
Nürnberg, Germany 69

O

O'Fallon, Ill. 47
O'Hara 82
Ober-Alton, Ill. 50
Oberfranken, Germany 69
Obermüller 39
Oglesby, Richard J. 119
Ohio 93, 131
Ohio (river) 96
OLSON, MAY E. 34, 57, 60, 61, 124, 125, 164, 167
Oppmann, Franz 41
Osterhaus, Peter Joseph 45, 58
Osterhaus, regiment of 57
Osterode, Germany 47
Ott, Ernst 153, 169
Ottawa, Ill. 54, 134
Our Penal Machinery and its Victims (Altgeld) 135
Over-the-Rhine district (Cincinnati, Ohio) 115
Oxford, Mississippi 27

P

Palatinate 22
Paris, France 6, 21
Paris, July revolution in 96
Patronage, Practice, and the Culture of American Science: Alexander Dallas Bache and the U.S. Coast Survey (Slotten) 37
Patterson, Dr. 25
Pea Ridge, battle of 45
PECK, JOHN M. 86
Peck, John Mason 67
Pekin, Ill. 132

Pennsylvania 31, 131
Pennsylvania Germans 54
People's Party 83
People's Party 82
Peoria, Ill. 16, 54, 132, 134, 164
Perthes and Besser (publishers) 49
Peru, Ill. 54, 132, 143
Pestalozzi, Johann Heinrich 19, 36, 50
PETTERCHAK, JANICE A. 167
Pfadler, Philipp 41
Pfeffer, Heinrich 41
Pfeifer, Sebastian 41
Pfund, Johann 54
Philadelphia, Pa. 5, 25, 26, 47, 110
Philipsburg, Pa. 38
Philosophical Society of Philadelphia 25
Pierce, Franklin 80
Pioniere, Die 133
Pittsburgh Convention 31, 38
Plattner 26
POCHMANN, HENRY 167
Poland 16
Political History of the United States during the Rebellion (McPherson) 89
political life in Illinois 43
Popp, Georg Adam 41
Popular Science Monthly 25
populäre Geschichte der Stadt Peoria, Eine (Bess) 167
population of German-born citizens 93
Portsmouth, Ohio 96
Portugal 26
postmaster of Belleville, Ill. 46
Prager, Robert P. 146, 147
Prairie Farmer 119
Prairie State: A Documentary History of Illinois, The (Sutton) 57
Preston 15
Price, General 45
Probst, Christian 41
Proceedings of the State Historical Society of Wisconsin 90
Prohibition 153
Protestant Seminary at Tübingen 71
Pruessing, Ernst 75, 78, 79, 80, 85

Prussia 12, 114
Public Library of St. Clair County 18
Puritanism 31, 83

Q

Quincy, Ill. 10, 11, 53, 134

R

railway system 50
Raith, Julius 13, 35, 43, 44, 46, 47
RANDERS-PEHRSON, JUSTINE
    DAVIS 113
Rangers 48
Rapp, Wilhelm 71
Rappauf, Peter 41
Raster, Hermann 55, 62, 71, 72
Rattermann, H. A. 104
RATTERMANN, H. A. 32, 39, 58, 104
Rauch, Georg 41
Rauch, Philipp 41
Reader Adler 38
Reagan, Ronald 155
reconstruction 79
Red River 13
*Reflections on Some of the People and
    Issues in the Early Days of the
    German Evangelical Synods of
    North America* (Schade) 169
*Refugees of Revolution: The German
    Forty-Eighters in America*
    (Wittke) 37, 115
Reichert, Lorenz 41
Reichert, Seb. Joh. 41
Reinhard, Joseph 134
Reinhold, Chrisoph 41
Reise, Aug. 134
Religious institutions serving the
    German-American population 132
Remann, F. 134
Reminiscences of Carl Schurz
    (Schurz) 38, 90
repeal of slavery 79
*Report on the Geology and
    Agriculture of the State of
    Mississippi* (Hilgard, E.) 27
Republican Convention of 1856 101
Republican National Convention 76

Republican Party 68, 69, 71, 73, 74,
    75, 81, 83, 85, 101, 102, 103, 111,
    123, 124, 130, 131, 135, 148
Reuss, Dr. Adolph 5, 17, 18, 30, 36
Reuter, Fritz 29
REYNOLDS 107
Rheinbaiern, Germany 29
Rheinhessen, Germany 16
Rheinkreis 16, 21
Rheinpfalz, Germany 22
Rhenish Bavaria 69
Rhine, fall of the 21
Richland Co., Ohio 135
Rilliers 49
Ringgold 45
Rio Grande (river) 11
Ritter, Georg 41
River and Harbor Convention in
    Chicago 55
Riverside farm 121, 122
Roberts 25
Robker, B. 41
Rock Island, Ill. 132
Rockford Republican 89
Roessler, Edw. 134
Roessler, R. 134
Roman Catholic episcopate 51
Romer's Hall 83
Roos, Jos. 41
Roosevelt, 144
Rosenstengel, Professor 122, 123
ROSKOTEN, OLIVER J. 169
Rummel, E. 135
Ruppelius, Michael 16
Russell, H. L. 123

S

Sachsen-Weimar, Germany 51
Salomon, Friedrich 13
salt deposits investigation 28
Saltillo 11
Sandher, Heinrich 16
Santa Anna 11
Santa Rosa, Coahuila (Mexico) 11
Sauer, Peter 41
Sauter, Karl 54, 65, 66
sawmill, first in Arenzville 52
Saxony-Meiningen, Germany 29
SCHADE, GERHARD 169

Schäfer, Adam 41
Schäfer, Joh. 42
Scheel, Johann 5, 13, 35, 42
Scheel, John 134
Scheirer, Georg 54
Scherer 26
Scheve, Julius 42
Schiller Theater in Chicago 133
Schiller's plays 133
Schillinger, Matthias 39
Schlaeger, Edward 74
Schleswig-Holstein, Germany 11, 84
Schleth, Heinrich C. T. 29, 37, 42
Schleusingen, Germany 29
Schmalenberg, J. N. 42
Schmidt, Dr. Ernst 69, 70, 71, 72, 74, 79, 85, 86
Schmidt, Dr. Otto L. 87, 141
Schnauffer, Carl 110, 113
Schneider, Georg 55, 61, 68, 69, 71, 74, 75, 78, 80, 135
SCHNEIDER, OTTO C. 87
Schneider, Otto C. 88
Schneider, Peter 42
Schneider, W. L. 51
Schoenlein 29
Scholl, Joh. W. 42
School of Design 153
schoolhouse, first in Beardstown 52
Schott, Dr. Anton 5, 17, 18, 30, 31, 36
SCHRADER, FREDERICK F. 88
Schraer, Heinrich 42
Schrag, Conrad 42
Schreiber, Karl 5, 16
Schulheiss, Franz 42
SCHULTZ, ARTHUR R. 167
Schultz, Daniel 39
Schurz, Carl 62, 75, 76, 80, 99, 102, 103, 135, 137, 140, 151
SCHURZ, CARL 37, 88
Schweppe, 51
SCOTT, F. W. 87
Seagram's Building (New York) 154
seat of government 5
Second Chamber 110
Second Illinois Regiment 11
Seibel, Georg 146
Selby, Paul 75
SELBY, PAUL 87

Senne, H. C. 134
Seventeenth Missouri Regiment 57
Seward, William H. 69, 76, 84, 102
Sherman 45
Shiloh 35
Shreveport, La. 13
Siebel, A. F. W. 151
Sieber, Martin 42
Siege of Vicksburg 13
Sigel, Franz 58
Sigel, Ill. 63
Sigel's command 45
Sixteenth Illinois Cavalry Regiment 131
SKILNIK, BOB 169
slavery, question of 100
SLOTTEN, HUGH RICHARD 37
Smithsonian Institute 26, 28
Smithsonian Institute 28
socialism 72, 87
Socialist Labor Candidate 70
Society of Danube Swabians 154
South Carolina 102
South Market Hall 74
southern Illinois 31, 32
Spain 27, 103
Spanish-American War 135
Sparks 30
Speier, Rheinpfalz, Germany 6
Speyrer 6
Springfield, Ill. 5, 29, 131, 132, 134
Spurensuche: German-speaking Communities in Chicago and in the Midwest 169
St. Clair Co., Ill. 5, 16, 29, 31, 32, 43, 46, 54, 93, 96, 131, 132
ST. FRANCIS CHURCH, TEUTOPOLIS, ILL. 169
St. Francois Co., Mo. 48
St. Louis *Neue Zeit* 68
St. Louis, Mo. 5, 10, 11, 22, 29, 31, 32, 37, 44, 49, 50, 51, 58, 68, 70, 96, 110, 112, 133, 138, 147
Staatsverband, Ill. 164
Stahl, Dr. 43, 53
Stanford University 141
STARK, SANDRA M. 167
state convention 19

Statistical View of the United States...Compendium of the Census, 1850, Table III 86
Steele, Gen. 13
Stein 95
Stein, Karl 54
Steiner family 6
Steiner, Bernhard 39
Steinheimer, Peter 42
Stern des Westens (newspaper) 53
STERN, MAX 168
Stibold, S. J. 135
Stollemann, 131
Stolz, Franz 42
Stose, Clement C. 65
Strassburg, France 111
Straussel, Martin 54
Struve, Gustav 109, 110, 113
Stuntz, John 134
Suppiger family 43, 49
Supreme Court of Illinois 98
SUTTON, ROBERT P. 57
Swiss immigrants 6
Switzerland 26, 29, 67, 99, 110

T
Taylor, Gen. 11
temperance 81, 82, 85
Tennessee 79
Tennessee River 47
Teutopolis, Ill. 63, 169
Texas 11
Third Missouri Volunteer Regiment 57, 70, 114
Third Reich 153
Thirteenth Illinois Cavalry Regiment 131
Thirty-sixth Illinois Regiment 131
Thomas 45
THOMPSON, C. M. 90
Thompson, Lawrence S. 113
Tilden 80
TISCHAUSER, LESLIE 169
Tittmann, Eduard 29
Tittmann, Karl 29, 42
Tittmanns 37
Tolzmann 61

TOLZMANN, DON HEINRICH 32, 34, 35, 36, 57, 59, 60, 61, 115, 129, 164, 165, 167, 172
Townsend, Andrew Jacke 144
TOWNSEND, ANDREW JACKE 65, 170
Transactions of the Illinois Historical Society 88
Transactions of the McLean County Historical Society 88
Transylvania University 96
Trapp, Dr. Albert H. 5, 29, 37, 134
Trautwein, Joh. P. 25, 42
Trenton, Ill. 111
Trier, 21
Trumbull, Lyman 101, 124
Tübingen, Germany 71
TUCKER, MARLIN TIMOTHY 170
Turkey Hill 6
Turner Cadets 76
Turnerbund 71
Turnvereine 132
Turnvereine 31
Turnzeitung 71
Tusculum 125
Twelfth Illinois Calvary Regiment 131
Twelfth Infantry Regiment 45
Twelfth Missouri Regiment 57
Twenty-fourth Illinois Regiment (Hecker Jaeger Regiment) 114, 131
Twenty-seventh Illinois Regiment 131

U
U.S. Census Report 86
U.S. Medal of Freedom 154
Ueber Deutschlands Nationaleinheit und ihr Verhältnis zur Freiheit (Hilgard, Sr.) 23
Ullich's block 78
Um die Einigung des Deutschamerikanertums: Die Geschichte einer unvollendeten Volksgruppe (Kloss) 38
Uncle Tom's Cabin 101
unification of Germany 155
Union Army 45

United German American Societies of Greater Chicago 155
United States 68, 99
United States Coast Survey 25
United States Corps of Engineers 25
United States Department of Engineers 28
University of Berlin 71
University of Leipzig 71, 141
University of Pennsylvania 25
University of Tübingen 141
University of Wisconsin, College of Agriculture 122
University of Würzburg 70
Unnigmann, Heinrich 42
Upper Alton, Ill. 50
Urban, Franz 42
Urbana, Ohio 141
Utah 146

V

Van Buren, Martin 15, 98
van der Rohe, Ludwig Mies 153
Vandalia, Ill. 5, 97
Vermillion Bay 28
Vicksburg 45, 57
Vienna, Austria 26
Vierheller, Christian 42
Vierheller, Ludwig 42
Villard, Henry 93
VILLARD, HENRY 104
vineyard and winery 11
Vinzens, Dr. 29
Virginia 77
Vocke, Wilhelm 80, 88, 134, 141
Vogel, Rev. Henry 122
von Kamptz family 44
von Wangelin. *See* Wangelin
Vorparlament 113
Vorwärts 87

W

Wacker, Frederick, Sr. 67, 72
Walsh, Diane 157
Walter, Kaspar 54
Wangelin, Hugo von 43, 44, 45, 57, 58
War of 1812 48
war with Mexico in 1846 47

Warsaw, Ill. 134
Wartburg Festival 96
Washington 21
Washington Co., Ill. 63
Washington, D.C. 15, 25, 26
Washington, George 30
Weber, Balthasar 42
Weber, Jakob 39
Weber, Wilhelm 10, 16, 31, 34, 38
Webster, 15
Wecker 71, 113
Wecker (Baltimore newspaper) 58
Weigler, 51
Weilbacher, Johann 42
Weilmünster, Martin 42
Weisbach 26
Wellmacher, John 65, 86
Werner, Nicolaus 42
Wesenheft, Charles 65
West Belleville, Ill. 22
West-Belleville, Ill. 33
Westermann, Conrad 42
Westminster Review 23
Westphalia, Germany 29, 69, 117
Wetzer, Jakob 42
Wezel, Franz 42
Whig Party 53, 101
Whigs 68, 73, 98
WHITNEY, ELLEN M. 167
Wichers, Anton 42
Wichers, Dr. 29
Wiesbaden, Germany 19
Wiesenborn, Joh. 42
WILDERMAN, A. A. 39
WILDERMAN, A. S. 39
Wildi family 6
Wildy, Rudolph 39
Wilhelm, Kaiser 145
Will Co., Ill. 132
Will County, Ill. 55, 117
Willich, August von 58
Wilson, Woodrow 143, 144, 148
Winter, Georg 42
Winter, John 42
Wisconsin 13, 56, 78, 93
Wislizenus, Dr. Adolph 29
Wittke, Carl 114
WITTKE, CARL 37, 115
Wolf 19

Wolf, D. 134
Wolf, Fritz 30
Wolf, Hermann 30, 42
Wool, Gen. 11
World Court 148
World's Fair 137, 138
*World's Best Orations: From the
    Earliest Period to the Present Time*
    (Brewer) 111, 114
Wright, John S. 119
Württemberg, Germany 71
Würzburg, Germany 70

Y

Yager. *See* Jaeger
Yates (governor) 102
Yates, Dick 119, 120

Z

Zieren, Heinrich 42
Zimmermann, Dr. G. A. 133, 141
Zimmermann, Wilhelm 42
Zschokke, E. 50
Zschokke, Heinrich 50
Zucker, A. E. 58, 59, 61, 62, 114
*Zur Feier der Goldenen Hochzeit von
    Gustav und Sophie Koerner (17
    Juni 1886)* (Rattermann) 104
Zürich, Switzerland 26, 29, 45, 50, 70
Zweibrücken, Germany 21, 24, 26
*Zwölf Paragraphen über den
    Pauperismus und die Mittel ihn zu
    steuern* (Hilgard, Sr.) 23